The Intellectual Roots of Independence

La definicion de Puerto Rico
a mi juicio, es este: una
nación de rehenes.

In my opinion Puerto Rico can best
be defined as: a nation of hostages.
—Zeno Gandía

The Intellectual Roots of Independence: An Anthology of Puerto Rican Political Essays

edited by Iris M. Zavala and Rafael Rodríguez
with an introduction by Iris M. Zavala

Monthly Review Press
New York and London

Library of Congress Cataloging in Publication Data
The Intellectual roots of independence.
    Translation of Libertad y crítica en el ensayo político
puertorriqueño.
    Bibliography: p.
    1. Puerto Rico—Politics and government—Addresses, essays,
lectures.   2. Political   science—Puerto   Rico—History—Addresses, essays, lectures. I. Zavala, Iris M. II. Rodríguez, Rafael.
JL1050.L513   320.97295   79-3021

ISBN: 978-0-85345-521-9

Contents

III. Under the Sign of Imperialism

IV. Culture and Politics

Foreword

We have not attempted to provide complete bibliographies for each author but rather to list their most important books and articles. Those works listed in the individual bibliographies do not appear in the Selected Bibliography at the end of the book. Footnotes are the editors', unless otherwise indicated.

We express our gratitude to all those authors who have given us permission to reproduce their essays; to Ricardo Alegría, Enrique Laguerre, Juana Meléndez Muñoz, Luis M. Díaz Soler for their generous help; and to *La Escalera,* and to the San Juan publishing houses Edil, Cultural, and Cordillera. Certain authors, such as Tomás Blanco and René Márquez, are not represented in this collection due to their indifference, not to ours.

Our readers may be interested to know that publication of this collection in Spain was prohibited by the Spanish government. This measure was occasioned by the inclusion of articles by nineteenth-century writers who attacked Spanish colonialism and by twentieth-century writers who expressed their own political radicalism as well as their disdain for official Spain. These authors, according to the censors' report, defend the Organization for Latin American Solidarity, OLAS ("a Castrista organization for the promotion of guerrilla warfare in Latin America") and the Communist Party. They also, the allegation continues, "speak in derogatory terms of the United States, express solidarity with Vietnam and Cuba, and characterize the Puerto Rican government as a puppet state."

Abbreviations

DIP—Departamento de Instrucción Pública
ICP—Instituto de Cultura Puertorriqueña
RICP—Revista del Instituto de Cultura Puertorriqueña
UPR—Editorial Universitaria, Universidad de Puerto Rico

1

Historical Chronology

Date	Event
1812	War in Spain. Spanish Cortes announces Liberal Constitution.
1816–1824	Wars of Independence in Continental Latin America. Puerto Ricans refuse to join military groups to repress Venezuelan patriots. Between 1816 and 1820, Ferdinand VII rules as an absolute monarch, repressing liberal thought both in Spain and in the colonies. In 1820, General Riego rebels, and the Constitutional Triennium starts; liberalism is re-established.
1825	In power once more as an absolute ruler, Ferdinand gives unlimited power to the military governors in Puerto Rico in order to repress independence fervor. These powers will subsist for forty-two years.
1831	Territorial Audiencia is created, independent from that in Cuba.
1835	Two Puerto Rican *procuradores* propose a set of reforms to the Spanish government, which are denied, while on the island Captain Loizaga rebels against the government to restore the Constitution of 1812. The *pronunciamiento* is uncovered and the leader and followers are punished and exiled. Import of black slaves is forbidden.
1837	Spanish Cortes approves special set of rules for Puerto Rico, after the 1812 Constitution is imposed upon the Queen Regent, María Cristina, who took

Date	*Event*
	power after the death of Ferdinand. Carlists and liberals clash in Spain; the era of *pronunciamientos* and military rule begins.
1838	A group of patriots plans a rebellion to proclaim Puerto Rican independence. The Spanish governor takes drastic and violent measures: one of the conspirators is found hanged in his cell in El Morro.
1840	More repressive measures are taken: foreigners are not allowed to enter the island, non-whites cannot walk the streets after 11:00 P.M., and moustaches and beards are forbidden, since they were worn by revolutionaries.
1845	Spanish Cortes legislates against slave traffickers. Puerto Rican government cuts smuggling of slaves to the island.
1847	Government of Juan Prim, well remembered for his liberalism in Spain and for his drastic repression of blacks in Puerto Rico.
1848	Government of Juan Pezuela approves the Laws of Pass-Books (*Libretas*), characterized by liberals as "white slavery." In contrast, it reduces the bonus for the redemption of slaves during baptism and repeats Prim's Black Decree.
1860	Betances is exiled because of his separatist ideas.
1862	Second exile of Betances. Primary education made obligatory.
1863	Julio L. Vizcarrondo creates the Spanish Abolitionist Society in Madrid.
1865	Spanish government invites Puerto Rican and Cuban commissioners to report on the consequences of the colonial special laws.

Date	Event

1867   After two years of hard work, commissioners return, disappointed. Artillery group rebels against the government; the leaders are executed and various patriots exiled. Betances proclaims the "Ten Commandments of the Free Man" from Saint Thomas soil.

1868   Spanish Revolution headed by General Prim dethrones Isabella II, "La Gloriosa" (September 10). Grito de Lares in Puerto Rico (September 23); Grito de Yara in Cuba (October 10). A decree in Puerto Rico frees all children born of slaves after September 17. International Workingmen's Association is organized in Europe, expressing the militancy of the proletariat.

1870   Amnesty for all those who participated in the Grito de Lares. All slaves who are state property are freed, as are those who served under the national flag and those not listed in the census of December 31.

1872   Puerto Rican representatives in Spanish Cortes succeed in winning equal civil rights for the colony.

1873   Abolition of slavery. First Spanish Republic, cantonalist, federalist, and anarchist uprisings in Spain. Conservatives in Puerto Rico organize a mutiny in Camuy, "La Estrellada."

1876   Atenéo of Puerto Rico is created.

1878   Zanjón Pact in Cuba.

1880   José Martí's (1853–1895) articles begin to be published in *The Sun* and *The Hour* in the United States.

1892   Partido Revolucionario Cubano is created to work for Cuban and Puerto Rican independence.

1895   **Cuban War; Manifesto of Montecristi, by Martí; the battleship "Maine" is sunk.**

Date	Event
1896	Revolutionary Junta is formed in New York, to work for Puerto Rican independence.
1897	Spanish government gives autonomy to Puerto Rico. First proletarian weekly, *Ensayo Obrero,* edited by Santiago Iglesias Pantín. Important tobacco worker's strike.
1898	Spanish-American War; United States declares war on Spain; July 25, General Sampson bombards San Juan and the American army occupies the island; December 10, Treaty of Paris—Puerto Rico and the Philippines sold to the United States for $20 million.
1899	American military government is imposed in Puerto Rico.
1900	Foraker Law establishes a civilian government; Puerto Rican Resident Commissioner in Washington will have voice but no vote. The law also allows for islanders to elect their own House of Representatives. Puerto Rican Socialist Party is created.
1904	Unionist Party is formed, offering three solutions to the Puerto Rican problem: autonomy, statehood, or a dependent republic. Iglesias Pantín allies with the workers.
1914	World War I. Puerto Rican soldiers fight under U.S. flag.
1917	Jones Act approved by U.S. Congress, decrees American citizenship to Puerto Rico. English will be official language; monetary devaluation sends waves of immigrants to the United States.
1922	Nationalist Youth Association and Nationalist Junta are formed.

Date   *Event*

1928   Creation of Nationalist Party.

1930   Albizu Campos heads Nationalist Party; CGT is formed. United States controls 44 percent of cultivated land; U.S. capitalism controls 60 percent of banks and public services and 100 percent of maritime lines. Economic crisis creates pauperization, immigration, strikes.

1933   Roosevelt Administration reverses 1917 policy of English as official language of Puerto Rico.

1934   Creation of Puerto Rican Communist Party.

1936   Spanish Civil War divides Puerto Ricans. Albizu is arrested and condemned to ten years; more than 100,000 people march on San Juan, while General Winship calls out the National Guard and police. The new Popular Democratic Party (PPD) is formed, headed by Muñoz Marín.

1937   Massacre of Ponce: 2,000 people meet to celebrate anniversary of abolition of slavery, while the police fire on the crowd, leaving 22 dead and 200 wounded.

1939–1945   PPD promises social justice and independence. World War II; Puerto Rican soldiers fight, mostly in the 65th Infantry Regiment. PPD wins elections (U.S. government still appoints the governor). A law passed by U.S. Congress imposes military service on Puerto Ricans.

1944   Muñoz Marín wins elections again and is leader of the Senate. Partido Independentista Puertorriqueño (PIP) is created; some PPD leaders, discontented with the mild reforms of Muñoz Marín, join it.

1946   Jesús T. Piñero, first Puerto Rican governor, is appointed by President Truman. Operation Bootstrap is in full swing (until 1960); U.S. factories with ten-

Date	*Event*

	year tax-exemptions flourish, thus ruining agriculture while rural zones are depopulated through massive emigration and immigration.
1947	PIP denounces the Puerto Rican colonial status in the United Nations. Albizu Campos released from prison.
1948	Elections for governor. Nationalist Party abstains, while PIP and other leftist groups are persecuted by the FBI. Muñoz Marín is elected governor (1948–1964). Republican Statehood Party founded on July 4.
1950	Commonwealth is proclaimed by U.S. Congress on July 3; October 22, Nationalist leaders are harassed through Jordan Plan; October 30, Blanca Canales Torresola and her followers proclaim the small town of Jayuya a republic (she will not be released from prison until the 1960s); another Nationalist group attacks the Fortaleza in San Juan, and there are small uprisings in Arecibo and Mayagüez. Albizu's house is taken by U.S. troops and he is imprisoned. Attack on Blair House in Washington by Nationalists. More than 2,000 arrests. Meanwhile, rich copper deposits are discovered on the island. Between 1950 and 1954 around 100,000 Puerto Ricans immigrate to the United States, and around 3,000 die during the Korean war (1950–1953).
1952	Muñoz Marín imposes a referendum and the Commonwealth (Estado Libre Asociado) is created on July 25.
1953	Muñoz Marín re-elected governor, grants pardon to Albizu.
1954	A commando unit headed by Lolita Lebrón attacks the White House in Washington, in order to draw attention to Puerto Rico's colonial status. Albizu is again imprisoned without formal charges.

Date   *Event*

1959   Cuban Revolution; Movimiento Pro Independencia
                (MPI) is organized. From this date a strong petro-
                chemical industry is developed in the south of the
                island (Ponce).

1961   Second Conference of Non-Aligned Nations in Cairo
                votes that the colonial status of Puerto Rico be pre-
                sented before the Decolonization Committee of the
                United Nations. April 17-19, Playa Girón (Cuba) at-
                tack, prepared by the CIA under President John F.
                Kennedy, is crushed.

1963   Cuba intervenes in United Nations to include the
                colonial status of Puerto Rico.

1964   PPD wins elections again, with Roberto Sánchez Vi-
                lella as governor.

1965   January, Albizu is granted pardon, taken to a hospi-
                tal, and dies in February; April 24, he is given a
                posthumous Honoris Causa from Havana Univer-
                sity. In February President Johnson sends the first
                troops to Vietnam; U.S. intervention against Domini-
                can Republic. Mass demonstrations against U.S. in-
                tervention in Vietnam and the drafting of Puerto
                Ricans on the island.

1967   Political referendum; only 65 percent of voting
                population participate: those for the Commonwealth
                and those for statehood (PNP). Thirty-five percent
                boycott referendum.

1968   PNP wins elections; industrialist Luis Ferré is
                governor.

1972   MPI becomes the Partido Socialista Puertorriqueño
                (PSP). PPD wins elections, with Rafael Hernández
                Colón governor.

Date	*Event*
1973	The right of the Puerto Rican people to decide their own future is approved by the United Nations. The decision is further approved by the Non-Aligned Nations meeting at Algiers.
1975	Puerto Rico's right to self-determination and independence is reaffirmed at the United Nations. The Lima Conference of the Non-Aligned Nations approves the UN decision. International Congress of Solidarity for Puerto Rican Independence is held in Cuba. Representatives of seventy-nine countries and eighteen international organizations meet under the auspices of the World Council of Peace. By initiative of the United Nations, the discussion of Puerto Rico's colonial status is postponsed until 1976.
1976	PNP wins elections with 48 percent of the vote; Carlos Romero Barceló is elected governor.
1977	Under U.S. pressure the discussion at the United Nations of the Puerto Rican situation is postponed until 1978.
1978	On Cuba's initiative, Puerto Rico's colonial status is finally recognized at the United Nations.
1979	Lolita Lebrón, Ramón Cancel Miranda, Irving Flores, and Oscar Collazo are released from prison. Struggle goes on in Vieques to get U.S. navy off the island. Vieques 21 case: Angel Rodríguez Cristóbal, a member of the Puerto Rican Socialist League working in Vieques, is killed in a federal prison in Florida. Twenty-one people are to stand trial before federal court. Fidel Castro addresses the thirty-eighth General Assembly of the United Nations on behalf of the Non-Aligned Movement.

Introduction
by Iris M. Zavala

The Spanish-American essay is characteristically a genre of de-
nunciation and protest. Intellectuals continually seek to affirm
and perfect a culture of their own, trying to distance themselves
from alien patterns and values. After centuries of colonization,
they aspire to provide urgent solutions to the many problems
reality presents. The countries which freed themselves from their
colonial past at the beginning of the nineteenth century immediately joined the march toward progress. While the new republics
felt their way along that road, examining their own possibilities,
affirming their personalities and capabilities, the two Antilles—
Cuba and Puerto Rico—were left along the wayside, still struggling for their emancipation.

Of the two, the most gloomy fate has been Puerto Rico's, whose
dramatic history led Eugenio María de Hostos to exclaim in 1891:
"The people of Puerto Rico are like a malleable wax ball; they
have taken on more shapes than any other people; they have, with
the most pious resignation, undergone the strangest transformations."[1]

It is precisely these changes and mutations that are reflected in
the essays collected here. The essay or the article is a useful
resource in the search for those political-cultural entities which
make up our world. Through discursive thought our writers have
explained, challenged, and attacked. In the essay, multiple problems—political, economic, social, cultural—interweave, along
with some that are impossible to define. But what predominates is
a concern with the political events in the island and with its future.
Our first liberal thinkers vigorously confronted Spanish colonialism, often demanding freedom of thought and an education
geared to understanding their own reality. What leaps from the
pages of their writings is a convulsive Puerto Rico where thinkers

11

gradually acquire consciousness and express their exigencies and their boldness.

1. Early Manifestations

In 1839, thirty-two years after the printing press reached Puerto Rico, the *Boletín Mercantil* (1839–1848?) boasted of having three hundred subscribers—at a time when the island's population was about 359,000. Whites, free blacks, and slaves were all in one way or another subject to colonial rule. It is impossible now to know with certainty the degree of illiteracy in the country. In 1824 there were thirty-four schoolteachers in the fifty towns and, judging from the 1867 census, illiteracy was widespread among black slaves and white day-laborers, among plantation owners and artisans. From the census we also know that of the 656,328 inhabitants, 548,857 did not know how to read or write. These statistics help us to understand the poverty of the country, which apparently existed as a subsistence economy. Pedro de Córdoba, secretary to Governor Miguel de la Torre (1823–1837), gives a rigorous accounting of this early period in our history: in 1829 there were 140,496 whites, 40,785 tenant farmers, 138,888 blacks, mulattos, and slaves; there were 14,435 houses in town and countryside, and 20,696 shacks. These figures were to vary very little: illiterate masses and a decaying elite, dependent on the colonial government and identified with the leisure classes and colonial institutions.

Despite these impediments, throughout the century a literature was developing which, although initially expressing the interests of the propertied class, had a progressive significance for the country as a whole. This first period culminated with Manuel A. Alonso (1822–1889) and Alejandro Tapia y Rivera (1826–1882). The creole group had not yet developed ideologically, and their ideas, which had to be expressed with a certain caution, could not tackle the most urgent problems of national life. The obstacles imposed by the censors, the lack of appropriate terrain for the cultivation of letters, and the dependent economic system in which luxury items, such as books, were produced abroad, all resulted in irregular and interrupted ideological development. The first creole authors began writing fragmentary works, which reduced existing tensions as much as possible; writers resorted to the popular cliché and the archetype.

These early days in our history are particularly important. Here the new colonial weapons of capitalist exploitation were being forged and the anti-colonial struggle was beginning to take shape. Tensions arose that were not to be resolved. On one side, the world of the military and civilian bureaucracy which controlled the dissemination of ideology, which imposed a culture and a language, a life style, and tried to eliminate "native" expression. Against this enclosed dead-end world stood the countryside, which was arriving in the city, people who were climbing over the walls erected by the civil and ecclesiastical administration—the muffled sound of social reality seeking its expressive current; the nonofficial culture face to face with the walled city. Official literature had its language and its ideology; and the creole intellectuals had two alternatives: to speak of the real problems of the colony and create a national consciousness—a progressive attitude—or to limit themselves to expressing official ideology within the framework of the colonial bureaucracy.

It is significant that the *jíbaro*, or peasant, theme appeared almost simultaneously with Governor Miguel López de Baños' Edict of 1838, aimed at procuring workers for the landowning classes. Any person without property or profession could be classified as a laborer, and he or she was obliged to work for the landowners as a wage-earner. This edict was repeated in 1841 and 1849. On April 13, 1842, *El Boletín* unblushingly expressed the interests of the landowners.

> Nobody is more concerned that the lowest and neediest class of people receive a good education than the comfortable and rich classes. For these latter to be happy it is not sufficient to have comforts and the good of fortune; they also need peace, tranquility, and security in the enjoyment of these. (p. 235)

Similar motives led *El Boletín* to praise the United States in the decade of the 1840s. The journal projects an idyllic image of that country, where everything is peace and harmony: "Millions of individuals, in the midst of the infinite diversity of their movements, all working without jostling one another and all prospering without injuring one another" (June 16, 1842, p. 243).

The creole bourgeoisie and the governors often complained about criminality in the countryside, about attacks on property, robbery, crime. Thanks to Frantz Fanon and other sociologists, we now know that these are primary manifestations of class struggle. The dependent creole bourgeoisie of the nineteenth century, mostly landowners, went out of its way to blame these ills on the lack of religiosity in the countryside, on immorality and vice; they advocated Bibles and Christian resignation.

The *jíbaro* slowly became a literary subject. Writers tried to move their readers but without changing the structure of society; they sought a fraternal collaboration among classes, and at bottom they aspired to know the countryside in order to exploit it. Despite this conservative ideology, they met with opposition among the ruling powers, and Alonso's *El Jíbaro* was put out of circulation by the civil authorities. In other words, even as a literary subject, divested of revolutionary ideology, it was feared that the Puerto Rican theme might awaken the people.

In Alonso's book we find both worlds, the official and the marginal. Perhaps the difference between conciliatory and progressive thinking is better expressed if we make a semantic distinction between "the *jíbaro*" (*el jíbaro*) and "*jíbaro*-like" (*lo jíbaro*). The first was a battle-cry, the second represented the picturesque and the social archetype, which served as a pretext to wipe out customs and vices. The first indicated opposition to the world of the colony by affirming a reality of one's own; the second was a criticism of that reality, which was seen as an inferior cultural expression. The peasant world appears as archaic and idyllic, where people dance and sing, removed from real problems. Despite the dichotomy, it *is* progressive literature. Alonso reflects that essential ambiguity. His book portrays customs with irony, mockery, and sarcasm: "To correct customs as one amuses." Alonso has a reformer's intentions: he is not describing something which is disappearing, but painting what he discovers. In *El Jíbaro*, we find two languages that represent two points of view: he uses correct and pure urban Spanish to propose reforms and censure the colonial regime, and *jíbaro* language to express the peasant world as he sees it—not with its tensions nor its heart-rending realities, but rather with its external folklore. Alonso creates archetypes; the *jíbaro* is dancing, cock-fighting, brawling, card-playing. That is, he describes the peasants with the characteristics that exploitation gave them. Nevertheless, the other Alonso is capable of openly mocking the governors: "El Bando de San Pedro" is a caricature of official edicts, and exposes the absurdity of persons and institutions. It is more than likely that he was alluding to Pezuela, whose edicts against popular fiestas and whose criticisms of the country's customs were notorious. Alonso mocks, deflates, satirizes.

At other moments, his attitude is more reformist and less of a caricature. In his *jíbaro* poems, however, Alonso drops his tone of sarcasm and mockery. He sees the laborer from the outside, but it is undeniable that in *El Jíbaro* there is an underlying cultural identity.

Alonso tries to understand history, become master—and make his readers masters—of a sharp and real historical sense. He becomes conscious of the roots which his society sinks in the people. He discovers the human and social landscape. But his vision is necessarily simplistic; he does not show the tension between the people and the rulers. He does not truly understand peasant life—he stylizes, he abandons the immediate plane of the real, he narrates only the externals. His is a literature without conflict, one which makes compromises; a domestic literature which poeticizes, romanticizes reality, disguises it. Nevertheless, he is progressive because he brings the spirit of the island to a literary work, he recreates from the nonofficial world, using nonofficial language. He brings the countryside to the city. Even more, he gives literary status to the marginalized; he exposes the country's reality and reveals it. Ambiguity, not alienation.

Alonso takes an ironic look at the social landscape; he aspires to reform, and in his eagerness to do so he is able to touch the roots of unease. He advocates progress, education, freedom of thought. Like many people of his generation, he saw industry as the basis for a new social order. Furthermore, he rejected all dogmatism and limitations. The epoch breathes in his short and incisive portraits, and it can almost be said that he gave life to progressive and democratic thought, which is shown with all its contradictions and erosion. His words about Santiago Vidarte, the first Puerto Rican poet, in large measure summarize his reformist intentions, namely, to encourage the arts and industry, to develop agriculture: "The writers of Puerto Rico should show the usefulness of artistic and industrial instruction which we sadly lack, and should brave, if need be, the worst of all criticisms, the acrimony of the ignorant."

Education and progress are also cures proposed by Alejandro Tapia y Rivera. In his *Memorias,* stories, novels, and articles he advocates the widest possible enlightenment; only this will do away with slavery, "which debases and corrupts." The *Memorias,* published posthumously, contain a skillful description of colonial life from 1826 to 1882, the daily life of a creole with cosmopolitan ambitions. He would like to have been born in many other countries, but it was his misfortune "to be born on that wretched island." With what sadness he informs us of the scarcity of books, the lack of secondary educational institutions and of universities, the abuses on the part of the rulers, and the civilian and ecclesiastical censorship! Few paragraphs better define the lethargic state of colonial life than this one: "In this miniscule portion of the earth, everything is lacking. . . . It is almost virgin in terms of life and the march toward enlightenment and good, compared with others. Three centuries of lethargy and routine ignorance, of unconscious but damaging egoism, could not have produced anything else."[2] At another point, he describes with successful irony the sadness of colonial life, as is the case in his entertaining "Puerto Rico, visto sin espejuelos por un cegato" ("Puerto Rico, Seen Without Spectacles by a Myopic Man") in 1876.

Tapia belongs to a generation of writers who investigated the roots of colonial imbalance; his sharpest darts were aimed at slavery and its consequences. In slavery he saw the element which destroyed the morality of the day-laborers. From among many descriptions, a few pages stand out which could be considered a sort of short political-historical essay. Here he comes out on the side of the "Antillean serf," whose fate is worse than that of the European proletarian because "he starts off by not owning even the property of his person." We must not forget that from among

Cubans and Puerto Ricans came the most energetic of abolitionist voices: José María de Labra, Julio L. Vizcarrondo, José Julián Acosta, Segundo Ruiz Belvis, and Eugenio María de Hostos. To fight against the pass-books and in favor of freedom for the slaves meant, as Hostos points out so well, to fight for "the emancipation of the Antilles, and their independence meant the ruin of all the privileges on which they live."

In few thinkers are the hopes and disillusionment of this first period in our cultural history reflected as they are in Hostos. Like Ramón Emeterio Betances (1827–1899) and Segundo Ruiz Belvis (1829–1867), almost unknown outside the country, Hostos was one of those proud Puerto Ricans "who did not wish to suffer the homeland's slavery." He was, as he himself called Ruiz Belvis, a vagabond of freedom, increasingly disillusioned, who often tried to convey reason's voice through caustic insults.

Out of Alonso's convulsive Puerto Rico, in the decades of the 1860s and 1870s, another, more organized, country emerges. Hostos' work is complex and all-embracing: education, progress, industrialization, freedom, independence, pan-Americanism. His reform program contained all the progressive and democratic ideas espoused by the ascendant philosophical schools of Europe and America: Krausism, positivism, utopian socialism. He always concerned himself with those doctrines which could best advance the interests of his country and his class. He belonged to a group of radical revolutionary nationalists, Puerto Rican and Cuban, whose thinking was based on concepts of radical and social equality. He was among the first thinkers to present the problems of the blacks, of the mestizos, of the Indians. Hostos, together with Betances (who was even more revolutionary), represents our nineteenth-century process and its objectives. His thinking reveals the contradictions of an entire epoch, our birth pangs. He was always inspired by a belief in America as the homeland of justice and liberty. Teaching, education, would be the basis of spiritual reforms and social betterment.

With the September Revolution of 1868 in Spain, he was naively confident that freedom and independence would come to Cuba and Puerto Rico. From his comrades-in-struggle in Spain he had received promises of autonomy. In the metropolis itself he saw how the problem of the two Antilles was ignored and post-poned; he then broke with Spain in an impassioned speech in the Madrid Atheneum, where he declared himself a federalist re-publican and, above all, an American: "Colonist, product of colo-nial despotism, restrained by this in my emotions, in my thoughts, in my actions, I avenged myself on it by conceiving of a definitive form of freedom and envisioning a political confederation. Be-cause I am an American, because I am a colonist, because I am a Puerto Rican, I am a federalist."[3]

In 1868 he found himself in agreement with other Puerto Ricans and Cubans for whom armed struggle, initiated with the Grito de Lares, was the only possible way to put an end to col-onialism. Despite his break with Spain, he still felt confident, with the advent of the First Republic, that his friends on the Iberian Peninsula would also proclaim a republic in Puerto Rico, or that they would at least be able to implement important reforms that would eventually lead to freedom. After a short time he felt betrayed. Pain then made him exclaim with sarcasm that the Spanish Republic was a "republic of charlatans," a "child's game." His beautiful essay entitled "En la tumba de Ruiz Belvis" contains a biting reproach to a Spain that was shaken by deep convulsions, prey to social and economic conflicts that would culminate in the Restoration.

Manuel Fernández Juncos (1846–1928), Salvador Brau (1842–1912) and Francisco del Valle Atiles (1847–1917) document some of the negative effects on the laboring classes of the last years of Spanish domination. In *El Buscapié* (1877–1896), Manuel Fernández Juncos made passionate attacks on the poverty, prosti-tution, and ignorance of the working classes; on emigration and the moral ambiance in which the workers and agricultural labor-ers lived. Brau wrote eloquent sociological pages about laborers and peasants in his polemical *Ecos de la batalla* (1886). Equally valuable and important is the work of Del Valle Atiles, *El campe-sino puertorriqueño* (1887). Here we find a type of social philosophy that complements Brau's *La campesina* (1885) and *Las clases jornaleras* (1882). The central theme of both thinkers is education: the social weaknesses of the field workers are the result of the lack of instruction, of isolation, poor nutrition, the climate. Games of chance, cock fights, concubinage, the lack of religiosity, can all be resolved through a good educational system. There is also an aggressive defense of the day-laborer; Brau even suggests the creation of cooperatives to solve the proletariat's problems.

Both authors seem to have been familiar with European sociological literature. The defense of the laboring classes, the need to attract them by advocating better working conditions, schools, consumer cooperatives, credit banks, forms part of an international movement in favor of workers' demands that was initiated by the French and English utopian socialists: Saint-Simon, Charles Fourier, Etienne Cabet, Robert Owen. Furthermore, in the period in which Atiles and Brau were writing, the First International had been formed and the socialist and anarchist movements had developed and gained strength in many European and American countries.

The date these studies were published is important: in the decade of the 1880s there emerged in Puerto Rico a strong separatist movement among all social classes, as a result of the sugar crisis. The *jíbaros*, or agricultural laborers, emerged as a social force and began to worry the reformist liberals who were anxious to attract them. In addition, in 1886 the agricultural crisis forced more than 30,000 workers to stop work. The peasants, who had not shared the progress gained by the ruling class, lived at subsistence level. The crisis flung them into unemployment and insurrection, and *jíbaros* participated in the emancipation movements of 1887, 1896, and 1898.

Brau and Del Valle Atiles exposed the poverty of the peasantry and demanded a speedy remedy. They felt they could help to raise the call for social justice; they denounced discrimination against peasants and day-laborers. A patriotic and rebel spirit predominated; in the most remote parts of the countryside they found an agrarian creed, a growing attitude in defense of the dispossessed. In 1895, another progressive liberal, Mariano Abril Ostaló, described in somber tones the life of these day-laborers in the pages of *La Democracia:* "The peasant is the *beast of burden* who suffers the whip and lowers his head and walks on, walks on until one day weakness prostrates him, work overcomes him, and he falls in the nearest corner, leaving behind him his miserable progeny who will follow him in their toil and in ill-treatment and in humiliations."[4]

These thinkers did not acknowledge the class struggle. Their writing was aimed at promoting happiness and well-being. They tended to reconcile classes and antagonisms; they wished to transform society on the moral plane. From positivism and naturalism especially, Brau acquired a kind of historic and ethnic determinism. When describing the Puerto Rican, for instance, he stated: "There you have the primordial sources of our character: from the Indian we adapted the qualities of indolence, taciturnity, selflessness, and hospitality; from the African, resistance, vigorous sensuality, superstition, and fatalism; the Spaniards introduced their gentlemanly earnestness, their characteristic haughtiness, festive tastes, austere devotion, constancy in adversity, and love for homeland and independence."[5]

The struggle among the political parties and (as of 1887) the power of the autonomists, as opposed to the assimilationists, the pressures of the radical groups, and, above all, the Spaniards' fear of another war like the one they were fighting in Cuba, finally brought about a Charter of Autonomy in 1897, but it came too late. The new legislation allowed for a certain degree of local initiative, and for commercial treaties that would favor the creole bourgeoisie. But in July 1898, the United States armed forces disembarked in Guánica, which is possibly where Columbus landed, bringing the first colonialism to America.[6] On October 16, 1898, Puerto Rico passed into the hands of the United States, whose expansionist aims had long ago fixed on the Antilles and had hit a responsive chord in a group of local plantation owners and landowners who had been asking Washington for help. They trusted they would find support from their partners in the north in their own struggle against the usurious practices of the Spanish commission-agents and thereby guarantee more secure trade. Betances' warnings had been in vain; he had said that only independence would be "able to save us from the American minotaur; I believe in the near-future independence of my country. . . .The powerful are powerful only because *we* are on our knees. Let us stand up."[7]

During the first months of U.S. military occupation, until the peace treaty was signed, some weak voices of protest were heard. An article published in *El País* stands out: "We do not want to disappear from the planet in an ignominious manner, and since after fifty years with *you* nothing would remain of our race, not a memory of it nor of its customs, its traditions, anything, *we swear to die before we become your slaves*."[8]

Another, equally valid, analysis came from Hostos, who in 1889 went before the U.S. Congress with Rafael del Valle, Julio H. Henna, and Manuel Zeno Gandía to present Puerto Rico's case and ask for a plebiscite. The delegates' speeches were published in a small book, *El caso de Puerto Rico*, and in the prologue Hostos reaffirmed his hope for freedom, his faith in justice. The conference was prepared, he says, "in order to show the people of the United States of America and the whole world that the people of Puerto Rico will not submit in silence to being treated as slaves, or as dependent beings. . . . The Puerto Rican people, on asking the nation to which they have been annexed to apply to them the principles of the first act of its own statutes, are not asking for grace; they are demanding justice."

But the prevailing attitude toward the United States was one which saw it as the "bastion of freedom and a center of progress." For more than half a century active trade with the United States had been developing, which made the landowners look with sympathy on the metropolis, as had happened in Cuba.[9]

Many liberal reformers believed that, with the mighty colossus of the north in command, progress, development, and independence would not be long in coming.[10] Between 1898 and 1900, the Island suffered a military government which did not change until the year after the adoption of the Foraker Law, which gave the president of the United States the right to appoint a U.S. civilian as governor. Charles Hubert Allen was followed by others, until finally in 1946, in the Fortress of San Juan, the first Puerto Rican governor, Jesús Teodoro Piñero, was installed, with Washington's blessing.

This first stage of Puerto Rican thought contrasts strongly with ideological and literary movements in the rest of Spanish America. The battle was prolonged in Cuba and Puerto Rico, the last colonial vestiges, and they struggled more tenaciously. Several years had passed since the last American country had freed itself from Spanish colonialism, yet the two Antilles remained subject to Spanish domination. As a consequence, literary creation and thought were given over to the polemical article, to topical works, and to party manifestos. In the rest of the Americas, however, a number of essayists had emerged at the beginning of the nineteeth century to give intellectual expression to the ideological revolution in the American world.[11] A large number of writers appeared who were bent on the task of discovering America, discovering themselves: Esteban Echeverría, Juan B. Alberdi, Domingo F. Sarmiento, Juan Montalvo. They threw themselves into the rediscovery of their own roots and their books demonstrated a consciousness of unity that would later take on a more nationalist character. In 1864, Francisco Bilbao published his *Evangelio de América*; in 1867 *La América*, by José Victorino Lastarria, appeared; in 1883 *Conflictos y armonías de las razas de América*, by Sarmiento. Finally, and within this end-of-the-century line, the words of few authors resounded as loudly as those of José Enrique Rodó, who gave expression to the Americanist spirit, to the values of our continent. *Ariel* (1900) is perhaps the most consummate example of idealism and the exaltation of values in opposition to the crude materialism of the north which was already beginning to show its fangs. Rubén Darío also challenged the other (Anglo-Saxon) America in such essays as "El triunfo de Calibán." What images and pointed metaphors are those of this wrathful Darío! In his hands the Yankee becomes a "red gorilla," a frightening and grotesque buffoon, a menacing monster. In his *Cantos de vida y esperanza* (1905), he includes his proud and combative ode to Theodore Roosevelt in which he challenges the "powerful and great" United States in the name of a spiritual supremacy. Rodó and Darío invite us to examine the Hispano-Christian sources of Spanish America against

> el futuro invasor
> de la América ingenua que tiene sangre indígena,
> que aún reza a Jesucristo y aún habla en español.

the future invader
of that ingenuous America which has indigenous blood
that still prays to Jesus and still speaks Spanish.

In the Antilles, two figures mark the end of the century—José Martí and Eugenio María de Hostos—figures whose vigorous mental freedom and noble actions were the very expression of American unity. In both we find a constant involvement with ethical affirmation, yet as part of transforming activities Martí went much further: his criticism of United States democracy and his crystal-clear observations on capitalist society place him among the first to denounce imperialism as such. Hostos often took a liberal-reformist position, although he did on occasion call for armed struggle, just as Betances did in 1898, almost on the eve of his death: "I do not want [us] to be a colony, either of Spain or of the United States! What are the Puerto Ricans? Why do they not rebel?"

Revolutionaries or liberals, with these first generations of Puerto Ricans a new realistic and critical sense of life emerged; they were a part of the liberal bourgeoisie, bent on gaining control of economic and political enterprises. They were the carriers of penetrating sentiments and thoughts, they accumulated and assimilated experiences which played a decisive role, although they were not able to reach the proposed historical objectives that were necessary at that time.

2. After the United States Invasion

After 1898, the same problems and solutions as those developed during Spanish colonialism continued. The ruling class continued divided between the autonomists and the annexationists, while among intellectuals a resistance to the total adoption of the values and features of the dominant country predominated. Despite the changes imposed on its culture and way of life, Puerto Rico continued a Hispanic country. The awakening in the decade of the 1930s would merely reaffirm this first spark of wholeness.

Cultural affirmation attracted both the left and the right, or, to put it another way, the separatists and the annexationists. The former opposed Hispanic and Catholic culture and invited everyone to a fond return to the Spanish past; the latter often maintained that the Hispanic-Christian base was so deep that annexation to the United States world would not endanger it. Luis Muñoz Rivera (1859–1913) and José Celso Barbosa (1857–1921) to some extent represent this group: they are ambivalent, wavering figures.[12] It is with them that the idea of Puerto Rico as "a bridge between two cultures" arose, an idea that was to have its most fervent defenders in the 1940s.

In the first years after the U.S. invasion, certain forms of writing abounded: polemical articles, political manifestos, calls to the people analyzing certain laws or other measures, and denunciations of colonialism. Each important historical moment is reflected in the arts: the Foraker Law of 1900, the protests against U.S. citizenship as imposed by the U.S. Congress (Jones Law), the emergence of political parties.[13]

The most notable liberal intellectuals of the first generation of Puerto Ricans under U.S. imperialism were defenders of the opposition within the regime. The creole petty bourgeoisie suffered from a lack of national consciousness, a fact which corresponded to its slow and irregular economic development within the stultifying structures of the Spanish colony. Rosendo Matienzo Cintrón (1855–1913) and José de Diego (1867–1918) fought from the ranks of the Union Party to gain the independence of Puerto Rico. They trusted in the magnanimity of the U.S. people, who would be the best guarantors of the island's sovereignty. With them we see the beginning of the interminable polemic and struggle for Puerto Rican citizenship, which was ultimately denied when U.S. citizenship was imposed in 1917 during the First World War as a solution to the U.S. army's need for soldiers.

De Diego and Matienzo Cintrón proposed a lukewarm and temporizing reformism; they saw the political struggle in terms totally lacking in social content. They did not make any deep economic analysis. Their best and most combative pages advocate political resistance and spiritual and cultural progress. With this generation, the voices of Spanish-Americanism languished: the visions of Martí and Hostos were extinguished, to reappear some years later.

De Diego maintains a constant dialogue, an open polemic with U.S. personages, although he does not express this directly. This gives an aggressive quality to his essays and articles: he seeks to affirm himself before the invaders, he accuses them, he besieges them. His best articles are informed by a spirit of political dialogues, in which the adversary's identity is implicit. "No" or "La Independencia" have a listener whom he confronts with his point of view, his beliefs. How passionate is De Diego in his struggles against the U.S. Senate, in his attempt to strengthen the dignity of the Puerto Rican people! His "Carta Cívica" to Senator Miles Poindexter is an example of his passion and his faith, but at the same time of his lack of understanding of the social and economic forces behind the U.S. occupation. "So, Mister Senator, you wish to make us citizens of an inferior and special kind, citizens whose country is not permitted to join you as an independent state, because the citizenship of the United States is incompatible with another national citizenship. If we cannot be one of your states, nor form our own nation, then we shall perpetually have to be a colony, a possession of the United States. Is that the citizenship you offer us? Well, that citizenship we reject! We reject it as an affront to the personality and the dignity of the Puerto Rican people and as a distortion of the justice and the democracy of the American people."[14]

The writers of the first generation under the dominion of the United States reflect the fluctuations and hopes which had characterized the island spirit after its occupation in 1898. Penetration by imperialism elicited a tone of disillusionment, even of bitterness. Matienzo Cintrón found occasion for irony, for ridicule, for mockery. In "La guachafita fá," he comments on citizenship with a festive and playful but always sharp tone: "*La guachafita fá* is American citizenship for Puerto Ricans. If you ask for it in good faith they won't give it to you, on the ground that you already have Puerto Rican citizenship in a union of Americans;

that American citizenship is a very bad thing that would ruin
Puerto Rico, since there are already too many niggers in the
United States to be adding a million more."

In the same calm tone, he puts a finger right on U.S. racism.
There would be, he says, three citizenships in the metropolis, two
on the continent, and the third in Puerto Rico: "The citizenship of
North American whites, of North American blacks, and of Puerto
Ricans. That of the masters, that of the freed slaves, and that of
the poor idiots in noncontiguous countries who don't speak English."

And he ends with a self-criticism that deserves to be quoted:
"We no longer want to be governed by you, either with or without
citizenship. There was a time when we thought freedom couldn't
be had without you. Later we thought we could get it with you or
without you. Now we think that true freedom, which brings with
it the sovereignty of our own government, can't be had with you
but only without you, perhaps against you."[15]

The second generation of writers is burdened with bitterness
and a sense of impotence. It is their concern with politics, the
party game, that stands out. Previous voices were immersed in
debate and polemics with the occupation forces; then a struggle
with the country itself, with their compatriots, began and this has
lasted to the present. Now we see the emergence of what seems to
be one of the fine qualities of the literature and thought of Puerto
Rico: the Island framework. The writers try to enamor, to seduce,
to attack, to torture. Their public is the Island reader; they try to
warn them or move them so that they will return to the right path,
so that they will not be misled or dazzled by fictitious and apparent realities. They denounce the sad social reality, the moral and
physical impoverishment of their people; often discouraged by
the lack of response, they hurl insults, they denigrate. This quality, I believe, lasts until the present; *El puertorriqueño dócil* (1960)
by René Marqués (1919–1979) is a good example of this type of
writing.

This need to speak with the Island world imparts a hybrid
character to Puerto Rican essays and literature: Island novels
become political and moral disquisitions, essays border on the
article or propaganda leaflet. What the writers try to communi-

cate is that, far from improvement of the country's economic and social situation, its problems have been exacerbated. The insertion of Puerto Rico into the U.S. economic orbit resulted in crisis and the ruin of the coffee industry and a 95 percent reduction in the sugar tariff. Then monoculture developed and with it the creation of an absentee industry that dominated the Island's coastal region. With the disappearance of small landowners and the technification of the sugar mills, which belonged to large foreign consortia, an impoverished proletariat earning starvation wages emerged. The United States did not bring the hoped-for development, but rather ruin and exploitation.

Miguel Meléndez Muñoz (1884–1965) gave voice to the life of this peasant in novels, stories, and essays. In 1916 he published his moving and penetrating *Estado social del campesino puertorriqueño*. He did not idealize the *jíbaro* world: he observed directly, along the lines of Brau and Del Valle Atiles, but in a different historical context.

Nemesio R. Canales (1878–1923) and the older writer Manuel Zeno Gandía (1855–1930) also protested poverty and exploitation. *Paliques* (1913) by the former and the novels and articles of the latter paint a somber portrait of colonial life and poverty. Let us recall the framework of Zeno Gandía's *La charca* (1894) and *Garduña* (1896), which he subtitled "chronicles of a sick world." Anticipating future writers, he analyzes social, moral, and human corruption. The Puerto Rican counterpoint of coffee and sugarcane is revealed; the novelist seeks its countenance through objective and scientific observation. The human document is the working people and their revolutionary upsurge, which is already beginning to be felt. Santiago Iglesias Pantín (1870–1939), a poor Galician immigrant, did in political reality speak for the new socialists in the Puerto Rican proletariat. At about this time he began the arduous task of creating consciousness, and he exhorted his comrades, introducing a new vocabulary. At that time, he wrote: "The word 'worker,' which elicits enthusiasm, respect, and even terror in Europe and America, is completely unknown in this country." With the end of the century, Puerto Rican worker populism already had its spokespeople.[16] Pantín brought the voice and conscience, Zeno Gandía offered in his novels a clear image of oppression and an as yet unorganized restless spirit.

Socialism began to sink roots. The Socialist Party was founded in 1900, but neither the problems nor the class antagonisms were resolved, despite a series of strikes that spread throughout the island in 1904, when there were about 8,600 organized workers.

Nemesio Canales reexamines these same antagonisms, with an ironic, biting, but well-aimed thrust. Among his polemical essays eight, published under the title of *Riqueza y pobreza*, stand out. Here he speaks in favor of the working class and against capitalism. With Canales, we might say, the concerns and dilemmas of the twentieth century are sharpened. The period of vague illusions, of unfulfilled hopes, closes, although Canales never presents remedies that might transform the situation. However, he dissects the social layers and classes and the interests of each. His vision of money as the instrument of oppression and conquest echos some of the ideas of José Ingenieros, Carlos Mariátegui, and Manuel González Prada. Take, for example, the following statements: "Poverty makes us weak, makes us ignorant and coarse, turns us into a permanent display of ugliness and filth, into a perennial nucleus of villainy and of sloth and of crime, into a tremendous and infectious virus in which all ills, all wretchedness, are latent." The influence of naturalist determinism can be seen here: "Because they are poor, our children grow up feeble and sickly, without blood in their veins, without light in their minds."

On another occasion, he defends radical social theories: the eighth and last essay of *Riqueza y pobreza* advocates state capitalism, the socialization of property and of work. These changes, he says, would stimulate the creation of "a new, strong, and beautiful society which I can already feel approaching like a hurricane."

Canales has socializing ideas, but according to what we know about him it would seem that he does not have a socialist ideology. Likewise, he displays an extensive knowledge of foreign thought and literature. Unfortunately, his work as an essayist was fragmentary; he was not able to structure his thinking in one, all-encompassing study. But he was, in large measure, a window on the world; he was a sharpshooter without too many followers.[17]

Zeno Gandía, who spent more than twenty years in silence, reemerged in this decade with new political and literary ardor, in order to attack imperialism. Furthermore, one can perceive a substantial change in his style—from his early realism and naturalism he moved to a vigorous modernist prose. For him, writing is not a way to worship art, but rather a sacred undertaking aimed at unmasking the alien life and the vast scabrous source of colonialism. Even in his first novels, written at the end of the century, Zeno Gandía had denounced exploitation; in his *Crónicas de un mundo enfermo* (a title which embraces his entire narrative work), he referred to peasant life and to his own country as a great organism beset by innumerable ills. Now he returns with renewed zeal; his two urban novels, *El negocio* (1922) and *Redentores* (1925), focus on the U.S. racism and contempt that had shackled the island's spirit and culture. He denounces errors and tries to present ideals to a repressed and drifting people. He was writing, he said, for the future. In the letter to Mariano Abril written in 1925, he commented: ". . . Puerto Rican books remain in the bookstores. . . . It seems that no one cares to know our own environment; and in the face of this ill, which would seem to be incurable, we have no alternative but to write for future times."[18]

El negocio refers, of course, to the sale of the country to foreign businesses and monopolies; the "redeemers" are the exploiters, the Puerto Rican allies of the invader, the sellers of the territory, the compromises, the greed. Few descriptions project this image better than this from the well-known chapter 18 of *Redentores,* which uses the Spanish fortress of El Morro at the entrance of San Juan harbor as a metaphor: "It was El Morro, the tremor of El Morro projecting shock waves, leaping of waves, cones of foam; the sea and El Morro the feared sea, turning over enraged as if boiling in the hatred of centuries among the impulses of high tide and the swoons of ebb tide, subjected to a formidable undertow, to an impetuous and docile current, to fierce and deafening northers, succumbing in spasms of convulsive swells; it was the sea, El Morro, fulminating whip lashes of chained rage, howling funereal psalmodies, furiously shaking the colony's bulk, as if to awaken it from its deep slumber of servitude."

Impassioned by events, the old liberal vociferates and writes with a furious pen. Also representative of his spirited thought is the answer he gave in a survey prepared by *Indice* in 1929. To the question, "What are we as a people?" he answered: ". . . Puerto Rico isn't a nation because it lacks the necessary conditions to be one. . . . [It] is a nation of hostages. . . . We were better off once than we are now. There is depression in our country. A misunderstood positivism seems intent on killing the legitimate aspirations that our people always had. One might think we were being corrupted by the clouded prisms, through which we look at life."

3. A New Consciousness

It was in these conditions of indecision and search that the Nationalist Junta emerged in 1922; finally the Nationalist Party was created in 1928, and Pedro Albizu Campos was elected its president in 1930. Contrary to the traditional way of carrying on political struggle through parliamentary methods and electoral decisions, under Albizu's presidency the new group advocated armed struggle in its commitment to independence. Although it did not achieve all of its objectives, there is no doubt that it signified a qualitative change in Puerto Rican politics and in the country's attitude towards the United States and the rest of the Latin American world.

The emergence of the Nationalist Party coincided, furthermore, with the development of workers' groups, above all the General Confederation of Labor (CGT, created in 1932), and the Communist Party, which was officially formed in 1934, and gained influence among the landless peasants and cane-cutters. The history of this stage of the labor movement is now being studied; in any case, Albizu Campos has always been recognized as one of the first political leaders to denounce imperialism in its economic, military, and cultural aspects, even though he embraced a heritage of Hispano-Christian values. From this vantage point he opposed imperialism, often on moral grounds. In commenting on the first thirty years of Yankee intervention, he explained: "Christian civilization has imposed the rule of law in the internal life and foreign relations of nations. There have been violent attacks on this rule but, out of fear of relapsing into barbarism, it is undeniably respected."[19]

The pro-independence upsurge is closely linked to the Wall Street crash. As a result of the crisis, poverty spread, followed by a wave of strikes. Politicization of the working sector and nationalist fervor culminated in the jailing of Albizu in 1937 and strong repression by the state, the best example of which was what has come to be called the Ponce Massacre (March 21, 1937): a bloody act committed against a group of some 2,000 persons who had come together in that southern city to celebrate the anniversary of the abolition of slavery. The colonial police fired on the demonstrators, dealing a severe blow to the nationalist movement and to the pro-independence movement in general.

But other forces had been at work. In 1936 Luis Muñoz Marín created the Popular Democratic Party (PPD) and it came to power in 1940. The party had a program of social reform and economic progress, and based itself on a populist and peasant base. Later it would intensify the process of industrialization. From 1940 on it became clear that for the PPD the Island was not a nation, but rather a peripheral fragment of the United States, separated politically and economically from the Hispanic world and from the socialist bloc. This support for neocolonialism alienated some intellectual sectors which, discontented with the definitively colonialist turn of events, created the Independence Party (PIP) in 1945; its electoral policy continues to the present day. Furthermore, in 1946 Operation Bootstrap was initiated and the Island became a great U.S. factory, to the detriment of agriculture and the rural areas. Time and again the *independentistas* (now divided into two factions after the Movement for Independence [MPI] was created in 1959) were to unmask U.S. colonialism before the United Nations, while the groups in power persecuted the various leftist groups.

These changes and perspectives are reflected in the essays written during those years. In the 1930s there was an upsurge in the area of ideas. A sign of this rebirth was the magazines *Revista de las Antillas* (1913–1914) and *Indice* (1929–1931), where many pro-independence intellectuals collaborated, most of them followers of Matienzo Cintrón and of De Diego. *Indice* pointed an accusing finger at the past and was a guide for the future. On August 13, 1930, Vicente Géigel Polanco (1904–1979), one of its young editors, wrote an important article, "La desorientación política," which was representative of the climate of opinion of the period: "It is not the time to formulate reproaches. It is the time to examine our conscience, to rectify erroneous plans, to trace a correct path for collective thought." Géigel would subsequently join the PPD and, discontented, abandon it much later on.

He there presents a brief analysis of the colonizing process at the cultural and political level, reproaching the Puerto Rican and the intellectual for having "cooperated for thirty-two years in a policy of deplorable deals."

The generation of 1930, which gathered around *Indice*, focused its efforts on the affirmation of Hispanic values and tried to alter national consciousness.[20] Since 1898, the United States had exerted pressure in order to impose its culture through schools, the university, the media, and propaganda, trying to impede indigenous cultural development in an effort to perpetuate its dominance. This generation tried to prod the country, warning that political annexation would be accompanied by cultural denationalization. Lost in the vacillations of the nineteenth-century reformists, who often hesitated between independence or annexation, electoral struggle or armed struggle, the young people asked in an important survey initiated in *Indice* in 1929: What are we? What are we like? The results of this analysis were not long in coming; by 1934-1935, the two most important books devoted to explaining Puerto Ricans and their future appeared: *Insularismo* by Antonio S. Pedreira, and *Prontuario histórico de Puerto Rico* by Tomás Blanco.

The magazine also represented a new opening toward the rest of Hispanic America. Contributions appeared from the Peruvian Juan Carlos Mariátegui, from the Cuban Juan Marinello, and from the great Argentine essayist Manuel Ugarte, one of the most impassioned critics of U.S. imperialism. Marinello called on Puerto Ricans to join with the Cuban people against the invader's capitalism. It is well known that Cuban anti-imperialism was intensified as a result of the struggle against the dictator Gerardo Machado. In 1927, the so-called Minority Group emerged, united around *Revista de Avance* (1927–1930),[21] composed of Marinello, Rubén Martínez Villena, and Alejo Carpentier, among others. *Indice* appeared, then, as a kind of counterpart in the other Antilles.

The Puerto Rican essay of those years reflects Spanish American ideas, although in a minor key. That first rediscovery of America, proclaimed by the intellectuals of the nineteenth century, was followed now by a movement of nationalist exaltation in all countries of the continent: Pedro Henríquez Ureña, *Seis ensayos en busca de nuestra expresión* (1928); Juan Marinello, *Sobre la inquietud cubana* (1930); Mariano Picón Salas, *Hispanoamérica, posición crítica* (1931); Ezequiel Martínez Estrada, *Radiografía de la pampa* (1933); and Samuel Ramos, *El perfil del hombre y la cultura en México* (1934).

The political and economic crisis resulting from the depression of 1929–1930 intensified the search for permanent, indigenous values. From north to south the question was: What are we? What are we like? From the Río Grande to Patagonia both the national oligarchies and the radical groups witnessed the end of the democratic experience, a disillusionment with revolutionary movements, and sank into metaphysical self-analysis. In Cuba, after the fervor of the 1920s, the efforts of the revolutionary movement against Machado failed; Argentina suffered the death-rattles of a world crisis, which began to destroy the structure of a cocksure Argentina; Mexico experienced internal chaos, a product of politicking and *caudillismo*, until in 1934 Lázaro Cárdenas took office and made important social and economic reforms.

In the Dominican Republic, Pedro Henríquez Ureña professed his faith in the continental destiny and in the possibility of triumphing over the United States: "If the spirit has triumphed, in our America, over internal barbarism, there is no danger that external barbarism will overcome it. Alien power does not dazzle us: power is always ephemeral."[22] And at another time he exclaimed: "Our America sails without a compass on the turbulent sea of contemporary humanity"[23]—an image which Pedreira was

34 *Iris M. Zavala*

to use a few years later, although limiting himself to speaking about Puerto Rico. In Argentina, Eduardo Mallea sought an internal balance in *Conocimiento y expresión de la Argentina* (1937). The cult of the gaucho, of Peruvianism, of the Chilean *roto*, reappeared, among many other expressions of nationalist rebirth.

Puerto Rico entered fully into this current. There, as in the other countries, the intellectuals sought a solution to its problems through the efforts of the educated minority. In the 1930s, they incorporated the people's demands into their programs as an aspect of the political struggle. It is important to understand this element when examining the Afro-Antilleanism of Nicolás Guillén and Luis Palés Matos, for example, [24] or the idealization of the *jíbaro* in Luis Llorens Torres, [25] or the short story collection *Terrazo* (1947) by Abelardo Díaz Alfaro, as well as the essays of Miguel Meléndez Muñoz and the novel *La llamarada* (1935) by Enrique Laguerre.

Around *Indice*, Llorens Torres, Pedreira, and Blanco met with outstanding young intellectuals: Juan Antonio Corretjer, Margot Arce de Vázquez, Francisco Manrique Cabrera, Palés Matos (he published his first poems in the magazine), Concha Meléndez. Later they were joined by Isabel Gutiérrez del Arroyo, Monelisa Pérez Marchand, Nilita Vientós Gastón, and María Teresa Babín. That is to say, Pedreira, Llorens, and Blanco, from the professor's podium, from the Atheneum, or from their books, guided those younger in their search for a Hispanicism, for some roots with which to confront an imperialism that was forcing the progressive deculturization of Puerto Rico and its assimilation into the United States. In Madrid, Mexico, and the United States, these young people studied Puerto Rican, Spanish-American, and Spanish themes. They battled in favor of their cultural values, in favor of their language, their spirit, trying to rescue them from the past. The university and the Atheneum (founded in 1876) provided their platform, until in 1976 the pro-independence majority left the Atheneum after a bitter struggle against a conservative leadership. Today, guardians of the voices of liberation are to be heard in the university and/or in activities of the Casa de Cultura and the magazine *Sin Nombre*, headed by Nilita Vientós Gastón.

Indeed, opposition in the cultural sector has been difficult, because the cultural aspect forms an integral part of the unsheathed weapons of domination. The invaders have tried to stop the development of culture, which always brings a consciousness of one's own capacity for freedom. The most celebrated triumph of the *Indice* generation was in the realm of language: in 1905, English was made compulsory in the Island's schools and did not cease to be so until 1948, although it has not been eliminated completely.

In Puerto Rico the somber background of social and economic reality is justified and defended by some political and educational institutions which reflect the efforts of the U.S. occupier to subject the island to a process of cultural assimilation. Today military bases occupy 100,000 acres of the best arable land, thus making the Pentagon the largest latifundist in Puerto Rico. In addition, there are some 800 factories which earn net profits of 80 to 90 percent, and some 50,000 North Americans hold key posts in banking, commerce, and industry. These forces stifle all manifestations of Puerto Rican personality: the imposition of values occurs parallel with a total dependency on the United States.[26]

Intellectuals from the 1930s to the 1950s most directly suffered the process of transculturation and the inadequacy of their ideological postulates. Once again, in 1950, there was an attempt at insurrection on the part of the Nationalist faction and since then the so-called "gag" law has been in effect, wiping out all possibility of opposition and struggle by dissident groups. Once again Albizu Campos was jailed, not to leave prison until shortly before his death in 1965.

In 1952, the Free Associated State (officially called the Commonwealth) was proclaimed, and consciousness of an increasingly limited autonomy embittered some sectors of the liberal and pro-independence bourgeoisie, which undertook a purely cultural struggle, at times only nominal, for Hispano-Christian values. Increasingly, however, it became clear that Puerto Rico could not function as a bridge between two cultures. The fruits in this sense are minimal and most unoriginal.

In recent years new alternatives to the national question have appeared. The Cuban Revolution in 1959, the formation of the

Movimiento Pro Independencia (MPI), today the Puerto Rican
Socialist Party (PSP), the clash with the counterrevolutionary
Cuban immigrants, the Latin American guerrilla movements,
have stimulated new generations of young people who are
emerging from a political and cultural languor. Poetry journals
have appeared, such as *Guajana, Mester, Palestra, Versiones, Zona de
carga y descarga* (1973–1975). Other journals have appeared that
are more political, especially *Claridad* (organ of the PSP), *Rebelión*
(Partido Nacionalista de Cataño), *El Socialista* (small group led
by Corretjer), *La Hora* (1971–1973, a weekly led by César Andreu
Iglesias), *La Escalera* (1966–1973), *Pensamiento Crítico,* and *Nueva
Lucha,* defending new historical alternatives. In contrast to the
passive or pacified Puerto Rican, to the cultural hybridism and
the return to the Spanish past, these young people represent a
vanguard movement struggling against the past, trying to understand and explain it; against colonialism, against capitalism, and
against sluggish and co-opted pro-independence movements.
The vision they project is that of a militant human being, conscious of the need to join with the Latin American and Third
World vanguard.

This new attitude has been expressed especially in poetry, the
short story, and drama.[27] In contrast to the political and cultural
positions of their teachers and of the previous generation, and to
their diffuse resistance, the new groups have established the
relation between imperialism and culture with greater critical
awareness, and have directly confronted its economic and social
aspects. Now the combativity grows; the new generation often
expresses innovative points of view which had heretofore not
been heard. These recent manifestations which contribute to the
struggle against political and cultural forms are without a doubt
nourished by all of our failures and lacunae. Their critical flavor
has been intensified and areas of knowledge and struggle are
being rediscovered which had appeared to be buried or forgotten. There is no break with the old, but rather an integration, a
purification, a new sharpening of weapons. Culture, language,
history are revived with renewed pride and confidence.[28]

The essays which we have collected in this volume reveal the
hesitations and concerns of the Puerto Rican intellectuals with

regard to the future of their country. While it is true that among our best essayists we can find other themes, such as those of artistic creation, the countryside, literary criticism, it is also true that historical, political, and sociological themes predominate.

The reader who reads this anthology to the end will see the image of a whole epoch, of a whole history, develop because each text in itself, and the order in which we have placed them, has a tendency to raise multiple confluent planes of reality.

In this selection, we have placed side by side reminiscences, debates, essays (in the broadest sense of the word), newspaper articles, fragments. That is, everything which might give the idea of a concrete multiplicity. We wanted to make the readers feel the heart-beat of history: its genesis, its achievements, its contradictions, its failures. The works which we have collected here appear before our eyes as a totality of the survivals and deteriorations of a world, which has a lot to do with our world, and they explain and clarify it.

Each text has notes which place it in perspective, and a bibliography for each author and each problem discussed. We are not writing literary history, but rather we are attempting to show the development of Puerto Rican intellectual consciousness. It is true that some writers and names who are doubtless important to the island's history have been left out, but their absence in no way alters the intention of this anthology. We have included the most significant authors, the key moments; others can and will write history and fill in all the gaps.

In the first part we include some of the most representative works from the period of the Spanish colony. Here are the attacks and the ups and downs which the nineteenth-century liberal reformists experienced in their struggle for autonomy and independence. Analogous themes reappear in the second part, wherein the transition from formal colonial status and the prolonged debates on sovereignty or annexation are examined. The third part marks a substantial change in attitude and even in style. Here we include only those articles that confront political themes, the solutions to economic and social problems. On the one hand, the manifestos of Albizu Campos, exhorting the people to armed struggle, and on the other, the declarations of Gilberto Concepción de Gracia (1909–1967), seeking national liberation through party elections. Here also are the observations of a good number of our intellectuals, analyzing various political alternatives: statehood, free statehood, revolution.

In order to present a broader panorama, we have also included an excellent analysis by César Andreu Iglesias (1915–1976) of the workers' movement and a very short, cogent essay by the anthropologist Eduardo Seda Bonilla (1925–) on the alienation of Puerto Ricans under the present system of government. Finally, cultural and linguistic concerns as such have been elaborated by the last three generations, and we have added some discussion on Puerto Ricans in New York (the divided nation), and on the role of women in the anti–imperialist struggle, which will help us to understand the new dimensions of reality even at the risk of error.

We witness the process of a revolutionary struggle which has already lasted more than one hundred and fifty years—first, against the Spanish metropolis, and since 1898, after the crisis in the colonial system, against the "colossus of the north." Thus, the cause of a free Puerto Rico has deep roots, and although the objectives have not yet been won (once again, the pro-statehood forces won the elections in 1976), the feeling in favor of independence has, for more than a century, been nourishing the resurgence of a nation.

Notes

1. *Diario de Cortes* (1891), Vol. II, p. 31; *Diario en Hostos* (México, 1944).
2. *Mis memorias o Puerto Rico cómo lo encontré y cómo lo dejo* (Barcelona: Ediciones Rumbos, 1968), p. 76. José María de Labra confirms this vision on describing, in 1885, a precarious Puerto Rico, lacking highways, factories, sugar mills, banks, normal schools for teachers, aqueducts, churches; see his *Puerto Rico en 1885* (Madrid, 1885). Thus, one can understand the necessity for positivist thinking under these conditions.
3. *Páginas escogidas* (Estrada, 1952), p. 59.
4. Cited by Lidio Cruz Monclova, *Historia de Puerto Rico en el siglo XIX* (1852; University of Puerto Rico, 1964), Vol. III, p. 358.
5. Salvador Brau, *Las clases jornaleras en Puerto Rico* (San Juan, 1882), p. 85.
6. There are doubts concerning Columbus' port of disembarkation. The different hypotheses are summarized by Loida Figueroa, *Breve historia de Puerto Rico* (San Juan: Editorial Edil, 1969), Vol. I, p. 55. See also Eugenio Fernández Méndez, *Proceso histórico de la conquista de Puerto Rico* (1508–1640), ICP,

1970; Arturo Morales Carrión, *Historia del pueblo de Puerto Rico (desde sus orígenes hasta el siglo XVIII)*, DIP, 1968.

7. It still remains for Betances to be thoroughly researched. See Carlos M. Rama, *Las Antillas para los antillanos* (San Juan: ICP, 1975), is an anthology of many of Betances' writings, letters, and speeches. See also Ada Suárez, *Obras del doctor Ramón E. Betances. II. Epistolario—1895* (Río Piedras: Ediciones Huracán, 1978).

8. Cited by Cruz Monclova, *Historia*, Vol. III, p. 220.

9. This North American attitude towards Puerto Rico can be seen in the following works: Edward Barbusse, S.J., *The United States in Puerto Rico: 1898-1900* (Chapel Hill, N.C.: The University of North Carolina Press, 1966); Henry K. Carroll, *Report on the Island of Porto Rico* (Washington, D.C.: Government Printing Office, 1889); William Dinwiddie, *Porto Rico: Its Conditions and Possibilities* (New York, 1889); Ramiro Guerra y Sánchez, *La expansión territorial de Estados Unidos a expensas de España y los países hispanoamericanos* (Havana, 1964); Walter La Feber, *The New Empire: An Interpretation of American Expansion, 1860-1898* (Ithaca, N.Y.: Cornell University Press, 1963). For other aspects, see Paul Nelson Chiles, *The Puerto Rico Press Reaction of the United States, 1888-1898*, Ph.D. diss. Philadelphia, 1944, and José A. Gontán, *Historia política-social de Puerto Rico hasta 1898* (San Juan: Editorial Esther, 1945). For the case of Cuba the works of Philip S. Foner may be consulted: *A History of Cuba and Its Relations with the United States*, 2 vols. (New York: International Publishers, 1962–1963); the work of Arthur F. Corwin, *Spain and the Abolition of Slavery in Cuba, 1817-1886* (San Antonio: University of Texas Press, 1967); and Franklin W. Knight, *Slave Society in Cuba During the Nineteenth Century* (Madison: University of Wisconsin Press, 1970).

10. See the excellent review by Gervasio García of the book by Manuel Maldonado Denis, *Puerto Rico: una interpretación histórico-social*, which appeared in *La Escalera* IV, no. 1 (June 1970): 23-31. It contains keen observations on commercial relations between Puerto Rico and the United States during the nineteenth century. In addition, the works of Eugenio Fernández Méndez should be consulted: *La identidad y la cultura* (rept. ed.; San Juan: ICP, 1965); *Historia de la cultura en Puerto Rico (1493-1960)* (San Juan: Editorial Rodadero, 1964); *The Sources of Puerto Rican Cultural History, A Critical Appraisal* (San Juan: Ediciones Cemí, 1967); *Ensayos de antropología popular* (Río Piedras: University of Puerto Rico, 1966); "Reflexiones sobre 50 años de cambio cultural en Puerto Rico," *Historia*, no. 2 (1955): 257-279; *Desarrollo histórico de la sociedad puertorriqueña* (San Juan: ICP, 1969).

11. It is not our intention to present a history of the Spanish-American essay; we merely wish to situate the Puerto Rican essay within a hemispheric context, which will permit it to be better understood. Interesting observations on the Spanish-American essay can be found in Carlos Ripoll, *Conciencia intelectual de América, antología del ensayo hispanoamericano (1836-1959)* (New York: Las Américas, 1966); Leopoldo Zea and Abelardo Villegas, *Antología del pensamiento social y político de América Latina* (Unión Panamericana, 1964); Solomon Lipp and Sylvia Ehrlich Lipp, *Hispanoamérica vista por sus ensayistas* (New York: Charles Scribner's & Sons, 1969); Martin S. Stabb, *In Quest of Identity: Patterns in the Spanish-American Essay of Ideas, 1890-1960* (Chapel Hill, N.C.: University of North Carolina Press, 1967); Harold E. Davis, *Latin American Social Thought* (Seattle: University of Washington Press, 1963). Among the

40   *Iris M. Zavala*

important studies are also William Rex Crawford, *A Century of Latin-American Thought* (Cambridge: Harvard University Press, 1961); Dardo Cúneo, *Aventura y letra de América Latina* (Buenos Aires: Editorial Pleamar, 1964); Jean Franco, *Culture of Latin American Society and the Artist* (London: Pelican Books, 1970); *Spanish American Literature* (Cambridge: Cambridge University Press, 1969); Antonio Gómez Robledo, *Idea y experiencia de América* (México, 1958); Raúl A. Inostrosa, *El ensayo en Chile desde la colonia hasta 1900* (Stanford, Ca.: Stanford University Press, 1966); Robert G. Mead, *Breve historia del ensayo hispanoamericano* (México, 1956); Arturo Torres Rioseco, *Ensayos sobre literatura hispanoamericana* (México, 1953); Medardo Vitier, *Del ensayo americano* (México, 1945).

12. The Instituto de Cultura Puertorriqueña published the *Obras completas* (Complete Works) of Luis Muñoz Rivera, with an introduction and notes by Lidio Cruz Monclova. See also Sebastián Dalmau Canet, *Luis Muñoz Rivera: Su vida, su obra, su carácter* (San Juan, 1917); Bolívar Pagán, *Historia de los partidos políticos puertorriqueños* (San Juan, 1959); and *Procerato puertorriqueño del siglo XIX* (San Juan, 1961).

13. On the Foraker Law, see Lyman J. Gould, *La ley Foraker: raíces de la política colonial de los Estados Unidos* (Río Piedras: University of Puerto Rico, 1969); Truman R. Clark, *Puerto Rico and the United States, 1917-1933* (Pittsburgh: University of Pittsburgh Press, 1975). There are also references to the repercussions of political problems on Puerto Rican culture and personality in Germán de Granda, *Transculturación e interferencia lingüística en el Puerto Rico contemporáneo (1898-1968)* (Bogotá: Instituto Caro Cuervo, 1968); Aida Negrón de Montilla. *Americanization in Puerto Rico and the Public Schools System (1900-1930)* (San Juan: Editorial Edil, 1970); as well as in Erwin H. Epstein, ed., *Politics and Education in Puerto Rico: A Documentary Survey of the Language Issue* (Metuchen, N.J.: Scarecrow Press, 1970).

14. Rosendo Matienzo Cintrón, *Obras completas* (San Juan: ICP, 1969), Vol. II, p. 221.

15. Luis M. Díaz Soler, *Rosendo Matienzo Cintrón: orientador y guardián de una cultura* (1960), Vol. II, pp. 110-112.

16. See the excellent book by Igualdad Iglesias de Pagán, *El obrerismo en Puerto Rico: época de Santiago Iglesias (1896-1905)* (Palencia de Castilla: Ediciones Juan Ponce de León, 1973), p. 30. *Claridad* has devoted several instructive essays to this redirecting of worker populism, among them articles by Alejandro Nogueras Salinas, "1904: Miseria y organización" (June 1978). See also Angel G. Quintero Rivera, "The Development of Social Classes and Political Conflicts in Puerto Rico," in *Puerto Rico and Puerto Ricans*, eds. Adalberto López and James Petras (Cambridge, Mass.: Schenkman Publishing House, 1974).

17. See by Servando Montaña Peláez, *Nemesio Canales: lenguaje y situación* (Río Piedras: UPR, 1973), and *Antología nueva de Nemesio Canales*, 4 vols. (Río Piedras: UPR, 1974).

18. Cited in Elena Zeno, *Manuel Zeno Gandía, documentos biográficos y críticos* (San Juan, 1955), p. 64. I include Zeno Gandía here because, although he belonged to the previous generation, he contributed greatly to the creation of an anti-imperialist consciousness from the decade of the 1920s until his death.

19. "Declaraciones sobre el informe del Instituto Brookings," Publicaciones de

Forum, n.d. On the Nationalist Party, see Paulino E. Castro, *Historia sinóptica del Partido Nacionalista de Puerto Rico* (San Juan, 1947). A profound analysis of the party is needed, as well as studies of Pedro Albizu Campos. For the time being, we can refer to the little book by Juan Antonio Corretjer, *Albizu Campos* (Montevideo, 1969). Also see the series of articles by Benjamin Torres in *Claridad,* April 29, May 8, and May 12, 1977, as well as the series by Georg Fromm, ibid. May 27 to June 30, 1977.

20. On the *Revista de las Antillas,* see Lisa E. Davis, "Revista de las Antillas: El modernismo como resistencia popular en Puerto Rico," *Casa de las Américas* 105 (November-December 1977): 54-61.

21. See the index of Carlos Ripoll published in New York in 1969. See also José Antonio Portuondo, *Bosquejo histórico de las letras cubanas* (Habana, 1960), and Ambrosio Fornet, "Revaluación del movimiento cultural del 30," *Casa de las Américas* 40 (1967): 29-34. The "Protest of the Thirteen" in Cuba is similar to that proposed in Puerto Rico by the *Indice* group.

22. *Seis ensayos en busca de nuestra expresión* (Buenos Aires: Editorial Raigal, 1952), "La utopía de América," p. 32.

23. Ibid., "Patria de la justicia," p. 28.

24. In this sense, a correct focus seems to me to be that of Arcadio Díaz in "La poesía negra de Luis Palés Matos," *Sin Nombre* 1 (1970): 7-25. On other aspects of Afro-Antillean poetry, consult the thesis of Florence Estella White, *Poesía Negra in the Works of Jorge de Lima, Nicolás Guillén and Jacques Roumain, 1927-1947* (Madison, Wisconsin, 1952), summarized in *Wisconsin Summaries,* no. 13, p. 389, and by Wilfred G. O. Cartey, "Three Antillean Poets: Emilio Ballagas, Luis Palés Matos and Nicolás Guillén. Literary Development of the Negro Theme in Relation to the Making of Modern Afro-Antillean Poetry and the Historic Evolution of the Negro," Ph.D. diss., Columbia University, 1965.

25. See the study of Arcadio Díaz, "La isla afortunada: sueños liberadores y utópicos de Luis Llorens Torres," *Sin Nombre* 6 (1975).

26. At the present time, fishermen from the island of Viéques are fighting to prevent the U.S. Navy from carrying out maneuvers there. The U.S. Navy controls 27,000 acres on the east and west coasts of the island, with 9,500 civilians living on 6,000 acres in the interior; see *New York Times,* January 28, 1979, p. 19. Also, thousands of Puerto Ricans born or reared in the United States are returning to the island; see *Los Angeles Times,* April 16, 1978, p. 5.

27. Juan Sáez Burgos reproaches his teachers in an ironic poem for having taught him that "lies are truth on the planet"; "Hate your brother as [you hate] yourself"; "Curse those who love"; "May horror go with you." See his book, *Un hombre para el llanto* (San Juan: Editorial Edil, 1969). Alfredo Matilla and Iván Silén have edited an anthology of the young Puerto Rican poets entitled *The Puerto Rican Poets* (New York: Bantam Books, 1972). Juan Angel Silén reflects, in his essay, these new points of view. See his *Hacia una visión positiva del puertorriqueño* (San Juan: Editorial Edil, 1970). In novels, José Luis González, Pedro Juan Soto, Emilio Díaz Valcárcel, and Luis Rafael Sánchez all discuss, with sharpness and art, the basic problems. Also notable are the essays, especially the work of José Luis González, *Literatura y sociedad en Puerto Rico* (México, 1976), and those of Manuel Maldonado Denis.

28. Data on the transformation occurring among young people can be found in Arthur Liebman, *Politics of Puerto Rican University Students* (San Antonio:

University of Texas Press, 1970), and in Ismael Rodríguez Bou, *Esbozo de un tema: las nuevas generaciones en Puerto Rico* (San Juan, 1965). To the insular factor we should add the transformation taking place in the United States, especially in New York. We exclude this aspect because none of the young people committed to the movement has expressed his or her ideas through essays. Puerto Rican studies programs have established themselves in many U.S. universities through pressure on the part of the students, and contribute to an awakened consciouness among Puerto Rican immigrants to the metropoli. In this sense, of great importance is *Puerto Rico Libre: Bulletin of the Puerto Rican Solidarity Committee in New York.* See the article by José Yglesias, "Right On with the Young Lords," *New York Times Magazine,* June 7, 1970. See also, M. Abramson, *Pa'lante: Young Lords Party* (New York: McGraw-Hill, 1971).

29. See the anthology of Mariana Robles de Cardona, *Búsqueda y plasmación de nuestra personalidad. Antología crítica del ensayo puertorriqueño desde sus orígenes hasta la generación del 30* (San Juan: Editorial Club de la Prensa, 1958); Margot Arce de Vázquez and Mariana Robles de Cardona, *Lecturas puertorriqueñas. Prosa* (Sharon, Conn.: Troutman Press, 1966); E. Melón and Masdeu Martinez, *Literatura puertorriqueña. Antología general (Siglo XIX)* (San Juan: Editorial Edil, 1970); Eugenio Méndez and Arturo Santana, *Puerto Rico y su historia. Lecturas escogidas* (San Juan: DIP, 1954); A. G. Quintero Rivera, *Workers' Struggle in Puerto Rico* (New York: Monthly Review Press, 1976) and the critique of the Spanish edition of this book done by Gervasio García, in *La Escalera* 4, no. 2 (May 1972). The department of Hispanic studies of the University of Puerto Rico has contributed significantly to the studies of Puerto Rican literature and thought, although many of the relevant theses are still unpublished. Equally valuable is the contribution of Ricardo Alegría, as director of the Instituto de Cultura. Many of the anthologies, re-issues, and studies owe their existence to his intervention. It is a pity that in some cases on publishing the complete works of some writers, exact bibliographic data are not given. Furthermore, as is to be expected, the Instituto cannot publish extremely radical works, since it is a governmental agency. In the past few years, CEREP and the Annals of Historical Research have undertaken an in-depth study of Puerto Rico's culture and history. Although irregular, its publications are of fundamental interest to those wishing to gain knowledge of the true history, rather than official versions.

I
Spanish Colonization

Alejandro Tapia y Rivera (1826–1882)

Born in San Juan and began his studies there. Was exiled to Madrid in 1850 after a dispute. In the Spanish capital he participated in the "Society for Collecting Historical Documents of the Island San Juan Bautista de Puerto Rico," along with the Puerto Ricans Segundo Ruiz Belvis, José Emeterio Betances, José Julián Acosta, and others. From 1857 to 1862 he lived in Havana. Back in Puerto Rico, he followed the teaching profession and contributed to magazines and newspapers.

He was a playwright, essayist, opera librettist, novelist, biographer, and historian. His outstanding poem is *La Sataniada* (1862), influenced by Byron. His historical works are most noteworthy, although his novels are still of some interest.

Selected Bibliography

Tapia y Rivera, Alejandro. *Obras completas,* ICP, 1968.

————. *Cofresí.* 1876; San Juan, 1944.

————. *Cuentos y artículos varios.* San Juan, 1938.

————. *La palma del cacique, Leyenda histórica de Puerto Rico.* 1852; San Juan, 1943.

————. *Mis memorias o Puerto Rico cómo lo encontré y cómo lo dejo.* 1927; San Juan: Ediciones Rumbos, 1968.

————. *Póstumo el transmigrado: historia de un hombre que resucitó en el cuerpo de su enemigo.* 1872; San Juan, 1945.

García Díaz, Manuel. *Alejandro Tapia y Rivera. Su vida y su obra.* San Juan: Editorial Coquí, 1964.

Gutiérrez del Arroyo, Isabel. "Biblioteca histórica de Alejandro Tapia." *Asomante* 4 (1954): 5-25.

Martín, José Luis. "Alejandro Tapia y su poema 'La Sataniada.' " *Asomante* 2 (1956): 78-94.

————. *Análisis estilístico de "La Sataniada" de Tapia.* ICP, 1958.

Meléndez, Concha. "Alejandro Tapia y Rivera." *Asomante* 1 (1945): 56-57.

Pagán, Juan Bautista. "Sobre el padre de nuestras letras: Don Alejandro Tapia y Rivera." *Artes y letras* (September 1953).

Puerto Rico, Seen Without Spectacles
by a Myopic

Recently I came across a geographical dictionary and, as you might expect, leafed through it for the article on "Puerto Rico." I perched my spectacles—an indispensable piece of equipment—on my nose and began reading this:

"Puerto Rico, smallest of the Greater Antilles, is situated in the Atlantic Ocean between parallels 17'54'00" and 18'30'40" north and between the meridians 59'20'26" and 60'58'52" west of Cádiz. Its capital is the great city of Puerto Rico or San Juan, a commercial depot of first importance for shipping from the main Antillean and South American centers, thanks to being an absolutely free port. The harbor, where up to the beginning of our century ships of the line anchored, became so obstructed as to be almost inaccessible to larger shipping; but thanks to more far-seeing interests it is now all cleaned up, the swamps in the southern part dried out, the mangroves formerly infecting and obstructing it cleared away. With drydocks, shipyards, and huge warehouses now occupying these areas, it has become one of the world's best harbors, thus deserving the name given it—no doubt for its natural excellence—by its first visitor, Juan Ponce de León. Within its spacious horseshoe may be seen today thousands of ships showing the flags of every country, while three-masters and steamships by the hundred are tied up at the piers and spacious warehouses of the Puntilla, in addition to smaller vessels to be counted in thousands.

"Cataño has become a fine commercial town, connected with the capital across the harbor by a service of a dozen small steam launches, and with Ponce in the south by three railroads, the Oriental, Central, and Western.

"The city with its lights turning nights into day; with its abundant water facilitating cleanliness and industry, where once drought haunted the inhabitants; with its beautifying and health-giving trees everywhere, its art gallery and services for poor children, now no longer wandering the streets; with its unsurpassable poorhouses and orphanages, its renowned lunatic asylum and its jail, run like all others in the island on the moral-rehabilitation lines of the world's most famous prisons—on top of all this contains magnificent buildings, among them the university, converted from one of its old monasteries; the bank; the public library with over a million volumes, close by the seminary; the Athenaeum, temple of all the sciences, located on San Francisco Street among the fabulous stores which, once barely reaching San Justo Street, now extend to the Plaza de Santiago. We do not mention the private discount, guaranty, and savings banks and the famous Territorial and Industrial Bank with operations running into the billions. The Campo del Morro and the rampart-free Puerta de Tierra are delightful areas to stroll, with pleasant shady squares, exquisite statues, fountains, and showy gardens. The Santiago port region spreads out into a community that reaches as far as Martín Peña, a part of the city connected with Caguas by railroad.

"There are also numerous schools of all types of instruction, an industrial conservatory, a Museum of Sciences and Fine Arts; newspapers which have contributed to this progress and, by vigorously and resolutely sustaining rights and duties and clearly demarcating state, social, municipal, and individual attributions, have destroyed all misgivings about a people only aspiring to just and natural progress: a progress guaranteed by the enlightened nationhood of their birth and within which, with goodwill, all advances have a place, as is happening today in that island. And if anyone still exists there so perverted by the old as to use progress for the condemnation of progress, that is as inevitable as the existence of shadows where the light ends.

"A dozen steamships connect the coastal towns all around an island that is small in territory but notable today for its wealth and the industriousness, virtues, and wisdom of its inhabitants, who as a whole, it may be said, enjoy all the benefits of civilization.

"It is impossible to meet there anyone who cannot read and write, and extremely rare to find a vagrant or a person without an occupation. Property, fairly enough distributed, unites its forces by association in all kinds of mercantile and industrial societies, while in the intellectual sphere there are societies for religious, scientific, educational, and moral purposes. Even animals are protected by this benign influence through associations for their betterment and the prevention of the cruelties of which they are victims in lands ignorant of the duties of cultures and civilization. Cock-fighting has been abolished.

"One can hardly find a town that is not linked to others by rail and telegraph, and that has insufficient banks, schools, newspapers, and public and private libraries. With the canalization of rivers, the formerly lost wealth of their waters is used in agriculture and the numerous hydraulic workshops; boards of experts see the towns seemingly made for the traveler's enchantment, where adornment, hygiene, and abundance meet the eye as one walks, along with commodious and cozy inns.

"In the peasant's house one finds educational and recreational books and furnishings worthy of the most decent urban homes. This *jíbaro* of Puerto Rico wears shoes and, on fiesta or town-meeting days when he foregathers to discuss the best distribution of local resources, dons a frock coat.

"Canalized rivers have put an end to the devastating floods of old, and the viaducts crossing them are so built and maintained as to dispel any fear. That is, swollen rivers no longer carry away bridges as formerly happened.

"Mayagüez, already a great emporium; Ponce, linked to its built-up beach by superb bridges that protect against floods without isolating it; Guayama, given new life by its irrigated fields; Arecibo, Aguadilla, Humacao, Caguas, and other towns which are not important centers, living a civilized life and competing nobly in material advances and intellecutal culture. Academies, great colleges, associations, theaters, avenues, open-air concerts, handsome cafés: in short, whatever beautifies the life of other towns is found in the abovementioned. And Ponce, once a mere sugar town, now looks like a suburb of some great European center.

"The railroads have speeded and smoothed the postal system, and linked the production of all parts of the interior with the culture that is the due of a fast-growing population in constant and varied communication. This contact expands culture and business, bringing increase of well-being and public wealth. Strange that no one thought before of the railroads' great contribution, in so fertile and populated a country.

"These arteries have carried life and abundance into every corner, and the rural farms and plantations have grown twenty times. Steam applied to the great sugar factories has separated cane cultivation from the fabrication process, leaving the former to small proprietors and consequently making use of an infinity of previously uncultivated lands. The same power discovered by Watt, applied to the plow and reaper and a thousand other agricultural uses—the great diminisher of labor—eases, cheapens, and expands production.

"The heights are crowned by the Yemen shrub—a specialty of today's Puerto Rico—whose flowers promise a harvest previously unusable for lack of transport. The tobacco plantations are striving to provide the world abundantly with the Comerio leaf, its cultivation improved by science and its processing by the intelligence of enlightened workers in the cities.

"Cattle of all kinds multiply in the green meadows of Yabucoa and other island plains, offering with skillful cross-breeding an appropriate variety of strains and species.

"A thousand previously unknown industries use the island's rich, diverse natural materials—yesterday unexploited—for textiles, farinaceous products, and preserves.

"Every center has been transformed there into an Athens for science, a London for industry and trade; every town and village into an orchard; every home into a garden; and the whole island into a paradise of plenty and well-being."

That's what the dictionary said. As I read it, astounded by this scintillating picture, I kept trying to see if my spectacles—perhaps misted over—were taking me for a ride into a dream! But my very astonishment, the yearning to reach the climax of this lovely intoxication, forced me to read on. Finally, though, I threw the book down, exclaiming: "That's how they write geography!" But the movement made my glasses fall off, and I realized. . . . they had no lenses! So I put on another pair and resumed my leafing; but then I couldn't find the famous article—the dictionary didn't even mention Puerto Rico! No doubt I had read the description of some other country and, in a fit of wishful thinking, had taken for Puerto Rico, Ponce, etc., the names and descriptions of other places.

That's what you get for trying to read without glasses!

A Myopic
1876

Cuentos y artículos varios, San Juan, 1938

African Slavery

During three centuries the Spanish colonial society not only was based on slavery but took responsibility for it; for while the institution was a worldwide one at the outset, here they tried to keep it going after a new epoch condemned it. Slavery, along with the lamentable system of colonial absolutism of which it was a part, made no small contribution to blocking any advance along the path of progress.

Everyone knows the lethal influence of that institution wherever it exists. It destroys the family, since marriage is contrary to its interests: a slave is easily transported and passed from owner to owner, but a family is harder to sell or buy, so that each of the children ends up with a different master.

Slavery debases labor and skills, for when free people see these in slave hands they generally tend to avoid being identified with the serf. Hence those fatal sayings, "Work is for slaves," "I won't work any more because I'm not a slave."

Slavery also lends authority to cruelty by the master through the punitive power it vests in him, leaving to the discretion of his character and interests the treatment, fate, and even life of the slave. And this not always indirectly but by express law, as in the edict of General Prim, governor of our island from 1847 to 1849, which authorized the master to kill, the hangman to mutilate, in cases that could only arise from slavery.*

On top of these atrocities, slavery is the perpetual robbery, bequeathed from fathers to sons, of a human being as if he were an animal or thing. His labor is the master's property during the life of the slave, unless he ends up abandoned in useless old age,

---

* Prim, ironically, headed the 1868 Revolution in Spain which dethroned Isabel. In the Peninsula, he was a liberal.

as has happened lately under the law of transition which furnished nothing more positive than another disadvantage for the institution.

I have always been sickened by the sophistry propounded in the masters' behalf, glorifying their "benevolent paternalism" by comparing the well-being of their serfs with the misery of the "proletarians," the poor free workers of Europe. To be sure, there are rare exceptions (often illusory), but these are generally attributable to the cold calculations of the exploiter: he looks after a machine that he wants to maintain in strict accordance with his own interests, that is, in the most economical way possible. For when the slave trade was flourishing and buying a slave was easy and cheap, it was customary in Cuba (according to a certain publicist) to calculate maximum production against the price of black lives: the number sacrificed and easily replaceable entered into the probabilities of increasing the crop. What did it matter if so-and-so many slaves were worked to death, if production grew to a compensating extent and slaves cost little?

To compare them with the free proletarian—what a nakedly lying parallel! And furthermore an insult to human morality and dignity.

If the Antillean slave were compared with the Antillean proletarian, whose lot he would share if he were free, the lie would be compounded. Clearly the slave cannot be imagined as sailing for Europe to become part of its proletariat. And the Antillean wageworker doesn't die of hunger unless he wants to, since there are mechanical jobs aplenty here, as in any fertile and new country.

Let them show me that by law the Antillean slave, like Europe's poor free proletarians, cannot be physically maltreated, nor bought and sold, nor deprived by his master of the fruit of his toil, nor left at the mercy of another man who forces him to work for the master's interest; that he can go where he likes in search of his own betterment; that he can acquire and dispose of savings not as a minor but as an adult without overlord; that he can have a legal personality, enlighten himself freely like the free whites of Europe, and like them freely choose and pursue a profession; that he can think and proceed as Europe's free whites, albeit poor and proletarian, can under law. Then, granted that equality, I will accept the comparison and say that those Europeans are worse off than our slaves. But today, as slaves, the only right they have is to be kept alive with part of what they produce—that is, treated worse than the pampered stable animal that doesn't have to live for work and produces nothing for the master. At the same time that animal has no active soul with aspirations to own something, while the slave who has one toils only to pile up property for the master, who starts by owning the person of the slave.

The poverty of the Antillean slave, who starts by not even owning himself, emanates from the rape of his labor; that of the proletarian in Europe from purely economic causes, from errors originating in vicious social organization, problems whose solution is under constant study.

The slave is outside of common law and subject to the arbitrary and mercenary will of one man, who calls himself master and is both judge and litigant—and what a litigant!

Please don't tell me that there have been officials to watch over the slave's pseudorights, for more often than not these officials were friends of the masters or upholders of the interests of the class they belonged or could belong to. Very rarely did the function fall to someone like Hernandez Arvizu, the liberal lawyer who opposed the slave traffic between Puerto Rico and Cuba. Certain "merchants," attracted by the better price of slaves in Cuba, began transporting slaves there as samples, separating them forever from their families and ties and selling them to the sugar mills. This developed into such a scandal, after one slave killed himself at the hour of embarcation, that the decent and compassionate governor-general Fernando de Norzagaray gave orders reducing and greatly hampering such trade.

I have named Arvizu and will name another, don Pólux Padilla, who a few years later (1872) opposed the shipping to Havana of child slaves to be sold there. To prevent this at all costs, he stood up squarely to the government; finally he bought the slaves and immediately freed them.*

* For more on these abolitionists, see Arthur F. Corwin, *Spain and the Abolition of Slavery in Cuba, 1817-1886* (Austin: University of Texas Press, 1967), Luis M. Díaz Soler, *La esclavitud negra en Puerto Rico* (Río Piedras: University of Puerto Rico Press, 1965), and Manuel Moreno Fraginals, *The Sugarmill* (New York: Monthly Review Press, 1976).

What kind of education could a young woman receive who was brought up seeing the procreation of slaves outside the marriage bond?

How could the sensibility proper to her sex not be blunted, constantly observing the use of the whip?

What respect for charity and human dignity could educators inculcate in a public habitually witnessing the cruelties inherent in slavery?

What love of liberty, what horror of tyranny could be engendered in a society thus trampling underfoot the most sacred rights of the free human community?

This was the more perturbing when one saw Christian ministers, as in the southern states of the North American republic, insisting from the pulpit that slavery was an institution of divine right. To our shame there was no priest among us who dared cry out against this antievangelical crime; and I have heard some defend it on the ridiculous ground of Noah's curse on his son Ham.

Among our first deputies to the Cortes was a cleric, Bishop Puig-Coll y Toste, who didn't dare speak for it in the debates but defended it with his vote, on the standard proslavers' ground of the prosperity of the Island (the masters' prosperity, he should have said) and the paradisical felicity enjoyed by slaves, their good fortune in comparison with the poor free people of Europe.

This idyll based on sacks of coffee and hogsheads of sugar, pictured by a priest without a mention of morality or the Gospel, brought from another Puerto Rican delegate, the liberal Sanromá, the comment: "After hearing this good gentleman's eulogy of the slaves' happiness, I am tempted to paint myself black and ask to be shipped as a slave to Puerto Rico."

On this point of kind treatment I must recall that one *hacendado* fretfully attributed the Toa Baja slave revolt to the bad example set by a señor Cantero, who treated his slaves too well.

And as for punishment, the courts were besieged with suits charging extreme cruelty and treatment leading to suicide and homicide. The suicides were committed by slaves seeking emancipation in death, and the homicides were acts of desperation against masters or foremen. There were even cases where slaves—a mother and her sons—would agree to kill each other. In one case there was an agreement between Victor and a fellow slave that one should kill the other (as he did) so that the murderer might then go to the gallows (as he did). The trial that followed was notable for the perplexity of the judges at a prisoner who had deliberately sought suicide at a rope's end.

As for the laws protecting the lives of slaves, they were often ignored on the ground or pretext that discipline must be upheld.

Some *hacendados* faced a series of lawsuits, or several at once, for extreme cruelty. Despite the normal understandings with the masters, the court saw no alternative to depriving one barbarous Ponce *hacendado* of the administration of his plantation. In one case that I saw, this monster was required to explain the death of a young slave named Elena. He had made her and other slaves walk barefoot over sharp rocks or gravel after the soles of their feet had been beaten to bloody pulp. For the punishment of Elena, who was pregnant, he had a hole dug in the ground to accommodate her belly, so that the embryo would not be lost while she was flogged on the buttocks.

I know of a notorious *hacendado* who had the teeth of a slave pulled out because the man used to eat sugar cane, and ordered twenty-five lashes for a slave cook because she didn't serve white rice with the part burned in the pot, which he particularly fancied.

Among the barbarities of another *hacendado* known to everyone, recalling the days of Tiberius, Nero, and Caligula, was walling up a slave.

A judge, don F. de——, who soon afterward was promoted, wrote and published a pamphlet to show that since the sugar mill or hacienda was worse for the slave than prison, slaves sentenced to jail should serve their time in the mill so that the master would not be penalized through loss of their services.

Such viciousness inevitably infected the spirit of legislation and the domestic and governmental practice of society. This infection makes it less than surprising that, in 1867, Governor-General Marchessi ordered the flogging of free men for this or that offense, in disdain of the Audiencia's protest and laws on the books. Such was his frenzy that, when the rich and influential *hacendado* don M.F. came to present the people's objections to these illegal and atrocious punishments, the governor gave him short shrift and threatened to have M.F. himself flogged. This the *hacendado*, full of righteous indignation, related to his friends.

I have more of the same kind to tell about this deplorable governor whom the people, for the love they bore him and the great floods and frightful earthquakes that followed the San Narciso hurricane during his adminstration, called "Mr. Calamity." He was indeed among the calamities and sizable one.

I knew one slaveowner who innocently complained of not having been able to prevent his slave escaping, in spite of having made him eat human excrement. . . .

One, in the French Antilles, cut off the eyelashes of a child between eight and twelve years to prevent him from sleeping during the all-night working hours of the sugar-grinding season. The wretched child could no longer sleep because the eyelash roots got into his eyes when he tried to close them. The resulting inflammation spread into his brain and this and the enforced wakefulness caused his death.

To sum up, the beatings and jailings stood at every moment as accusers of the institution. It can be said that for every hundred civil prisoners sent to the gallows in any given period, two-thirds were slaves, committers of offenses arising from their condition and the despair in which they lived. Some killed a major-domo or foreman whose brutal conduct aroused their hatred, to find on the gallows the only escape from their miseries.

There were cases where the slave, trusting in his master's honesty, amassed some small savings from his toil in hope of freeing himself and deposited them in the master's keeping. The master would then deny it before a judge; for lack of proofs which a helpless and ignorant slave couldn't produce, the case could not be established, and the black, his money lost, had to find another master to avoid the fury of the first one for having been brought to court. This sort of thing was done without a blush.

Not that there may not have been rare cases of fraud or false accusation on the slave's part; but this is less likely than the other situation considering the subjection of the slave, who, however shrewd, would with difficulty swim in such deep waters. He knew from his own and others' experience that he could expect to come out on the losing end. His testimony was hardly likely to weigh against that of the all-powerful, against the class to which those who were supposed to give him justice belonged. Such justice had to be crookedly administered to maintain the obedience and discipline that the system required. Those who tried or would have liked to defend the slave against the interests and solidarity of a whole society, did so with the fear arising from their isolation. They tried not to insist too much, to avoid the hostility and even punishment that rewarded advocates of so-called abolitionism, synonymous at the time with separatism. Actually this last crime could more justly have been charged to some of the slaveowners, who were so influential and fanatical about the institutions that all other interests, including the national, had to take a back seat. As in the south of the United States, there existed a majority favoring separation to assure retention of their slaves. Nor was Cuba lacking in people who, while slavery continued on the mainland— before and even during the Civil War—dreamed of annexation to the southern states. But once slavery was abolished there, such people became furious partisans of national integrity.

At one point, after there had been talk of abolition in the Cortes, the ranks of Cuba's filibustering annexationists were swelled by many creoles and some Spaniards; and one of these was heard to remark that "if the metropolis attempted to free the slaves, they would throw themselves into the arms of the United States." Everyone will recall the annexationist effort by Narciso Lopez—similar to those of Walker in Nicaragua, supported by the South and the slaveholders—and the attempt that cut short the life of Pinto in Havana.*

By no means all were proslavery— the Cuban annexationists included a number who were not—but all got mixed up in a common class front. But it can be said that annexationist tenden-

* The references are to the Cuban López, the North American William Walker, and the Cuban Ramón Pinto. They all rebelled against Spain and fomented annexationism. Walker helped Cuban émigrés; in 1856 he revoked the Nicaraguan antislavery decree. See Philip S. Foner, *A History of Cuba and its Relations with the U.S.*, 2 vols. (New York: International Publishers, 1963).

cies melted away or ceased to be active as soon as abolition began
to loom up in the United States.

During the U.S. Civil War these people were boosters of the
South, and when slavery collapsed nearly all turned their eyes
back toward Spain. This evolution was particularly marked
among some of the few annexation sympathizers in Puerto Rico.
When agitation for the reform and abolition program began in
Madrid, they vowed to contaminate the new tendency there in
every way possible. Only an annexationist would deny that Puerto
Rico had some of the most ardent and persevering champions of
the antireformist cause, speciously invoking nationalism to conceal their love of slavery.

Since separatism could not possibly have room for slavery,
these people were not for independence; and they took fright at
the events of Lares, as with good reason did most of the Island's
top people.

Mis memorias, o Puerto Rico cómo lo encontré y cómo lo dejo, 1928

Fernando de Ormaechea

Poet and dramatist. Details of his life have not been obtainable, but he is the author of the following: *Revista de Puerto Rico* (1880) (drama); *Cuatro menguante* (Ponce: El Comercio, 1885) (drama); *Quejas y risas* (Madrid, 1881) (poetry); *"Potpourri" de aires puertorriqueños* (Puerto Rico: Imprenta de El Agente, 1884) (folkloric sketches).

Antillean Types: 1. The Patrioteer

I, Spanish by the grace of God and the Constitution, simple and open as a good son of my earth, obedient and patient to be more in character—for none is better at suffering and shutting up than we blessed Spaniards; I, who have crossed the ocean three times to come and make a fortune in these ancient colonies, today most reasonably aspiring to be Spanish provinces; I, having fulfilled all the required desiderata, clauses, etc., to be tranquilly Spanish in this country, consider myself fully entitled to speak out about what I think and the way I see things. And what I am going to say in the exercise of this legitimate right will be certain weighty truths, in the frankest and most unvarnished way of which I am capable. For as a pure and unadulterated Spaniard, beating about the bush has never made me happy; on the contrary, I like to consider myself as plain, or bare-faced if you like, as the opposite wall; and when I speak of the wall, let me say that I am not thinking of the honorable censor of printed material.

So here I go:

There isn't a motherland any more.

Don't be alarmed by this first truth which I have uttered. I said there is no longer a motherland, and will proceed posthaste to demonstrate it.

There isn't one because those who have customarily presided over her destiny, have been swallowing a chunk of it every day, so that bit by bit she has been lost to us.

There isn't one because, just as in more innocent and less mischievous times it was an everyday thing to sacrifice oneself for the motherland, now it is she who is sacrificed and her sons who preside over the sacrifice—politically speaking, of course.

There isn't one because self-congratulation for serving and defending her is now the order of the day; and everyone knows that when people keep congratulating themselves for a virtue, it is precisely because they don't possess it.

Finally, there isn't one because patriots have become very scarce while we have a superabundance of patrioteers whom I accuse, publicly and solemnly, of the great crime of matricide, since they use every means to destroy her by sickening her to death.

The motherland—something so sacred as the motherland, so worthy of consideration and respect, so venerable, so sainted, so deserving that everyone claiming to be decent pays her homage—has dwindled in this petty epoch into an object of speculation, a source of lucre, a pretext to commit with impunity any kind of villainy and swindle.

The motherland, noble and venerated matron, tender and most loving mother, had the misfortune to bear a few ungrateful and sickly children—luckily only a few. But being so few among the vast majority of her good children, they make more noise on their own than a legion of demons or a gaggle of mothers-in-law.

These spurious and denaturalized children are known as patrioteers: they seem to have been born for the sole purpose of disgusting their poor mother, yet they insist they love and adore her and would give their life's blood for her. In reality it is they who feed on the blood of her to whom they owe everything—not on its nectar sweetness but on the bitterness that is in her for having suckled them at her breasts.

Humbugs and speculators of the worst and most bogus type, foetuses that never developed human characteristics, they pose before the gullible as the motherland's guardians and defenders against her good sons whom they portray as attacking and tarnishing her. Their stunted brains invent conflicts and disorders; they continually sound the alarm when not a straw is moving and the only disorder is in their contemptible heads, the only conflict what they themselves stir up as they fish in muddy waters.

A fine type, the patrioteer! I know him well. Gradually through years of studying him I have learned to strip off the masquerade bit by bit and inspect him in all his revolting nudity.

Your average patrioteer tends to be an ordinary fellow of obscure origin and mean intelligence who by one of fortune's aberrations has come to play a certain role in society, if an unsavory one. Thanks to a position not always legitimately won, to some greasepaint that protests at being put to such ignoble use, he aspires to the society of decent folk and passes himself off as well-bred and educated—which doesn't faze him when sticking his nose in everywhere.

The thoroughbred patrioteer—that is, thoroughly unbred, as all of them are—will always tell you, whether or not it's to the point, that he's more Spanish than Pelayo,* that the motherland is first in his heart, that he would make any sacrifice (except pecuniary) for her; that the country is lost, that national fervor is becoming sadly lukewarm; and that patriots must unite and stand shoulder to shoulder (they call this maneuver "touching elbows") as all patrioteers do among themselves on all great occasions, especially when a good business deal is in the wind. He will use every available medium to scatter within peaceful societies the seeds of mistrust and alarm, and will then pose as the ever-watchful sentinel to see that nobody makes a move or utters a word without his permission.

A Quixote of a new species—incomparably more ridiculous than Cervantes', armed from head to foot with helmet and roasting spit—he fancies his fingers and toes to be enemy hosts and is constantly waging tremendous battles against wineskins and windmills which he most solemnly insists are terrible giants and formidable enchanted castles.

After the manner of Juan Palomo, he is both the one who cooks and the one who eats: that is, it is he who hatches the conspiracies, who sounds the alarm, and who rushes into combat—metaphorically, of course; who conquers, who pacifies, who proclaims himself a hero and then nominates himself for a medal with which he proudly struts, deluding himself that he has really won it. In short, he does it all while the supposed enemy stays home, quiet as a mouse and without starting anything with anybody.

Meanwhile, peaceful, sensible citizens who dislike noise contemplate all this elaborate hubbub and dazedly ask each other: what goes on here?

* A figure of speech which means ultranationalist or patrioteer.

What should be going on? Nothing. It's the patrioteers who have gone off the deep end.

I have seen people shut up in lunatic asylums for much less.

The patrioteer is a valiant hero, yes; but a hero who never fights. A pacifist hero, you might say—he won't tangle with anyone who shows he means business. I compare him with one of those peacetime fire-eaters who, when the first shots are heard, are to be found eating—not exactly fire, which they know to be indigestible, but a good beefsteak by the kitchen stove while others get into the action.

"A thousand bombs on their hides! If the enemy shows his head, you'll see what I'm made of! I'll eat ten of them alive as I would eat a sour apple! Thunder and lightening! Let them come, you'll see what they'll get!"

And look: here comes the enemy—and these types take off into a nice quiet corner.

Oh, yes, I understand it up to a point. Because the patrioteer is a philosopher who says to himself:

"In peacetime, good patriots should go armed to the teeth, shout a lot, and make frightening faces. But from the moment when peace is disturbed, shots ring out, and the action starts, it would be antipatriotic and antidigestive to expose oneself to a whack that would put one out of commission to continue serving the motherland."

After all, if you come to think about it, they are preeminently men of order who owe themselves to their families and their interests. So it would hardly be proper for them to go and expose their hides like any poor sod—the kind who does nothing and doesn't even move while they shout themselves hoarse in the motherland's service, so that but for their patriotism and sacrifices God knows where we would be by now.

Furthermore, we must do them justice. The others may fight for their country like heroes and emerge victorious with powder-blackened faces leathered by sun and wind, their clothing in shreds from the heat of the battle, presenting the rude image of pride in heroism and satisfaction in victory. But meanwhile these patriots never stop inflating and dislocating themselves out of joint, whooping and hollering, yelling and cheering in patriotic frenzy, brandishing the flag, exhibiting themselves everywhere as if they too were banners, adorning their houses with bunting. That, yes: plenty of bunting and tinsel.

Banners and bunting are two things a patrioteer is never without. They are, as it were, the currency of his species, the family coat of arms—so identified with him that one comes to realize they are the symbol of his patriotism: pennant patriotism.

For sensible folk, valiant indeed the role of this type!

But just imagine: in spite of all, there are still some people who take him seriously. You'd better believe it . . . and their name is Gullible!

"Potpourri" de aires puertorriqueños.
Tipos, costumbres, impresiones, aventuras y desventuras, 1884

Salvador Brau (1842–1912)

Born in Cabo Rojo, distinguished himself as dramatist, poet, journalist, and historian. His poetry is romantic, often philosophically oriented. He also published sociological works in which he studied his country's economic and social aspects. His interest in rural themes is shown in the novel *La Pecadora* (1890), dealing with religious and social intolerance. His reformist and contentious works appeared mainly in *El Buscapié, El Agente,* and *El Asimilista,* liberal-progressive journals.

Brau also produced important historical studies. In 1894 he went to work in Seville's Archive of the Indies, collecting documents on the colonial past. Most of his articles remain scattered and his novel has not been republished.

Selected Bibliography

Brau, Salvador. *Historia de Puerto Rico.* San Juan: Editorial Coquí, 1966.
————. *La colonización de Puerto Rico.* San Juan: ICP, 1966.
————. *Las clases jornaleras en Puerto Rico.* San Juan, 1882.
————. *La campesina.* 1885.
————. *Ecos de la batalla.* 1886.
————. *La pecadora.* 1890.
————. *Puerto Rico y su historia.* 1894.
Córdova Landrón, Arturo. *Salvador Brau, su vida y su época.* San Juan: Editorial Coquí, 1968.
————. "Salvador Brau, maestro de periodista." *Asomante* 5 (1949): 49-51.
Fernández Méndez, Eugenio. *Salvador Brau y su tiempo.* Río Piedras: UPR, 1956.
————, ed. *Disquisiciones sociológicas y otros ensayos.* Río Piedras: UPR, 1956.

In Full Daylight*

Continuing its discussion with *El Clamor del País*, *La Integridad Nacional* alludes—in a perfectly honest way—to one of the editors of the former journal. Having to the best of my ability functioned as its principal editor for some time, and the articles it addressed to *La Integridad* having come from my humble pen, I feel obliged to accept the allusion, publicly acknowledging the generous distinction conferred on me.

I could have fulfilled this debt of gratitude and courtesy without abandoning the reserve with which I have persistently chosen to guard my name. However, certain persons, finding no other charges to offer against me, and clearly lacking any notion of the value of modesty, have sought to throw this reserve in my face, succeeding only in giving me notoriety even in the metropolis. My incognition having thus worn so thin, I may as well tear it up completely for the benefit of he who, on the sole basis of reports about my private life, has shown me tokens of consideration—a consideration vouchsafed in most singular ways by other people whom my pen has long served and who were under some obligation to me.

The passages about myself in *La Integridad* are indeed honest, and I receive them with great satisfaction, not out of vanity but because they are limited to my social actions in general, in terms of which my political opinions have to be understood.

Whatever worth and dignity my conduct may show, I learned it

* Neither the character of this article nor its date of publication justify its appearance here [in *Ecos de la batalla*]; but summarizing as it does my basic political principles, I believed it could serve the average reader first opening this book as an advance indication of the spirit informing its pages. If anyone, unconcerned about my reasons for opening that parenthesis in a polemic of a general nature, finds its biographical reminiscences irritating, he can get rid of his irritation at small cost. Simply turn the pages without reading them. (Author's note).

from my good father. My father was not a foreign colonist. A son
of virile Catalonia, he was driven to this peaceful corner of American soil by the terror unleashed there in the Carlist wars, when
bloody Carlos of Spain, aided by the followers of the guerrilla
leaders Cantillón and Oñate, sowed mourning and desolation
through the ancient principality.*

In Puerto Rico he married a saintly woman, also of Spanish
parentage, who had likewise sought asylum in this hospitable land
from the continent's revolutionary storms, and who was the ember
of that modest, work-sanctified home where my heart and spirit
warmed into their first sensations and unfoldings.

There I learned to love Spain. The language I spoke was
Spanish, I stammered out prayers in Spanish to the God of Spain
whom I was taught to worship, and Spain's customs, traditions,
glories, and feats suffused my childish imagination, awakening
the desire to know the marvelous land where such things happened.

Thus I got to know Spain, studied her history and learned to
respect her flag. The cult of nation, the spirit of race, and venera-
tion of my ancestors were injected into me along with the cult of
virtue and work.

But when the man who gave me my existence turned his thoughts
back to his native land with its happy memories, that return in
spirit to the soil of his fathers inevitably brought a bitter sigh from
his breast and a silent tear to his eye. That sigh and tear bespoke
a protest against the brutal despotism which had torn him from
the beloved motherland he would never see again. And that
despotism was Spanish too, so that it darkened the image for me as
it did for my father.

When my father's silence turned me to my mother to satisfy
childish curiosity, she also recalled a night of horror when she was
carried along strange paths by her parents, as they fled like
hunted hares from the distant flash of rifles, the lethal bullets
whistling over their heads. To save themselves from the fury of
this bloodbath heralding a time of grim tyranny, they left home,

---

* The Carlist wars were fought by ultrareactionary rural guerrillas, headed by
priests and traditionalists under the slogan, "Christ and Carlos."

fortune, peace, and happiness behind in fertile Cumaná. This tyranny was also imposed in the name of Spain.

These were the conditions in which my character was formed, this the basis of my political beliefs. I loved Spain because my Spanish parents taught me to love her; I hated tyranny because I saw two of its victims in those who gave me life. Within those principles my ideas were formed, and when I turned to History to confirm them—that "teacher of truth" as Herodotus called her— she taught me not to confuse the national spirit, which throbs with the incarnation of the motherland, with the individual spirit where injustice is wont to lurk.

As I turned History's pages I found Spain battling manfully against the Roman empire; achieving that eight-centuries-long epic called the reconquest; bleeding herself to civilize a world, giving it all she then had; rousing herself to shake off an invasion of treason and deceit; fighting to recover her trampled rights and scorned liberties. And I recognized a Spain my father worshipped, the Spain he had taught me to love and to bless. But then I saw her squandering in Flanders the treasures America produced for her, killing commerce with the expulsion of the Jews,* ruining agriculture by banishing the Moors,† decimating the population with the *autos de fe*,†† oppressing the Indians and introducing African slavery to the New World. And in all this I saw not the Spanish genius but the profligate ambition of a few royal tyrants, the fanaticism of a devouring theocracy, and the moral subversion of a few selfish plunderers.

Yet loving Spain as I did—respecting her precepts and proud of speaking her language—I found one day that I, the son of Spaniards, was not a Spanish citizen because I wasn't born on metropolitan territory. I had Spanish family over there in the old country; my father's brothers and all their children were Spanish; but because of my birth in America I was a "colonial." This I found ridiculous: that my Spanish father could give me blood, language, beliefs, and name but not his citizenship rights—it was

* The edict signed in Granada in 1492.
† The expulsion carried out between 1609 and 1614.
†† The inquisitorial tribunals set up in 1480 to persecute converts to Christianity. See Henry Kamen, *The Spanish Inquisition* (New York: Mentor Books, 1965).

incomprehensible. Many others were in the same case, and children of foreigners who had renounced their nationality to become Spanish also took offense. The protests rose, and when the Republic heard them in 1873 it resolved them by applying to us the general Constitution of the State. I blessed the new government for that because I saw it as reflecting the principles in which I had been raised. As I see it, the democratic spirit of that political code is what Spain needs to maintain her influence in the New World.

There were of course those who complained that democracy would bear no fruit in Spain. But hasn't it? The Cortes of León are seventy years older than Britain's Parliament, and inclusion of the Third Estate in the national assemblies has been an unquestionable fact since 1113.

Furthermore, wasn't the Justicia Mayor of Aragón* above the king? Wasn't the organization of the Council of 100 in Barcelona a manifestation of pure democracy? Wasn't it democracy that gave life to the guild brotherhoods in Valencia and to the Castilian communities that Carlos V crushed at Villalar? Wasn't it the democratic spirit that animated Jiménez de Cisneros to look to the popular militias to curb the arrogant aristocracy?†

Doesn't Castelar†† tell us today that "Spain is filled with a democratic spirit as deeply rooted as it can be in America?" And face to face with that absorbent, cosmopolitan Anglo-Saxon democracy, will Spain seek to maintain her influence in America by barricading her overseas provinces against the metropolis' "democratic spirit" of which the great orator speaks? Don't we proclaim every day the need for closer intellectual and material ties between Spain and the republics which violently threw off her dominion, so that a great league of Latin American peoples may be forged to counter the drives of the northern republican

---

* Aragon's supreme council of five, arbitrating between king and vassals and between ecclesiastics and laymen, issuing decrees in the king's name and seeing to their implementation.
† Francisco Jiménez de Cisneros, regent of Castille in 1506 and of Spain in 1516, founder of Alcalá University.
†† Emilio Castelar (1832-1899), conservative republican famous for his oratorical gifts.

colossus? And will that be achieved by exclusiveness, by the centralization and unification of Antillean consciousness?

No. North American democracy, the influence of that nation which derives its strength from liberty, cannot be opposed by tyrannies and mistrust and doctrinaire traditionalism. Liberty must be fought with liberty; and in every latitude liberty, like humanity, is one.

As Labra* said in one of his talks at La Unión Mercantil, "politics is not only the science of ideals, but the most difiicult art of incarnating ideas in customs and practices."

If Spain's policy in America must be one of attraction, throughout the vast continent that speaks her language and is inspired by her beliefs and has inherited her customs, then attention must be paid to Blanco'st remarks in his *Venezuela heroica*: that in the struggle that deprived Spain of those territories, "the new triumphed over the old; the monarchy bowed its head and the republic arose. The victory, in synthesis, corresponds to the idea." Torquemada did not triumph over Luther; the *Syllabus* did not shackle Fulton; no gags could smother Gutenberg; a brighter and more civilizing nimbus surrounds Washington and Franklin†† than the halo of horrors embracing the Duke of Alba and Philip II.

These are my convictions, these the ideas that can drive my pen. By following them I serve liberty's cause, and by serving that, I believe I serve my race and my flag.

If I am wrong, it is late in the day to mend my ways. I would have to deny my parents and forget the lessons I had from them. There is in my conscience no shadow accusing me of such forgetfulness; as I received their precepts, so I profess them; as I expound them, so I will transmit them to my children.

If the *Integridad Nacional* people find this information useful, I trust they will put it with their previous data about my private life and judge them all together, and may justice aid them in the task. I am confident that even should their judgment be adverse, my

* Rafael María de Labra (1841-1918), Cuban abolitionist.
† Eduardo Blanco (1838-1912), Venezuelan politician and writer.
†† The allusions are to the impossibility of religious fanaticism drowning the spirit of progress and liberty.

consideration for the journal and its learned editor will not thereby be diminished. For I am of those who believe that social culture should be a bond of attraction in the vast field of ideas. And the educational principles received from my parents do not forbid me to extend a friendly hand to a generous adversary—a hand which he can clasp because I have kept it unstained, so that in blessing my children I might not have to hide it in shame.

Puerto Rico, October 29, 1885

Ecos de la batalla, 1886

The Way We Are

The Puerto Rican people have great qualities of character. Some of these are shared by all of Spain's extended family but are very specially ours. Others are so special that one would seek them in vain in any other branch of the Spanish tree in the enormous neighboring continent.

Originating in southern Spanish provinces, the first colonizers of Puerto Rico brought us the lively imagination and delicate feeling peculiar to that region, but by no means its vehement way of doing things.

This fact stands out so forcibly that anyone knowing little of our origins, observing our niggardly performance of many social actions, would think we had come not from the south but from the north of Europe.

In truth, expansiveness of character, generosity and long-suffering, and the propensity to resign oneself with a promise — sometimes with a simple formula of courtesy (which we generally see as a happy augury) — sufficiently describe the dreamy richness of our fantasy and reveal where it really comes from. But in spite or perhaps because of just this, we are a special people, easily led and very addicted to letting someone else do it, little concerned when we find that it isn't done after so much was promised.

In view of our origins it seems strange that the dominant quality of the Puerto Rican character should be independence; but so it is.

Whether because of the isolation in which we have lived, or because of the habits of rural life, or out of ignorance of certain social arrangements, the Puerto Rican values his individual liberty very highly and shows no disposition to sacrifice it for conventional labels and formulas.

79

And whether this is good or bad, we won't try to ascertain, nor is it necessary for our purpose. We describe, let others undertake to judge. And there is no doubt that we are describing from the life.

Of course we Puerto Ricans have the least courtly manners on earth. We say this as a generalization, aware that there must be those among us who enjoy frequenting spacious salons and know how to behave in them with that exquisite refinement proper to palace etiquette. But the collective cannot be judged by the individual, especially when the individual has been able to modify himself through circumstances foreign to his peers.

Study the Puerto Rican in any part of the Island and you'll see him eloquent and merry at his gatherings, but circumspect and even withdrawn in public life; very respectful toward authority but avoiding involvement with it to the utmost, even in matters that are important to him. If authority summons him, he responds quickly, but can hardly wait to leave its presence and return to his tiny bit of land and his chores.

If the occasion arises for you to enter a Puerto Rican's house—we speak of the genuine, not the adulterated article—you'll see how scrupulously he performs his duty as a host, however little you know him; but don't expect him to come to yours to return the call.

In his national duties he is a model. Is the ancestral soil in danger? At once you'll find him defending it. Is there suffering among his brothers in remote provinces? His purse is open to help them. Does the nation celebrate some glorious anniversary? He joins spontaneously in the general rejoicing.

These are typical characteristics of our people; but at the opposite pole, does some calamity befall him? He asks no one for help. If someone gives it, he accepts; if it is offered, he is wary; if his hopes are dashed, he resigns himself.

Somebody may say: "If only one could add to these conspicuous attributes a certain measure of tractibility, and less of the tendency to retreat into solitude when it comes to attending official gatherings and public offices, these people could get more benefit from those entrusted with administering and leading them." The observation may be pertinent, but what can we do?

We're like that. Brought up in solitude, we don't do well in the bustle of the court.

The colonial regime did much to deepen these solitary instincts, and if the deceptions we have suffered are not enough to diminish our innate loyalty, they suffice to make us cautious and suspicious.

It is true that this habitual withdrawal from the orbit of authority, resulting from our characters and the political education we receive, has led certain people to think us willful and at odds with the powers that be. But that is our way and we continue believing in good faith, and in spite of all, that peoples should be judged by their history, not by the misrepresentations of bad counselors.

And we're so addicted to our customs that we show no signs of turning over a new leaf.

Do we get a governor? We put down the red carpet for him. Does he vouchsafe us four flattering sentences? We enthrone him in the seventh heaven. Does he show signs of doing something for our country? We proclaim him our benefactor, our savior, and there is no place worthy enough for his name to be engraved there; yet we always stay at a respectful distance, like mariners setting their sails so that the ship won't move. Some say this is no way to act; maybe so, but it does have its advantages.

If the governor keeps none of his promises, sides with the political speculators, and takes us for a big ride, we see no need to get excited but just say, like the fox: the grapes are sour anyway. Our attitude of reserve keeps us from getting hurt. So one shouldn't look only at the obverse side of the coin.

It can happen—and has happened—that a reformist governor becomes a rabid conservative, or that, giving ear to fantastic counsels and traditions (fear being contagious), he ends by overwhelming us with gubernatorial decrees or stupefying us with stentorian cries of abuse, after which he departs in peace to collect a marquisate or similar reward. For such situations the Puerto Rican character seems to have been expressly created.

We listen to the abuse with stoical calm, and with admirable *sang-froid* observe the outpouring of lucubrations about imaginary plots. And when we hear that the hero has awarded himself the honors of victory over there in the Capitol, or when he entreats us for our votes to put him in a parliamentary seat, we permit a wry smile to play on our lips and enliven our faces. That's how we are.

El Domingo, September 9, 1883

Manuel Fernández Juncos (1846–1928)

Writer of vignettes of Puerto Rican customs, legends, and traditions, also a poet, biographer, and journalist. Born in Asturias, whence he emigrated as a child to Puerto Rico; a Puerto Rican by devotion and preoccupation. Founded and edited the weekly *El Buscapié* and the *Revista de Literatura, Ciencias, y Artes* (1887–1893), which contributed notably to the island's literature and culture. Works appearing in both publications have not been collected.

His accounts of our customs are ironical and of great pictorial value: not mere esthetic descriptions or nostalgia for the past, but portraits of subtle irony, sometimes bordering on sarcasm, of popular and representative colonial-world types—the ticket vendor, the newspaper dispatcher, the schoolmaster. He is more concerned with reforming customs than with defending the past.

Selected Bibliography

Fernández Juncos, Manuel. *Semblanzas puertorriqueñas*. 1888.
————. *Cuentos y narraciones*. 1907.
————. *Galería puertorriqueña. Tipos y caracteres. Costumbres y tradiciones*. San Juan: ICP, 1958.
————. *Obras literarias*. San Juan, 1882.
————. *Habana y Nueva York*. 1886.
————. *De Puerto Rico a Madrid*. 1886.
————. *Varias cosas*. 1888.
————. *Sátira contra los vicios y malas costumbres actuales*. 1893.
Carrino, Frank G. "Manuel Fernández Juncos: Pivotal Force in the Insular Movement of Puerto Rico through 'El Buscapié.' " Ph.D. diss., University of Michigan, 1955.
Conde, Pedro. "La vida y los tiempos de don Manuel Fernández Juncos." Ph.D. diss., University of Puerto Rico, 1933.
López, Julio César. "Algunos temas en los cuadros costumbristas de Manuel Fernández Juncos." In *Temas y estilos en ocho escritores*. Barcelona: Editorial Rumbos, 1967.
Mercader, José. *Datos biográficos de don Manuel Fernández Juncos*. Madrid: Imp. Editora, 1913.
Pedreira, Antonio S. *El periodismo en Puerto Rico*. Habana, 1941; San Juan: Editorial Edil, 1969–1970.

Political Iconography

Even the most cultured peoples show a marked tendency to personify the abstract to give ideas tangible and material form, and to use certain external and conventional symbols for beliefs, affections, and sentiments.

In olden times religious ideas were manifested in the form of stars, fruit, flowers, and animals of various kinds.

Mythology came later to provide human images for the beliefs, sentiments, vices, and virtues of more artistic but no less idolatrous generations.

Modern religions which vaunt their spirituality portray the supreme good in human form, equipped with long ash-colored whiskers, summer dress, and sandals in the Hebrew style; and the spirit of evil with tail and horns, long claws, and the look of a predator.

The same occurs with respect to moral or juridical ideas, and thus we often see equality represented by a spirit-level, death and the teaching profession by a skeleton, verbal patriotism by a chock-full-of-nuts confection, infidelity and abundance by a horn, justice by a scale, and the colonial regime by a funnel.

From the way we externalize any abstract idea or nonmaterial sentiment by appropriate and perceptible images, one might conclude that humanity abhors the abstract as nature a vacuum.

But where one especially notes this picturesque and amusing custom is in the intercourse of political life.

The history of all ages and nations affords many curious examples of this truth.

And with that, I think, enough of metaphysics and introduction.

85

☆

Puerto Ricans, a Spanish people and hence impressionable, still new to political combat and more artist than philosopher in the diverse manifestations of their political life, cannot escape from the general rule concerning externalization of ideas and using—and abusing—*images* to proclaim opinions and beliefs.

Since the national revolution of 1868* gave real vitality to politics hereabouts, our society started dividing into two groups, one reformist and the other stationary, corresponding with the two great systems into which the art of governing is wont to be divided.

This division of ideas with respect to politics was immediately followed by the division of hats, clearly and precisely distinguished ever since by the greater or smaller width of the band. Conservatives liked them narrow and tight, liberals broad and loose, thus providing a certain analogy with the programs and procedures of each group.

Once these insignia came into general use, the state of public opinion was easily ascertained. One could survey the electoral "heads" in any town and see whether the broad silk band or the narrow patent-leather one predominated. Having observed the hat, one already knew what the wearer had in mind. This remains true: the hat is the man.

Apparently in other times and places it was with the coat that a person displayed his political notions, if we can credit the proverbial "turncoat" epithet for people switching parties. Here the word has purely metaphorical significance.

"So-and-so changed his hat!" That is the correct expression here when someone lapses into the ugly crime of apostasy.

☆

In communities of the interior, especially small ones, people still take very seriously the question of the hatband and of other

* Referring to what was called "La Gloriosa." Puerto Rico experienced an attempted revolution called "The Cry of Lares," and Cuba called "The Cry of Yara." Concerning "La Gloriosa" and its effects, see Clara E. Lida and Iris M. Zavala, *La Revolución de 1868. Historia, pensamiento, literatura* (New York: Las Americas Publishing Co., 1970).

outward signs of political opinion, and this strongly influences all of a person's public and private acts.

An inch more or less on the width of said hatband often decides the success of a business, the fate of a man, the happiness of a couple in love, the future of a family.

Nothing is more efficacious than a hatband in tune with the prevailing political breeze to win good fortune without deserving it, to avoid trouble one does deserve, to get an innocent person punished, or to obtain credit with the firm intention of not paying.

If, for example, the mayor and the judge are conservative (as they will tend to be), it is very important to appear before them on certain occasions in a fine straw hat, with a band so narrow as to be almost invisible and a highly visible cockade.

This helps explain the affection shown by certain people for protective insignia, which in the stormy days of General Sanz were known as lightning conductors.*

In commercial operations the politics of the hat has been much used, and still is, although now it pays off less than it once did. Time was when a narrow hatband presented at the strategic moment was a sure letter of credit, and still alive in memory are fatal hatbands which drove custom away from certain merchants, disastrously multiplying the left column of the profit and loss report.

Experience, that great teacher of businessmen, has notably modified their assessment of these symbols as credit indicators; still, there is no doubt that, other things being equal, some merchants give more consideration to narrow-banded than to broad-banded customers.

For their part, the customers (very few of whom wear the sign of Cancer) generally prefer shopping at stores where the broad band is favored and patent leather is conspicuous by its absence.

So it's no surprise in these parts to come upon a philosophical merchant with two hatbands: a narrow one for making his purchases, and a very broad one for wearing outside the city.

---

* José Laureano Sanz y Posse, governor in 1868–1870 and 1874–1875, under whom was launched a wave of repression against separatists.

☆

What I am saying about hats and hatbands only has exceptions in a few neighborhoods, where due to local circumstances politics has not yet intruded on dress. Also in large centers where the vogue of the authoritarian stovepipe hat lends an equalitarian touch, where fashion levels classes and parties through the democratic derby, and where the budget imposes symmetry on its favored one through the official cap.

☆

Many other ways of showing political views are adopted and recognized here.

In the average community there are two barber shops: a liberal one where everyone roots for the reformists, and a conservative one where the razor or conversation thoroughly scrapes and plucks friends of the *Boletín.**

Generally, too, there are two casinos, one liberal and one conservative, where people dance the *merengue* to their favorite political tune.

The liberals dance it forward and the conservatives dance it backward.

For the cure (pardon the expression) of diseases, there are likewise two doctors in each average-sized community.

One takes the conservatives' pulses and the other the liberals', displaying in each case a certain analogy between their political stance and their professional technique.

The conservative is partial to diets, bleedings, leeches, and the Broussais antiphlogistic method. The liberal one goes for the heroid, resolute, radical approach. The latter dashes in with the knife and then thinks about cauterizing, the former resorts to plaster, unguents, poultices, and dilators. When the time comes for a consultation, it is fascinating to hear the discussions and polemics of the two medics concerning the state of the patient and the superiority each attributes to his curative method.

In the frequent cases of disagreement, a third discordant voice

---

* The *Boletín Mercantil* (1839–1872), reformist newspaper.

is sought in some nearby town—an empirical and neutral Galen without either a cockade or a broad band, something between Broussais and Brown, a dabbler in both systems who can't decide for either. A physician of the order of ducks, as popular political jargon has it.

This new character's intervention in the dispute rarely brings harmony between the two original contenders. Rather, he tends to raise their temperatures higher or ally them against him, further deepening the confusion.

The head of the household then pays for the time invested in all this argumentation and chooses from the three the one to attend the bedside, after having made sure (by their hats) of the politics of each one.

"Right or wrong, so be it," he says for his own consolation. "If God will that the patient be saved, let him owe his life to someone with decent politics. If he dies . . . at least let a doctor of our own party collect the fees."

☆

Politics similarly rears its head in almost all private activities, even domestic service.

A conservative's servant displays the insignia of the master to distinguish himself from the liberal's. If domestics of both camps have a tendency to pilfer, at least let it be on the political level, each one wearing a hatband in harmony with the boss's. If one of them leaves the service of a reformist to enter that of a conservative, or vice versa, he makes a quick switch, keeping the old band in his pocket for when he will need it again.

When looking for a new boss without knowing in which camp he may find one, he carefully keeps both bands in his pockets, leaving the hat nudely neutral to indicate its adaptibility to whoever offers him the most.

☆

When a community is big enough to sustain a café with sweets, desserts, and drinks, two competing ones are set up, one liberal and one conservative.

The first offers water in abundance and, to anyone requiring coffee, serves it black*; the customers read liberal papers and have enthusiastic discussions, and the cigarette brands sold and smoked are La Honradez, La Reforma, La Autonomía, El Siglo, Astrea, and Castelar. The second serves a cocktail with a straw to be sipped slowly, and hot chocolate with toast; cheap, strong Indiscutible cigars are smoked, and cigarettes of Tres Coronas, ¿Quién Vive?, El Momio, and Zumalacárregui brands.†

☆

Another of our country's popular ways of showing political views is in the use of colors.

One need only observe the hangings in a casino or private home, the shades in a barber shop, the window of a store, the dress of a lady, the collar of a dog, and even the harness and bridle of a horse, to identify the party favored by the casino, home, barber shop, store, lady, dog, or horse adorned with these particular colors.

Government loyalists use a mammee shade of yellow to symbolize their opinions. The opposition uses red (the shade of a harassed taxpayer), and thus the colonists under our national flag show how they divide up.

Neutral "ducks" show their preference with a lilac color that really isn't a color.

Even in the romantic department the party spirit has its influence, although to tell the truth politics isn't the best love-conductor.

Certainly conservatives' and liberals' daughters are most apt to marry narrow- and broad-hatbanded suitors respectively; but this preference originates in the constant socializing of similarly oriented families, the subordination of social intercourse to the accident of politics, the gatherings in the respective rival casinos where couples dance to one party's tune and it is almost sinful to be promiscuous.

Yet love, which has no political affiliation and exercises in all

---

* Milk was an upper-class item, and coffee became a symbol of "Puerto Rico for the Puerto Rican" circles.
† These cigarette brands and drinks exemplify the insular vs. the foreign, i.e., separatism vs. annexationism.

parties a capricious and dictatorial influence, often does very dirty tricks to diehard families, fomenting mutual passion between a charming and subversive-eyed libertarian and an upstanding youth with susceptible heart and conservative headgear.

And it is well known that when the naughty children of Aphrodite set themselves to achieve such fusions, neither the autocrat born under the sign of Cancer nor the Central Committee itself has power to stop it. Politics simply has to be shoved aside for the time being while they work the thing out in a Vergara-type embrace.

The priest blesses this kind of armistice, whose duration may be longer or shorter according to the phases or eclipses of the honeymoon. Finally a day will come when for this or that reason the spouses remember that they belong to two different parties, that they have lived among hats with different bands and danced in casinos with different-colored adornments.

From that day both begin to recover their former political inclinations, but without great harm to domestic peace and conjugal harmony.

He subscribes to the *Boletín Mercantil,* she to the favorite newspaper of Puerto Rican ladies, *El Buscapié.*

Galeria puertorriqueña, 1888

Francisco del Valle Atiles (1847–1917)

Noteworthy writer and essayist. Studied in Spain and France. Was one of the founders of the Ateneo Puertorriqueño (1876). In 1884 published *Inocencia,* the first realist-naturalist novel written in Puerto Rico. In it he uses all his knowledge of the countryside and rural life to present a magnificent brief in defense of women and against guilty society. He also wrote short stories (which remain uncollected) about the ambiance of the island. Interested himself in sociological themes and often described social evils: hunger, disease, prostitution. His books and studies need republishing. At the end of the century he joined the ideologists of annexation and was among the founders of the Republican Party (1899).

Selected Bibliography

Valle Atiles, Francisco del. *El campesino puertorriqueño, sus condiciones físicas, intelectuales y morales, causas que las determinan y medios para mejorarlas.* 1887; reprinted in Eugenio Fernández Méndez, *Crónicas de Puerto Rico: Antología de autores puertorriqueños.* San Juan: Ediciones del Gobierno, 1957.

—————. *Un estudio de 168 causas de prostitución.* San Juan, 1919.

—————. *Inocencia.* Puerto Rico: el Asimilista, 1884.

—————. *General Antonio Maceo.* Ponce, 1899.

Gómez Tejera, Carmen. *La Novela en Puerto Rico. Apuntes para su historia.* San Juan, 1947.

Martínez Roselló, M. "Don Francisco del Valle Atiles, novelista." *Puerto Rico Ilustrado,* October 6, 1928.

The Spiritual Life of the Jíbaro*

Let us say something about the *jíbaro*'s language—that "total expression of the life of the spirit," as Revilla† calls it, which can provide this part of our work with valuable data.

The speech of the peasant has the imperfections of those who never had any education; he still uses words that modern Spanish has forgotten, and the impurity and barbarism of his language are notorious. Of his defective pronunciation we will speak later; but added to this is a certain negligence in his way of speaking—a negligence shared in greater or lesser degree by all inhabitants of Spanish America and even of the Canaries, and thus by the Puerto Ricans in general, but especially among the *jíbaros*.

Our peasantry confirms the observation that all persons used to living in the country tend to shout, but such intensity and vigor of speech are often seen to be less marked here than in most rural folk. This, while not universally true, may be explained by organic pauperization, to which corresponds a rather weak respiratory apparatus. Deep sounds do not predominate in the *jíbaro*'s tone of voice; rather he may be described as ranging from baritone to tenor and even contralto, and the falsetto voice is no rarity.

In his phonetic illiteracy the peasant lacks the soft *c* and the *ll, v, x,* and *z*. The *c* followed by *e* or *i,* and the *z,* almost always come out as *s,* for example *serro, simarrón, sanja, sumo.* He changes the *ll* into *ñ* and sometimes into *y,* as in *ñaman, cabayo;* the *v* into *b* as in *bira.* The final *d* and terminations of the preterite participles are not

---

* This text reflects what Frantz Fanon calls the alienation of colonized people. Cf. *The Wretched of the Earth* (New York: Grove Press, 1968).
† Does this refer to Manuel de la Revilla (1846–1881)? He wrote articles of literary criticism and philosophy at the end of the nineteenth century. It should also refer to José de la Revilla, teacher, writer, and publicist.

95

96 Francisco del Valle Atiles

pronounced, as: *mitá, comprao.* Often he makes an *rr* sound like a *j*, as in *ajroj* for *arroz*; changes the *r* into *l* or *j*, as in *amol, cajne*; and finally—as our good friend and fine poet don Luis Muñoz Rivera has pointed out to us—he almost always sounds an *s* like a soft *j*, for example *loj, pejroj, ejtán.* Sometimes he will do the same with a *z*, as when he says *ajoraoj* for *azorados.* The *h* is always a strong *j*, as in *jacer* for *hacer.*

If physically speaking the *jíbaro's* language is full of defects, from the physical-spiritual standpoint it reveals not only the poverty of his intellectual development but a sharpness of intelligence that could easily be cultivated.

After this brief examination let us look into the state of the useful arts among the rural classes, and start with the most beautiful of them all, poetry. The product of imagery and sentiment, we find it—if not in its most resplendent array—beautified by the natural clothing of spontaneity and simplicity that everywhere adorns popular verse. Many *cantares* of the *jíbaros* reveal a poetic genius rich in fantasy and not without imagination and wit. Considering these people's descent from southern Spaniards, who possess those precious gifts in rare measure, it could hardly be otherwise.

If this source of beauty falls short of its potential, we might ascribe it to the *jíbaro's* lack of learning, for imagination, after all, is not enough to produce the beautiful: other powers of the spirit, duly cultivated, should come to its aid. This deficiency causes the peasant to lyricize subjects of little worth; indeed his songs sometimes contain such absurdities that, to judge by them, one would have to doubt even the common sense of their authors. One comes upon explanatory stanzas full of obscenities; others are extravagantly headless and footless, as the saying goes—nothing more than words devoid of sense, although the author presumes to describe them as "argument."

Yet at other times the uncouth poet brings it off. We have heard some quite beautiful and ingenious carols—what they call *aguinaldos,** and some of their *cantares* can awaken esthetic emotion.

* Ivette Jiménez de Báez has published an important study of the Puerto Rican popular lyric: see *La décima popular en Puerto Rico* (Mexico: Veracruz University, 1964).

Their theme is nearly always love and its passions, but other themes can also inspire them. Their couplets recall the rich popular verse of Spain. Their Andalusian derivation is generally clear but many *cantares* can be traced to the influence of other Spanish provinces with their prodigality of carols, merry *seguidillas,* picaresque ballads, etc.

To give a slight idea of our popular poetry, here are a few *cantares:**

> Puse en tu puelta un letrero
> Y el letrero dice así:
> —Pasajero, pasajera,
> Cuando pasej por aquí,
> Si no quierej sel cautibo
> Pasa sin miral siquiera;
> Yo miré una vej, y bibo
> Ejclabo jajta que muera.

> I put on your door a writing
> And this is what it said:
> Passerby, passerby,
> When you pass by here,
> If you don't want to be a captive
> Pass without looking;
> I looked once, and live
> A slave till I die.

A gallant thought worthy of a lady of most delicate taste. And these *cantares* express well the intensity of love:

> Nunca me digaj adioj
> Cuando pol la caye baj,
> Que parese que me disej
> Adioj para nunca maj.

---

* In the text, these verses have misspelled Spanish to convey *jíbaro* pronunciation.

You never tell me goodbye
When you walk off down the street,
But to me it seems you're saying
Goodbye for evermore.

Si doblasen laj campanaj,
No preguntej quién murió:
Ausente de ti, mi bía,
¿Quién pué sel si no yo?

If the bells toll,
Don't ask who died:
Away from you, my love,
Who can it be but I?

The obstinancy of true love is depicted in this *cantar* no less naturally than the sentiments in the previous two quatrains:

Buscando boy pol la Ijla
Quien quiera haselme un abol:
Ajrancal de mi memoria
El recuerdo de tu amol.

Through the island I wander
Seeking who will do me a favor
To tear from my memory
The remembrance of your love.

And here is a beautiful quatrain in which the poet uses periphrasis to warn a sweetheart whose suitor doesn't seem very faithful:

Quítate de esa bentana,
No le baya a jasel daño
A la flor de tu ilusión
El biento del desengaño.

Get away from that window,
Your dream is a flower,
You shouldn't let it be bruised
By the wind of disenchantment.

These *cantares* throb with the jealousy and contempt for life which unhappy lovers like to display, sometimes genuine, sometimes just a ritual:

> Ayá ba mi corazón,
> Abrele con esa yabe,
> Y veraj si dentro dél
> Solo tu recueldo cabe.

> There goes my heart,
> Open it with that key,
> And see if it has room
> For anything but your memory.

> Dejde que pagaj mi amol
> Con el odio del dejden,
> Boy buscando una dolama
> Que mate de una vej.

> Since you repaid my love
> With the hatred of contempt
> I seek everywhere some infection
> That will finish me off.

> Si me quieres dimeló
> Y si no dame beneno,
> Que no es el primer amol
> que le da muelte a su dueño.

> If you love me, say so
> If not, give me poison,
> It won't be the first time
> That love killed the lover.

The *jíbaro* poet also knows how to express in song that ironic kind of pessimism so often found in Spanish popular poetry. Some examples:

Si quierej ejtal contento
Manda comprar, buen amigo,
Un quintal de indiferencia
Y dos arrobaj de olvido.

If you want to be happy,
Good friend, go out and buy
A hundredweight of indifference
And fifty pounds of forgetfulness.

El honol es un tesoro
Del que lo sabe gualdal.
Le he bijto cambial pol oro
Ejto no se ha de admiral.

Honor is the treasure
Of him who knows how to guard it.
I have seen it bartered for gold
Which is not to be admired.

There are epigrams like the following, which neatly shield the idea while they hurt:

Disen que tienej un nobio;
Disen que le quieres bien;
Disen que disen que yoraj,
Pero no disen por qué.

They say you have a lover;
They say you love him well;
They say that you're crying
But they don't say why.

Others are more open and obvious, such as:

Eso seloj de tu amante
Me dan ganaj de reil.
¡Pobresito del que pasa
Por onde han pasao mil!

This jealousy of your lover
Makes me want to laugh.
The poor sap, going
Where a thousand have gone before.

And here is a somewhat boastful expression of patriotism, inspired by the English invasion of which our histories tell:

¿De que le bale al ingléj
El ponel tantaj trincheraj,
Si sabe que Puerto Rico
Tiene lanchas cañoreraj?

What good does it do the English
To dig so many trenches,
Don't they know that Puerto Rico
Has gunboats?

Enough examples to show that, despite his poor intellectual development, the unhappy and anemic *jíbaro* keeps poetry alive in his soul, has a feeling for beauty, and sometimes knows how to produce it.

To round out our survey with another form of poetic expression, we will say the *jíbaro*'s tales and fables suffer from too much phantasmagoria, and have little worthy of note. Goblins, birds of ill omen, magic wands, miraculous transformations, instantaneous and effortless rags-to-riches mutations; in a word, nothing, at least in the ones known to us, to show intellectual distinction.

A few words are called for about these rural folk's musical instruments: the *maraca*, an Indian kind of tambourine, comparable by its name and the sound it produces with the *matraca*, the crude wooden rattle known to nearly all primitive peoples; the *güiro*, a gourd which, scraped on its lined surface, produces a dry sound very harsh to unaccustomed ears; and some variations of the guitar and cittern. These include the *tiple*, a small guitar with five strings of which the first and fifth are inexplicably the same, producing an anomalous combination of sounds; the *cuatro* with five double strings placed two by two, which is tuned and played like the cittern; the *bordonuá* with six strings and the *vihuela* with

up to ten, according to the maker's whim. None of these instruments conforms in its construction with a rational artistic idea;
having little material value, they are only made by the *jíbaros*
themselves, generally with ill-adapted implements. It would be
interesting to trace how these national string instruments have
gone off the track. The general idea of guitar and cittern construction persists in them, but the lack of proper tools to make
them like the models which the Spaniards brought from the
metropolis must largely account for their imperfection.

Yet with all the imperfection pleasant tunes can be played on
them. Skillful hands know how to draw graceful melodies from
such crude instruments, although modulations must be very difficult to produce on them. There are players of surprising skill
who can make a great show with them despite the difficulties they
must present, producing especially with the *cuatro* melodies one
could not imagine possible.

Accompanying himself on these rough instruments, the *jíbaro*
sings his languid erotic couplets or his animated carols during the
Christmas season. And this limited orchestra suffices him for his
dances, some of which it is sad to see falling into disuse. The
seis—perhaps so-called from the *seis* once danced before the altar
in a forgotten Christian rite—is a rather elegant figure dance
which may be losing its relationship to the old dance, with figures
like the old *españoleta* now substituted by the *merengue* to which the
seis is adjusted. The *sonduro, cadenas, caballos, puntillado, fan-
danguillo,* and perhaps some other variations unknown to us, are
being relegated to most unjust oblivion.

The dance called *caballo* requires the dancers to execute dizzy
waltz turns. The *sonduro* calls for such noisy footwork that sometimes the dancers will put metal plates on their shoes to make
more din. The *cadenas* is a dance with very pretty combinations
and music, accompanied by singing. The *puntillado* is a tapdance
to the most agreeable five-eight music, seeming to combine
three- and four-time rhythms with delightful effect. It too is a
figure dance only surviving in some communities of the interior.

Modern dance tends to wipe out all these; in urban society the
figure dance has disappeared, and in the country the same is
happening—to the injury of the essence of dance, since apart

from being good exercise it has its spiritual aspect. It has served to express musically the higher sentiments—of religion, of love, of war; today it only expresses amorous passion, but in a gross way, as represented by modern dance. In the figure dance the wooing process was more sensibly pantomimed: lined up face to face, the couples greeted each other, paraded around, clasped hands, and finally, after various figures, came the more intimate dance of whirling waltzes. The *merengue* eliminated almost all preliminaries: the man invites the lady and they immediately go into an intimate embrace, which lasts a long time little distracted by physical effort. For this dance requires none of the movements which, tiring the body, remove as much as possible of the voluptuousness—especially since it is done to languid, sweet, and tendentious music.

We don't suggest that this always happens in modern dance, but the danger of it cannot be overlooked. It is possible to dance the *merengue* innocently and correctly, but it is danced under circumstances against which it is well to be forewarned. If dance is to be conceded any usefulness, that can only be on condition that it give healthy pleasure rather than enervate. Dance the *merengue* by all means, but not so exclusively as to cut out more beautiful and spiritual dances.

From *El campesino puertorriqueño*, 1887

II
Independence or Annexation?

Luis Muñoz Rivera (1859–1916)

Poet and journalist. Founded the newspaper *La Democracia* and *El Diario de Puerto Rico,* and in New York *The Puerto Rico Herald.* Was resident commissioner in Washington where he fought for annexation. Intensely active politically. Also notable as poet and patriot. Most of his work consists of articles, lectures, and political speeches.

Selected Bibliography

Muñoz Rivera, Luis. *Tropicales.* New York, 1902.
————. *Campañas políticas.* 3 vols. Madrid, 1925.
————. *Obras completas.* 9 vols. San Juan: ICP, 1964.
Arana Soto, Salvador. *Luis Muñoz Rivera, savia y sangre de Puerto Rico. Patria y Pensamiento.* San Juan, 1968.
Cruz Monclova, Lidio. *Luis Muñoz Rivera, los primeros diez años de su vida política.* San Juan: ICP, 1959.
Dalmau Canet, Sebastián. *Luis Muñoz Rivera, su vida, su obra, su carácter.* San Juan: Tipografía Boletín Mercantil, 1917.
González Ginorio, José. *Luis Muñoz Rivera. A la luz de sus obras y de su vida. Estudio biográfico-educativo.* New York, 1919.

What I Was, Am, and Must Ever Be

On May 27, while I was absent in Washington, this touching item appeared in *El Heraldo Español* of Puerto Rico:

"We have never said that Sr. Muñoz Rivera, after having been leader of the Puerto Rican offshoot of a metropolitan monarchist party, said at two banquets honoring the King of Spain's saint's day—one in the park, one in the Inglaterra Hotel—that his ideas had always been republican."

But yes: by conviction rooted in me since I was barely fifteen, and by constant affirmation as I studied man's progress through history, my ideas were always profoundly republican.

I could never conceive that a man, with no other qualification than birth in a palace and inheritance of a scepter and crown, should rule and impose his sovereign will on others. I have believed that, solely by virtue of entering into life, all of us have the right to intervene in the functions of supreme power with our votes. In a word, that neither aristocracy, theocracy, autocracy, nor any other form of personal government or government by class, caste, or oligarchy, was compatible with human dignity. Hence my preference and partiality for democracy and the Republic.

But the prior reality for me was that I came into the world in a diminutive island, lacking the means to fight with weapons, subjected by bitter fate to the laws of a mother nation. The sons of our soil could never break that yoke but they conducted an almost unanimous struggle for their collective honor, calling themselves reformists in 1867, assimilationists in 1877, autonomists in 1887. The masters, the señors with their baptismal faith in the Spain that belongs to Europe, maintained their monopoly of public affairs. This was only natural for them; what was sad was that they were supported by a few sons of our soil who set themselves against their brothers' noble impulses, calling themselves "unconditional Spaniards" and helping to enslave Puerto Rico.

What a tough job, to fight successfully against the unconditionals of both countries! In that unequal struggle our most honest patriots expended their lives: Padial, Freire, Goico, Acosta, Baldorioty, Celis, Corchado, Brau, Marín, Córdoba, Alonso, Morales, Quiñones*. . . . The best minds of our land.

It was hopeless. When they defended the Island's cause they were accused of rebellion, of anti-Spanish activities; the Civil Guard took them by remote routes to iniquitous jails; they were placed outside the law, punished like criminals. Hopeless.

And as I watched the sinister show from my observation post in Barranquitas, there was formed in me a sentiment higher than scholastic philosophies, juridical systems, and forms of political power: a regional sentiment, the pure, noble, exclusive devotion to country.

I had seen my teachers fall, my brothers agonize, my people— the Puerto Rican people—divided in desperate, Dantesque contention. I continued to be a republican; but above all I wanted and had to be a Puerto Rican. And to be that effectively, to free the colony from colonialism, to shake the old tree of tyranny and break the monolith of secular privilege, I had to lean upon one force: the metropolitan parties.

Upon what party? Upon those who were putting up the same futile fight as myself for the Republic, or upon those in the citadel of monarchy who had power to establish autonomy, improbable as that was? I had not a minute's doubt. And on July 1, 1890, I founded this newspaper and raised in it the banner of an alliance

* Luis Padial Vizcarrondo, advocate in 1870 of Canadian-type autonomy; José Ramón Freire, editor of the reformist newspaper *La Razón* published in Mayagüez; Pedro Jerónimo Goico, abolitionist; José Julián Acosta, abolitionist; Román Baldorioty de Castro, abolitionist and politician, autonomist; José Celis Aguilera, chairman of the Liberal Reformist Party; Manuel Corchado Juarbe, liberal reformist who called in 1867 for a university in Puerto Rico; Salvador Brau, historian and critic; Francisco González (Pachín) Marín, member of the Borinquen Club, one of José Martí's group in New York; Santiago de Córdoba, advocate of eliminating customs dues and land rights; Manuel A. Alonso, the *jíbaro;* Luis Sánchez Morales, autonomist; Buenaventura Quiñones, who tried to proclaim independence in 1838.

with the Liberal Party. I worked, and I won. Autonomy ceased to be a philosophic abstraction and became a concrete fact. Puerto Rico was governing Puerto Rico!

Let those who object listen well. If any nation on earth—not Spain the discoverer and civilizer but any nation, Italy, England, Russia, Turkey, the monarchies with their kings and emperors and caesars and sultans—had guaranteed self-government for my poor little tropical rock, I would have been Italian, Russian, English, Turkish, whatever. Because that would not have made me a Turk, a Russian, an Englishman, or an Italian, but just what I am and all that I am—what most satisfies my native and reflective longings—a Puerto Rican!

Between the redemptive republic and the redemptive monarchy, what choice was there? I would have opted for the Republic. Only that the Republic didn't arise in Spain. And I wasn't going to sacrifice Puerto Rico to my preferences, to my ideal theories. In my heart and will, Puerto Rico takes precedence over Spain, over the United States, over all Europe and all America. So that when Puerto Rico needed and needs to save herself, I went to Spain and I will go to the United States; I don't stand on my own pride. Up with the interests of my Island and down with the beautiful things I learned from books, the illusions on which I fed my soul. If need be, down with the popularity arduously won in three decades of effort and sacrifice.

Today there is no danger in being a republican. I am one. I am thankful for this compatability between my political dreams and my patriotic duties. But if another monarchy were to triumph at the doors of Washington, like Catiline at the doors of Rome; if a Theodore Roosevelt were to create an American empire as Isabella built a Spanish one; if the circumstances arose again in which I didn't serve monarchy but went to monarchy in my country's service, I would accept union from Roosevelt as I accepted it from Cristina,* though it meant embracing and forgiving my enemies and forgetting the day when my plant was broken into with pickaxes, demagogy threatened my home, and reaction

---

* Reference to the Queen Maria Cristina, from 1885 to 1899, until Alfonso XIII became of age.

put me in the prisoner's dock. But that is nothing—less than nothing, since it is my own pain and sorrow, since if I felt otherwise it could be my vengeance or my pride.

This I was, this I am, and this I will be until I fall into my silent and restful grave. This, I believe, is how my good and perceptive compatriots should be. And because of it I am for union and clearing away Habsburgian obstacles, for the salvation and redemption of Puerto Rico.

And the rest . . . ? The rest is my country.

La Democracia, July 12, 1910

Rosendo Matienzo Cintrón (1855–1913)

Born in Luquillo, studied in Lérida, Barcelona, and Madrid where he was in close contact with the abolitionist group headed by Labra. Returned to Puerto Rico in 1884 and began to pursue his career as a lawyer. Contributed to *El Buscapié, La Conciencia Libre,* and *La Democracia.* In 1898 he belonged to the Republican Party which favored annexation to the United States. Later changed his political orientation and defended independence. His best writings from this point of view appeared in the dailies *La Correspondencia de Puerto Rico* and *La Conciencia Libre.* Most of his work remains uncollected.

Selected Bibliography

Díaz Soler, Luis M. *Rosendo Matienzo Cintrón. Orientador y guardián de una cultura.* UPR, 1960, 2 vols.

Medina Ramírez, Ramón. *Patriotas ilustres puertorriqueños.* San Juan, 1962.

Anonymous. "Nota Necrológica. *El Día,* 29 Dec. 1913.

The Guachafita Fá

La guachafita fá is American citizenship for Puerto Ricans.

If you ask for it in good faith they won't give it to you, on the ground that you already have Puerto Rican citizenship in a union of Americans; that American citizenship is a very bad thing that would ruin Puerto Rico, since there are already too many niggers in the United States to be adding a million more.

If you don't want it, if you want independence for your country, they'll tell you: ask for citizenship and you'll get it. Why not? Ask Congress for it again and if Congress won't give it the people will, the noble American people. Don't be downhearted. Within a century or two you'll be able to form a state. Meanwhile we Puerto Rican Americans will enjoy here the pure and honest delights of a colony—not just any old colony but a charming colony. To appreciate what the American colony of Puerto Rico is and will be like, remember the slaves of slaves who won their freedom any way they could.

The Americans say among themselves: boy, we oughta help those *espiquitis** get American citizenship, it would fit them like a pair of slippers on a church Christ. For obviously Puerto Ricans are sentimentalists, and American citizenship is all they need to feel like Americans, the way a stick over the shoulder makes kids feel like soldiers.

But it won't work out quite like that because an American citizen is a sovereign citizen, and this the Puerto Rican will never be albeit clad in the citizenly toga. There would in fact be three American citizenships, the two continental ones and the Puerto Rican: that is to say, the citizenship of North American whites, of North American blacks, and of Puerto Ricans. That of the mas-

* Possible deformation of the English "spic."

115

ters, that of the freed slaves, and that of the poor idiots in noncontiguous countries who don't speak English.

The black man in the United States has his own problems, into
which we can't enter for the time being except on the general
human level. Whether by his own or others' fault, he isn't a real
citizen of the United States. He is a dog, an ox, privileged to the
extent that he can own property; but he isn't a citizen that matters,
or he is the mere matter of citizenship. Not really a citizen.

If the whites so desire, the black man votes; if not, he doesn't. If
the whites think he should survive, he does; if not, he is lynched
on a tree or stoned or shot to death like a rabid dog or wolf.

So if you are going to have a third citizenship, as degrading for
Americans as Puerto Ricans, you will get a citizenship granted for
convenience, a concession calculated by and for "business." A
business negotiated between spic shamelessness and Yanqui
greed. Citizenship without sovereignty is citizenship acquired not
to ennoble but to demean oneself. The toga loses its prestige on
the back of a sick whore and, even as she puts it on, it changes into
a slave's tunic. By this weird process citizenship is debased without
elevating the recipient.

We know that the game is to swindle the country by conceding
"citizenship with colonialism," that is, without sovereignty: a sort
of empty nutshell given to a monkey to play with. Can the good
"boys" who live here believe we'll fall into such a farce?

No, friends, no. We don't want your citizenship because it's
third-class. We didn't want the citizenship Spain gave us because
it was third-class, so why should we want yours?

You denied us citizenship in bad faith so you could exploit us
with impunity, and now you offer this lovely third-class kind, and
perhaps will force us to take it—also in bad faith, like the old
identity cards—to go on exploiting us and to still the clamor
against you in the Island. A citizenship that will cover the people
like the flowers with which victims used to be led to the sacrifice.

But time rushes on. We no longer want to be governed by you,
either with or without American citizenship. There was a time
when we thought freedom couldn't be had without you. Later we
thought we could get it with you or without you. Now we think
that true freedom, which brings with it the sovereignty of our own

government, can't be had with you but only without you, perhaps against you.

As long as you who mystify freedom and your own country's precepts continue to govern, Puerto Rico will be governed by the lie, by dirty business deals, and by the trusts.

La correspondencia de Puerto Rico, November 21, 1911

"Pancho Ibero"

John Bull means England, Uncle Sam the United States, Japhet the whole European race, Shem the Asiatic, etc. Why doesn't the Ibero-American race, too, have a name to individualize it?

Pérez Galdós in his *Episodios nacionales* typifies the Spanish people as the family of Santiago Ibero—that valiant soldier, physically handsome, full of resolve, lover of liberty, well tempered to achieve extraordinary adventures.* I just read that the great novelist plans a trip to Cuba to write up the disaster of Santiago in the recent Spanish-American War. A good opportunity for the author of *Trafalgar* to get to know Pancho Ibero, a product of that *celtíbero*† stock about which he has written so lovingly.

We will call him Pancho because the number of Panchos in America is prodigious. It can be said to be the most popular name and the one that particularizes the New World, because here it is the familiar form of "Francisco" but nowhere in Spain does that transformation occur. In Spain, when you say "Pancho" or "Pancha," you immediately evoke in the listener the idea of a native of America.

To this Pancho we could attach various names which would more or less describe him. We could call him Peláez to suggest his descent from don Pelayo, hero of the reconquest for his race of the Iberian peninsula. Or to designate his language, one of the world's most beautiful, and the great master who did most to immortalize it, he could be called Cervantes.

But these names lack the breadth of Ibero, which embraces

---

* This character appears in some *Episodios* of the second and third series. He stands for liberty and progress.

† *Celtíbero* is the term used for a "true" Spaniard.

118

Pelayo and Cervantes and not only the language immortalized by
the author of *Don Quixote* but the one Camoëns* immortalized in
Portugal's epic poem, *The Lusiads.*

Our Pancho would appear in caricature eternally clad in white,
with his famous straw hat tipped over the face. Sometimes reining
in a small, nervous, fancily harnessed colt which could serve
equally to carry his lady love behind on its rump in the style of his
Andalusian-Arab forebears, or to pursue over the broad pampa
the unruly steer, the unbroken wild horse, or the giant ostrich, or
to perform Homeric military epics under the orders of a Páez, a
San Martín, a Máximo Gómez.† At other times he would appear
in clothing extravagantly bordered and fringed, a long machete
hung from his belt, tough cowhide boots with silver spurs, in the
horrific pose of one who has just brought down a government by
revolution or strangled a revolution on behalf of a government.

But this man whom the poncho, lasso, and machete fit like a
birthday suit is equally at home in the professor's hood, the
magistrate's gown, or the aristocratic formals of the diplomat or
man of the world.

Physically he is like this: medium stature, broad shoulders,
strong and sinewy legs, small hands and feet, big dark eyes, hair
the color of a crow's wing, fine mustache on lip to set off the pallor
of his skin, gait at once nervous and firm. Such will be the
representative of a people occupying the largest area on earth,
who will learn to control mankind's destiny in eighteen republics
beside whose great capitals of Babylon and Nineveh, Paris and
London will shrink into insignificance. And this not in the far
future but by the end of the present century.

By then Ibero-America will probably be more than 400 million
strong, all under one flag with three colors: yellow recalling
Spain, green recalling Portugal, and white to symbolize her aspirations, uncontaminated by those hateful appetites so hostile to

---

* Luis Vaz de Camoëns (1924–1580), Portuguese poet.
† José Antonio Páez (1790–1873), Venezuelan leader against the Spaniards and
first president; José de San Martín (1778–1850), revolutionary general and statesman, chief liberator of Argentina, Chile, and Peru; Máximo Gómez y Báez
(1836–1905), general of Cuba's liberation army in 1895, who after victory refused
the presidential nomination.

other people's liberties. That great country will have two official languages, Spanish and Portuguese, and English will be taught in every school as the third language of our southern continent. Letters will be addressed thus:

"Señor Manuel Cabral, Rio de Janeiro; or perhaps señor don Francisco beresaba, Santiago de Chile"; and below, after the style of U.S. of A., this glorious abbreviation: EUIA, meaning *Estados Unidos Iberos-Americanos.*

La correspondencia de Puerto Rico, January 5, 1911

Vicente Balbás Capó (?)

The only biographical data we have been able to turn up about Capó are that he edited *La Integridad Nacional* (1885–1898) defending the interests of Spain in America—he was an outstanding member of the Spanish Unconditionals party; and that after 1898 he launched *El heraldo español* (1900–1912 or 1915?), which first appeared three times weekly and later daily. In this paper he firmly opposed the North American invasion. Balbás represents the Creole intellectual group that stoutly attacked the new imperialism in the name of Hispanic-Christian values.

Selected Bibliography

Balbás Capó, Vicente. *Puerto Rico a los diez años de americanización*. San Juan: Tipografía del Heraldo, 1910.

Pedreira, Antonio S. *El periodismo en Puerto Rico*. Habana, 1941.

Aren't We Capable
of Governing Ourselves?*

Important Americans are so insistent on Puerto Rico's unpreparedness to govern herself, despite our belief to the contrary, that the matter calls for our urgent attention and serious thought.

Both mainlanders who hold the key positions in this island and top U.S. government people who have come to visit us dedicate papal-bull-like eulogies to our culture, proclaim that our island enjoys more prosperity than before, and add that self-government is beyond our capacity.

How does one statement tally with the other?

Why don't they tell us honestly just what failings they see in us, so that they may see their errors if the failings don't exist, or help us correct them if they do?

Whatever our defects, there is no doubt that our culture and political capacity are much superior to those of the peasant colonists from Great Britain who took up arms to win independence and were able to consolidate that great nation, the United States of North America, of which we are now an appendage.

Those heroic peasants could not at that time have had the cultural level we have now; they had no political life; political science being unknown to them, they could not be more capable than we of self-government. Yet they knew how to obtain it with that pure patriotism that made them sacrifice lives and property to win their rights and set up a great motherland. We, on the other hand, call people patriots who are only able to sacrifice their conscience, abasing themselves with hypocritical adulations and

---

* This resonant and well-written article has reached us with no signature or return address; and although we do not normally publish anonymous contributions, this one is so interesting, its subject so timely, and our approval of its ideas so complete that we do not hesitate to give it the most prominent position in our paper. (Note in the *Heraldo*)

fawning complacencies before the strong man in charge of the People's Treasury—so as to win and keep a fat salary, satisfying all their lusts and providing a luxurious life at the cost of Puerto Rico's wretched people.

Let us examine the reasons why we are flagellated before the whole world with assertions that we can't govern ourselves; and since they don't tell us what our faults or defects are, let us meditate deeply and look into the matter. Whatever the reasons, the people have the right to know them. And we should tell people "the truth, the whole truth, and nothing but the truth" so that we may take the energetic and patriotic steps that seem necessary to remedy our ills.

We must recognize that, continuing as we are now, we will never get what we want: our full rights and the true happiness of Puerto Rico. Our aspirations will be ignored, and if we express them we will be told in an almost imperious tone "not to concern ourselves about what we don't have," as if denying us the most natural and inalienable right of man, to aspire to progress and perfection!

It is imperative that the independent press and the true Nation—the one that pays, not the one that collects—awake from their deadly lethargy and stop abandoning Puerto Rico's fate to bad patriots and bureaucrats. This they must do if they don't want an interminable continuation of the tutelage that weighs us down, a tutelage which would end by suffocating our noblest aspirations, dragging us into degeneration and complete extinction of our own personality.

Let us not lose sight of the fact that, if we want to be respected, we must give up all hypocritical language and beggar's whining and adopt the tone of virile peoples who know their own worth and demand their rights. Let us not try to fool the American people, for they are a serious and shrewd people and this would only rouse their contempt. We have to tell them the plain unvarnished truth if we want them to pay attention!

To the American government and people we have to say honestly: we can't possibly feel happy and satisfied to be Americans as long as you don't treat us as such, as long as you don't recognize our rights to govern ourselves and get out from under the tutelage unjustly imposed on us for these eight years. That while you let our country be exploited by the "trusts" who corner what wealth remains to us and take out most of the wealth it produces, and while you make us consume basic necessities that are dearer than and inferior to what we had before, it would be humbug to say we are happy. How can we say it when the ruin of our once enviable coffee wealth is viewed with Mephistophelean indifference, and those who can and should prevent this do nothing about it? When we see extending everywhere the tentacles of the hungry centralizing octopus, sucking our anemic and exhausted blood to fill the belly of the Treasury with our tax money, pitilessly despoiling taxpayers who can no longer pay the assessments on their houses or hovels and on land they have fertilized with their sweat? These cruelties which are eating up our people are inflicted to satisfy the vices and necessities of "patriots" who thus serve as choristers for the intoners of that bogus chant about our present prosperity.

Finally, we see the prodigal squandering of the people's money on the unnecessary and on lush and exorbitant salaries, and the budget giddily mounting instead of introducing economies that would lower the onerous taxes. And while nothing serious is done to end such injustice and cruelties, how can we possibly feel content? How enjoy the prosperity we once had when our personality was recognized and enhanced, when we enjoyed all rights like other citizens of the metropolis? In those days our products had no lack of profitable markets, which supplied us with goods often cheaper and better than those we are now obliged to consume.

Furthermore, can a people without personality or nationhood, a people who have been turned into virtual helots, feel happy or satisfied?

Puerto Rico a los diez años de americanización, San Juan, 1910

The Emigrants

June 7, 1907

¡Pobrecitos, pobrecitos!
Miradlos cómo se van,
Porque en su tierra se mueren.
Porque en su tierra no hay pan.

Poor souls, poor souls!
Look how they go,
Because in their land there is death,
Because in their land there's no bread.

Popular song

Once again there is talk of workers emigrating abroad.

To tell the truth, while we never shared the notion that we were swimming in prosperity, as chanted by our politicians and governors, we never dreamed that at this point—eight years after the hurricane, nine since the American invasion—people would be talking to us again about this dismal thing.

A truly patriotic and honest article in the Mayagüez newspaper *La Bandera Americana,* reproduced yesterday in the *Heraldo,* demonstrates quite clearly that our much-vaunted progress is a myth—a lie that damages us by paralyzing regenerative action; for, to hear the optimists tell it, we have everything, we are happy, we have wealth and work for all, and so forth.

Showing that he feels in his own heart the pain of his country, my republican colleague in Mayagüez refers to the *bracero* emigration now being organized in Aguadilla and asks with perfect justification:

"What is the significance of this emigration by Puerto Rican natives, leaving behind their country and loved ones?

126

"It means," says my colleague, "that in our island there is no bread, no shelter for the poor because there is no work; that on this rock of ours the worker is exposed to death by hunger; that our economy is *in extremis*. It proves that what is said about our development is a lie, that there is nowhere to earn honest bread with honest toil."

This appears in a republican paper, member of a group cultivating the optimistic note under the stars and stripes, and for good measure carrying the name *The American Flag*. Coming from such a spokesman, it carries twice the authority of such a statement by a journalist less compromised in the present order of things.

True, *La Bandera Americana* goes on to insist that this state of affairs is due to "the Unionist Party situation"; and this strange assertion makes us think we are in the twilight zone of swindles and fictions and don't appreciate our true situation.

We differ with our esteemed Mayagüez colleague, because in our view no party here can be held responsible.

Here parties are not *power*: they are government parties, whether or not they enjoy official protection, with no power to act. They do what the governing power and Executive Council want them to do, without an infinity of zeros added on the right of a decimal fraction.

Since the parties are not power, they have no responsibility, neither Republican nor Unionist.

There is no government responsible to legislative chambers.

The delegates are mere provincial deputies, lacking the administrative attributions and faculties of those who made up the defunct *Diputación*.

So it is unjust to make the "Unionist government" responsible for this state of things, because the "Unionist government" doesn't exist.

The "Republican government" *never* existed, unless one can call "government" a purely auxiliary function in which the president's representative uses the parties as instruments, to pretend that he is vesting in the country faculties which the governing power and the Council members reserve absolutely to themselves.

Well may my Mayagüez colleague ask at the head of his article: "In what sense are we progressing?"

In none, colleague, in none. For this phenomenon of worker emigration that is now being repeated is clearest proof that the worker earns too little to cover the most urgent necessities of life.

And when the worker leaves a country because he has no bread, progress is a lie, a wicked farce, invented by those who have bought silence with a few crumbs in the budget.

After all, it is a pleasure for a dominating country to have such docile subjects, who think they have power because they are given a few official jobs and legislative functions—ridiculous and spurious since here all that is legislated is what the Executive Council wants.

Responsibility for this emigration is the American government's alone, and the country's sole responsibility is indirect: not the responsibility of either the Unionist or Republican Party, but of both. The members of both are guilty because they haven't known how to form the only party possible in this country—the party of Native Personality.

Illusions of official favor, palace predilections, and infantile jealousies have been exploited with skill by those who shrewdly appraise the frailty of our pride, our fascination with public office, our yearning for power. Meanwhile they entertain us with now-you-see-it-now-you-don't sideshows or dog fights, as at our baptismal parties where the kids amuse themselves by swatting each other, allowing the adults to enjoy the ceremony in peace.

On the day when a party is formed here that expects nothing from the government, that despises handout jobs and those who give them, and stands on its own feet; on that day my Mayagüez colleague can demand an accounting for such deep national calamities as these shiploads of emigrants—hungry, pallid, crushed, weak, sad Puerto Ricans whose heads are bowed, like men condemned to death, yet whose only crime is having shown themselves too "easy."

Poor bastards!

Puerto Rico a los diez años de americanización, 1910

José de Diego (1867–1918)

Born in Aguadilla, studied law in Barcelona where he founded the newspaper *La Universidad* and wrote for such republican and free-thinking magazines as *Madrid Cómico, Verán Ustedes, La Semana Cómica.* Also contributed to the Puerto Rican publications *El Buscapié* and *Palenque de la Juventud.* Went to Havana where he received his law doctorate in 1892. In San Juan he founded the Instituto Universitario José de Diego, and in 1916 the Academía Antillana de la Lengua. Was also a notable politician and founder of the Unionist Party (1904).

His poetry is often romantic, rhetorical, and grandiloquent. Its main themes are political and civil, especially in the poems collected under the title *Cantos de rebeldía* (1916), one of his best books. He completely rejected the idea of art for art's sake and defended the utilitarian concept of poetry. His essays are combative, often based on particular events; his deep concern for the Island's political future predominates in all of them.

Selected Bibliography

Diego, José de. *Obras completas.* San Juan: ICP, 1967.
————. *Sor Ana.* Mayagüez: Tip. Comercial, 1887.
————. *Pomarrosas.* Barcelona, 1904.
————. *Jovillos.* Barcelona, 1916.
————. *Cantos de rebeldía.* Barcelona, 1916.
————. *Cantos de Pitirre.* San Juan, Instituto de Literatura Puertorriqueña, 1949.
————. *Cuadernos de poesía.* San Juan: ICP, 1959.
————. *Nuevas campañas.* Barcelona, 1916.
————. *El plebiscito puertorriqueño.* San Juan, 1917.
Arce de Vazquez, Margot. *La obra literaria de José de Diego.* San Juan: ICP, 1967.
Corretjer, Juan Antonio. "En torno a José de Diego." *Indice* 3 (April-May 1931).
Cruz Monclova, Lidio. "José de Diego, poeta." *Puerto Rico Ilustrado,* December 18, 1920.
Dalmau Canet, Sebastián. *José de Diego.* San Juan, 1923.
Ferrer, Canales, José. "Huellas de José de Diego." *Revista Iberoamericana* (México) 22, no. 44 (1957): 323-32.
Maldonado Denis, Manuel. "La idea de la independencia de Puerto Rico en el pensamiento de José de Diego." In *Puerto Rico: Mito y realidad.* Barcelona, 1969.
Meléndez, Concha. *José de Diego en mi memoria.* San Juan: ICP, 1967.
Rodríguez Morales, Luis M. "El tema religioso en la poesía de José de Diego." In *Ensayos y conferencias.* Barcelona: Editorial Rumbos, 1962.
Rosa-Nieves, Cesáreo. "José de Diego. El modernismo en Puerto Rico." *Aguinaldo lírico de la poesía puertorriqueña.* San Juan, 1957.
Asomante 12 (1966) and *Revista del Instituto de Cultura,* September 31, 1966, are devoted to diverse aspects of de Diego's work.

No

Crisp, solid, decisive as a hammer blow, this is the virile word that should inflame our lips and save our honor in these sad days of anachronistic imperialism.

Two or three years ago Dr. Coll y Toste* wrote some brilliant passages to show that Puerto Ricans don't know, and need to know, the power of an energetic affirmation. The learned doctor erred: our greatest moral affliction is an atavistic predisposition to acquiescence without thinking, to that softness of will which makes lovers bend like roses to a breath of wind.

It is true that affirmation has set in motion and determined great undertakings in science, art, philosophy, and religion: all the miracles of faith and love; the death of Christ and the life of Columbus; holy prodigies of affirmation that lifted into divine light the glorious peaks of the spirit.

In political evolution, in the struggle for freedom, the affirmative adverb is almost always useless and always deadly—so soft in all tongues, so sweet in the romance languages which say it better than the Latin mother tongue. *Certe, quidem* lack the brevity and harmony of the Spanish, Italian, and Portuguese *sí*—likewise of the French *oui*—in the most expressive phrases whether of song or music, of flute arpeggio, of a bird's trill. The *sí* is noble and good for melody and rhythm, for fantasy and love; but for protest, for impetus, for laying hold, for anger, for anathema, for dry and explosive hatred, the lightning-flash *NO*. The harsh O reverberates roundly and volcanically like a lion's roar, like the chaos that produced life through the conflagration of all the forces of the abyss. . . .

Since the almost prehistoric risings of savage tribes against

* Cayetano Coll y Toste, historian.

131

Asiatic empire-builders, the refusal to submit, the protest against
the tyrant, the NO of the oppressed has been the genesis word of
the people's emancipation. And today, when as in our country the
ineffectiveness of means and transcendence of ends subdue revolutionary fire for the vision of the ideal, NO should be and is
the only word to save the enslaved peoples' freedom and dignity.

We don't know how to say NO and are instinctively, uncon-
sciously, almost hypnotically drawn to the *sí* of word triumphing
over thought, form over essence. Thus has our character—
artistic, weak, good-natured—been formed by the beauty and
generosity of our land. In general terms, your Puerto Rican never
knows how to say NO. "We'll see," "I'll think about it," "I'll decide
later": when he uses these circumlocutions, it should be understood that he doesn't want to. In fact he unites the *sí* and the NO,
joining affirmative and negative adverbs into one conditional,
ambiguous, nebulous alloy which leaves the will afloat in the air
like a homeless, directionless bird over a desert.

They, the masters, have without any special effort taught us the
word that marks the painful process of our evolution. Affirmation is the norm for legislative bodies, even in the bicameral
system: it results from the dynamic equilibrium between different counterposed forces. In our legislature, where one branch
is the instrument of a foreign government's oppression and the
other is the only instrument of the country's will, the virtue of
both bodies is simply a negative when the interests of people and
government are incompatible. Thus, solely due to the Chamber
of Delegates' weakness in the first Legislative Assembly, we could
lose within an hour legislation full of the wisdom of the ages,
conforming with the historical life and development of Puerto
Rico; and an administrative system could be imposed which
broadens the government's constitutional powers and narrows
the sovereign power of the people. The Chamber said SI, sur-
rendering its will. It could say NO, continue saying NO, and with
that formidable and persistent negative preserve the elements of
our national life; instead of agreeing to broaden a tyrannical
regime and, before God and history, leaving the tyrant to exercise
all alone the power with which he has violated the natural and

supernatural right of our people—of all peoples—to sovereignty over their own destiny.

We must learn to say NO: arch the lips, relax the chest, tense up all the vocal muscles and powers of will, and shout out that O of the NO! It might resound through America and the world, and to the very heavens, more effectively than the roar of guns. . . .

Yes, than guns—for guns are powerless to disturb the light or the course of a single peaceful star!

Nuevas campañas, 1916

Independence

It is high time that we lovers and partisans of national independence set down in black and white what needs to be submitted to the next assembly of the Unionist Party.

I withdraw no word of my estimate of our people's readiness to fight and die for their race, honor, and freedom, if fate were one day to demand of us the same sacrifice that all the New World peoples have made. But no one is so sublimely stupid as to think that we should immediately start gathering in the forest with our machetes. What we have behind us are ideas rather than arms— our faith, our hope, and our right. We have the support of our brothers in Latin America. We have the good traditional instincts of the people of the North against colonial tyrants unworthy to have been born in the land of democracy. All this we have and know we have. What we also have without knowing it are the unforeseen, the unexpected, the invisible—the mystery that germinates in the nebulous distances of the future.

We have God, who orders everything for the best. This is no religious invocation but a positive truth: a ray of light, a snake, a misfortune, a crime, a sun, an ant, a monster, a rose—all are concerted for the final harmony of the good, in action and reaction, contrast and affinity, in clashes and interferences, and in the prodigious secret of life's complexity. This isle emerged free to the winds and waves; freedom is good, and our island will again be free as it was created. Puerto Ricans should have the absolute conviction, the unbreakable faith, that it will be so against every obstacle, because divine and natural forces are at work to impose freedom as an element of the good and the good as a synthesis of the sole object of creation.

It is not true that *natura non facit saltum:* nature does at times make a leap, as with winds and rivers and the mighty rearing-up

134

of mountains. But true it is that the normal development of physical and moral forces is gradual and continuous—slow, rhythmic evolution only interrupted in abnormal conditions when time's infinite currents are halted and cannot continue forward without violence. If our right to emancipation has to take a leap one day, it will leap. And it will leap with all the force of that which must either disappear or, like the weakest of rivers or strongest of winds, proceed on its way. For there is nothing so small that it can be isolated from the grandeur of the universe.

But meanwhile our ideal must be *pursued* with all the perseverance and serenity that the sacred exercise of a sacred right demands. We must simply proclaim our right to Independence in a wisely conceived and ordered program for a collectivity which excludes or rejects no one, in which no one sets himself up as the sole director of ideas; which welcomes all Puerto Ricans as to a mother's breast, with infinite love and justice for all her children, including the bad ones. This will be the beginning, the coming to birth of the ideal which we must immediately surround with all the care necessary to preserve its life; to preserve the circumstantial elements for its growth and fulfillment, adapting it to the environment according to the laws of development, of the death or survival of all organic species.

Some creatures in our world are born limited in their movements, some in spaces too confined to move at all; later they get wings and roam everywhere, nimble and free. Our ideal of Independence will be born with the limitation of a protectorate, because that limitation is in the environment and necessary to supervise the ideal. Forever? No. Till when? Until the environment and the ideal themselves put an end to it; until wings grow and space extends, in the evolution of means toward the ends of life.

With our thoughts thus dedicated to the assurance of survival, the immediate realization of the ideal is not in our power and to obtain it we need a period of constant struggle and effort in the course of which we broaden our means of action. Thus we must also establish a temporary, intermediate, transitory solution of greater freedom—as transitory as possible, with the greatest freedom possible—permitting us to intervene in our own affairs for the fastest attainment of the definitive solution as we advance through a form of autonomy toward national Independence.

The more clearly we can say it, the better understood: we will oppose autonomy in any permanent sense—no matter how radical the system of colonial government—and any citizenship or sovereignty that is not ours, our very own. We will oppose the adoption of any foreign flag and the recognition of any other motherland than the soil where we were born and for which we should bravely, happily, and gloriously die when her liberty demands it.

Nuevas campañas, 1916

Looking at the Antillean Ideal

Anyone who has fixed his eyes on the sun sees a circle of flame wherever he looks. In the same way I see wherever I go the green water of the bay, the sky aflower with cirrus clouds, the heroic walls of the fortresses, the white semicircle of the town, the rigid spears of the palm trees—all of that luxuriant panorama that astounds and enchants the traveler from the monotonous and solitary sea. And between water and land and sky, like the wing of a marvelous bird emerging from the boundless air, the flag of the Cuban Republic triumphantly waving.

My patriotic stirrings, *my* first greeting, *my* first word, and *my* first love belong up there with that flag illumined by the flashing swords of our captains and the songs of our poets. For the Cuban flag, like the Dominican and the Puerto Rican, is mine, too: proud symbols all of the three-in-one motherland of the islands that extend and join together beneath the ocean, in the setting and spirit of the Antilles.

One of those Antillean flags, the free emblem of Puerto Rico which shines within me, looked to one journalist like the flag of the United States: a happy error affording me the best of excuses for explaining just why I have returned to this beloved city of my student joys and patriotic dreams.

My flag is not the flag of the United States. That is a flag of honor; mine a flag of love. I respect the ensign of the brave founders of the first American motherland. But mine is the last, and for me the last and the first and the beloved.

My painful struggles for Puerto Rico's freedom have not been undertaken in any aggressive campaign of hate or vengeance against the noble people of Washington. On the contrary, they look for the recognition of the Puerto Rican Republic by the · United States Congress, in a transcendent spirit of harmony and

137

coexistence between the two civilizing and redemptive races of the American world.

I might proclaim — but will leave it to a fitter occasion — that the United States Congress has already conceded Puerto Rico's independence and that its explicit recognition is not necessary. That it will come about by virtue of the Constitution that rules us, after a brief progressive evolution of our system of government toward our national sovereignty.

We should not even suspect the North American people of contemplating a betrayal of their democratic traditions by turning to their advantage the doctrine of American immunity against conquest. If this should happen, if the powerful eagle chose to torment so weak a captive as the Puerto Rican lamb,* if all roads of legality and horizons of hope were closed to us, Puerto Ricans would offer the ultimate sacrifice to their native land's dignity and liberty. But our hearts are still buoyed by faith in the North American people's justice, and we fight bloodless civic battles for the triumph of our natural right.

Whether hope fulfilled or despair beyond endurance be our destiny, we sense and we know that our brothers of Santo Domingo and Cuba — and in the continent beyond — will be with us in our joy, our anger, and our pain. But however noble it may be, we must not intrude our selfishness into the generous yearning for the Antillean union.

This brotherhood must not be forged as an instrument of Puerto Rican independence; nor do its aims and efforts lead directly to the Antillean Confederation, even though this is the natural realization of the vision of a future nation — a great and strong nation that will spread arches over a forest of columns for the triumphal march of new Antillean generations.

This institution of tomorrow, cradled by the mother-island of the New World's Christian civilization, cannot nurse suspicions, jealousies, and hostilities even in spirits most susceptible to fear of imaginary conflicts; for it removes all obstacles, conciliates all interests, satisfies all desires, binds together all wills, warms all hearts in a flame of love.

---

* Referring to the Puerto Rican coat of arms.

We look to the press to publish the basic principles approved in Santo Domingo for constituting the Antillean Union, and for immediately setting to work in those fields of social, economic, literary, scientific, and artistic life which bind and benefit our islands' relations and prosperity.

These are real and practical roads to the incarnation of the magnificent dream of Martí, Gómez, Hostos, and Betances: a radiance that burns in my eyes, that I see everywhere in a circle of fire, like he who has looked long at the palpitating sun. . . .

Flag of Cuba! Ensign of Santo Domingo! Standard of Puerto Rico! Roses of the Antilles! Rising constellation of the divine ideal!

Nuevas campañas, 1916

Nemesio R. Canales (1878–1923)

Born in Jayuya. After a short stay in Spain, moved to Baltimore where he completed his law studies. On his return he opened a law office with Luis Llorens Torres and Miguel Guerra Mondragón. Wrote for island magazines and newspapers and belonged to the young vanguard group around the *Revista de las Antillas* (1913). Later he founded with Llorens the weekly *Juan Bobo* (1915). Also wrote for *La Semana* and *El Día*.

His essays, collected under the titles *Paliques* (1913), are in vigorous modern prose. His modernism as they reflect it has two aspects: on the one hand, ideological, couched in an incisive, satirical prose, sketching political caricatures, and attacking the government and the parties in power, reflecting influences of end-of-century German philosophy (Max Stirner, Nietzsche); on the other, sentimental, tender, melancholy, musical.

He traveled extensively in Latin America and the United States and lived for a time in Buenos Aires and in Panamá where he edited *Cuasimodo*, an inter-American cultural review.

Selected Bibliography

Canales, Nemesio R. *Paliques*. 1913; San Juan: Ediciones Isla, 1967.
————. *Mi voluntad se ha muerto*. Buenos Aires, 1921.
————. *La leyenda benaventina*. 1922.
————. *El héroe galopante*. 1923; San Juan: Editorial Coquí, 1968.
————. *Nuevos paliques y otras páginas*. San Juan: DIP, 1965.
Babín, María Teresa. "Canales y Llorens Torres. Reencauzadores. Patriotismo y cultura de puertorriqueños." *El Diario La Prensa* (New York), April 23 and 26, 1970.
Géigel Polanco, Vicente. "Nemesio Canales." *Asomante* 1 (1945): 67-70.
Montaña Peláez, Servando. *Nemesio Canales: Lenguaje y situación*. Río Piedras: UPR, 1973.
Quiñones, Samuel R. "Humorismo en Nemesio R. Canales." In *Temas y letras*. San Juan: Biblioteca de Autores Puertorriqueños, 1955.

Wealth and Poverty

II

As promised, I return today to the question of "The Virtue of Money" on which I ventured in former chats. We were considering money as a synthesis into which everything of any value in our world may be fitted, and I was marveling at the fact that no one claimed any merit in being poor.

Having arrived at this point, consistency compels me to marvel also at the absurd and abominable social system that rules our lives.

Our present society is based on the exploitation of all by a few, without real benefit to anybody. Millions of people all over our planet toil and sweat and go without the most primitive needs, to fatten a dozen privileged beings in each country who don't even appreciate their privilege.

And here I differ from most of those who approach this question in a humane and liberal spirit. Far from spurning and cursing those absurdly privileged to possess too much of everything while others lack everything, far from invoking God's wrath upon the privileged ones, I praise and applaud them for it. I even confess without blushing that were I to find myself afflicted with a load of millions, all the sermons and diatribes on earth wouldn't make me let them go. Yes, I believe the rich do very well to get away with all they can under the shelter of a society that consents to it and even rewards it.

There is nothing wrong—how can there be?—with having many millions. As I have said, the only sin, the only crime, is to be poor. The dilemma is this: either one is poor, or one is rich; either one is exploited or an exploiter; either a lamb or a wolf. The choice is clear, at least for me. Hear ye one and all: between the two roles, that of defenseless and resigned lamb and that of wolf, I unwaveringly choose the latter: I proclaim myself a wolf, and if I

143

have anything to say about it, my children and grandchildren will be wolves! But the fact that I say nothing against the rich nor against wolves doesn't mean, as someone may think, that I accept the existing social system which dedicates all its activities to the defense of the rich against the poor.

It is not sentimentalism and pure compassion for the poor that bids us try to reform what exists and put something else in its place. It is for pure self-interest, for the advantage of all, for love of what is healthy and esthetic in life that we should suppress the poor, since from them come all the dirt, the plagues, and the evil scattered across the world.

We spend our lives organizing schools to wipe out ignorance, passing more and more sanitation laws to wipe out disease, establishing and maintaining prisons and courts and paying an exorbitant army of officials—judges, prosecutors, police, jailors, hangmen—to wipe out crime. . . .

Yet every day the evils we fight increase in numbers and cruelty; invincible brutality, disease, and crime share out the kingdoms of this world.

The truth is that we treat these social evils in the same way that some physicians treat organic diseases.

One complains to certain doctors that one's body is becoming covered with tumors, and the doctor proceeds to prescribe plasters and lavations for each tumor, as if the disease were in the skin and not in the blood.

Society does the same. Schools here, sanitation there, jails and courts and cops and hangmen everywhere to combat ignorance, disease, crime, without realizing that all these things are but symptoms, tumors, manifestations of a virus that resides not on the surface but in the essence—the very blood and marrow of the social organism. What is this virus? Give ear to my next chat and you will see and know.

VI

Someone will tell me, too, that without the poor—without laboring machines—neither rich nor poor will be able to survive.

And I reply: how nice that our own pockets contain the guarantee of the life of the poor. A gilt-edged guarantee, the pocket!

But seeing that the poor must continue existing, how to perform the miracle of ridding ourselves of poverty without finishing off the poor? How do we cure the pip without killing the fowl? How save ourselves from rabies without killing the dog?

I don't think it's quite as hard as it looks. What has prevented it till now has been man's ignorance, that accursed source of all the prejudices afflicting us. Furthermore, it has always kept us far from the root of the question, our mania for obfuscating the simplest problems, wrapping them in the fog of doctrinaire philosophy which poisons and putrefies everything.

On both sides—among the phlegmatic, well-heeled bourgeoisie and in the opposing camp of the hungry proletariat—much time has been lost in futile affectations of reverse dialectic as to whether property is or isn't an inalienable right, whether we do or don't have a right to the fruit of our labor, and a hundred thousand quibbles of the kind.

Our mania for believing we can't make a move in life without the benediction of some abstract principle, religious or metaphysical; our prodigious obstinacy in thinking that we men come into the world to serve principles: these are to blame for our snail's pace toward apprehending how easily we could cure the scabies of poverty if we wanted to.

If we approach it with the sane criteria of every man's advantage, of a judicious housewife sending out for the groceries, we will see how easy and simple the question becomes. Do we want the poor to stop being the eternal point of filth, violence, depravity, and crime? Then let us make money as cheap as water from the faucet. Why are we at such pains to supply everyone, even the wretchedest hovel, with water? Because the voice of our own interest tells us that the absence of water exposes us to the horror of an epidemic.

So let's do likewise with money. Not let anyone go without it, but make it flow—spread it all around like a jubilant, kindly rain. Then we'll save ourselves from poverty, the evil of evils, mother of all epidemics.

Let us desist from the notorious idiocy of striving to cheapen essential commodities like bread, codfish, and sugar while allowing money—the essential need par excellence, the most indispensable for bodily and spiritual health—to lie stagnant without benefit to anyone in a few millionaires' brimming coffers.

Ah, you witless governments everywhere! What good are your strivings to offer us cheap bread or sugar or fish if at the same time you don't stir a finger to provide us with money to buy them? Of what interest is the price of a pound of bread or sugar or meat to one with empty pockets?

Obviously, then, the first thing we have to cheapen, ahead of bread or fish or water, is money. For without money there is no bread, no fish, no water, however little they may cost.

But here is the rub: how do we cheapen money? How make it flow like water in the pipe?

Since the answer won't fit the space left to me, we will leave it for the next chat.

I really never thought that the question I am raising, without frills or circumlocutions, would turn out to be so long. But I wanted to explain my article "The Value of Money" so no one would bring false charges against me—and see where it has landed me.

See what you take on when you dive into the simple question of making money cheaper than water. . . !

VIII

I was saying that the State could prevent people from fighting each other for money.

How? Very simply: by the State becoming the only capitalist. Instead of one capitalist here and another there cornering and monopolizing all the money, one capital, one cashbox in the State's hands, and all citizens becoming pensioned wards of that State. And all maintaining the State with daily labor which they would only be obligated to perform up to a certain age, and which would certainly involve no more than two or three hours of each one's time. The State in exchange guaranteeing each one full enjoyment of his life through a daily money pension sufficient not only for his elemental and animal needs, but for needs arising from the tenderest and noblest parts of his being.

Once upon a time sluggish mankind smiled when anyone talked about such a State. Today the "trusts," those huge omnipotent "trusts," have demonstrated its possibility and viability. For if a corporation is possible in which thousands associate themselves under a collective name for this or that enterprise, there is no reason why a whole people can't unite to constitute, as the State or by any other name, a formidable "trust" for the grand task of socializing property and guaranteeing everyone his ration of life.

But, you will say, if you guarantee everyone a pension very few will work. And I say that in the State I envisage, *based precisely on the labor of all,* all would have to give their ration of work to have a right to their ration of life.* The professional loafer—a candidate for poverty—would not be tolerated for an instant. Just as we guard ourselves from a rabid dog by the immediate and instinctive alarm of the whole community, with no need for courts or cops, in the new State the same alarm would be raised by the presence of a loafer—a man who wants to live as a parasite like today's plutocrats and bureaucrats, to consume without producing. And the bum would suffer the same fate as the rabid dog. The motto of the new State would be just that: "Neither bums nor paupers."

But, you will object again, if the frugal few start saving part of their pensions they will soon accumulate money, and we would be back where we started, in the same old capitalism with its natural consequences of ruin and poverty for the many.

And I say that just as the community itself would shake off the bum from self-interest for fear of his contagion, so would all react with instinctive alarm against a case of avarice. A man caught *in flagrante* betraying the community by keeping for himself the part of the pension he didn't want or know how to spend, with the evil intent of snatching from State funds, would be treated without consideration—with the same implacable severity as the bum or the rabid dog.

* An obvious defense of socialist states.

We know that anything that is fundamentally hostile to the tranquility, health, well-being, or prejudice of a collective is unfailingly eliminated from that collective without need for police or judges. A State can pass laws for years and years but if they don't take root in some crevice of the collective soul, the soul of the people, neither judges nor jailers nor guards nor anyone can prevent them being laughed at, trampled on, and forgotten by everyone. On the other hand, when a law is based on a need or feeling of the collective, every citizen, every street, every home becomes its jealous guardian.

So much for the knotty problem of cheapening money. Here you would have money, instead of being the curse it is today, paying periodic visits to each citizen, shining like the sun for all, not for just a few; flowing like water into each house to slake all men's thirst for life.

One further objection remains: the lack of that stimulus that generates progress. I hear someone saying that when the ambition to accumulate money dies, human activity dies, too, and there is no progress.

Let us suppose, I answer, that progress dies. What does progress matter? Did we come into the world to serve progress? No, we came to serve ourselves. If we are served and satisfied, progress can go to the devil.

But I deny that the only stimulus that drives man into activity is the accumulation of money. And I add that for me money is a purely artificial stimulus, whose removal would leave all the energies of the human machine in full function.

Today we fight over a fistful of cash, because we have unhappily come to value the symbol more than the thing, the cash more than the man. But tomorrow, once the specter of poverty is banished forever, all the natural ambitions that move us today will remain in operation. Who dares deny the potential in man, even in today's man, of the ambition for knowledge, for love, for glory—those potent, indestructible, precious springs of the human soul in all epochs?

I have run out of paper and come to the end, but there is

material here for a million chats; the above is a mere sketch, not a definitive and complete portrait, of a social system. Of a vigorous, beautiful new society that I see advancing toward us with the stride of a hurricane. . . .

Paliques, 1915

Miguel Meléndez Muñoz (1884–1965)

Writer of essays, short stories, and novels. Lived all his life in Cayey; worked there in grocery stores and later became administrator of an agricultural concern. Finally became a landowning farmer but in 1928 lost his land because of the tobacco slump. His functions put him in contact with the campesino, and few writers have produced better work on the Puerto Rican countryside.

He began his writing with contributions to *El Heraldo Español*, then contributed to *La Democracia, La República Española, El Carnaval, Pica Pica, El Imparcial* and *El Mundo*.

A sharp interpreter of Puerto Rican reality, he was concerned about spiritual values and social problems. Began publishing his work around 1904. Between 1915 and 1917 wrote some modernistic sketches and stories which he collected in *Lecturas puertorriqueñas* (1919). In these the lyrical tone predominates when he is describing nature, but he looks with penetrating insight at socio-economic realities. He also reflects the confusion of values which characterizes our history since 1898.

Selected Bibliography

Meléndez Muñoz, Miguel. *Obras completas.* San Juan: ICP, 1963.
—————. *Retazos. Boletín Mercantil,* San Juan, 1905.
—————. *Lecturas puertorriqueñas.* San Juan, 1919.
—————. *Estado social del campesino puertorriqueño.* San Juan, 1919.
—————. *Retablo puertorriqueño.* Barcelona, 1941.
—————. *Fuga de ideas.* 1942.
—————. *Yuyo. Boletín Mercantil.* San Juan, 1913.
—————. *Cuentos del cedro.* 1936.
—————. *Cuentos de la carretera central.* 1941.
(All of these were reissued by Ediciones Rumbos in 1963.)
Arce de Vázquez, Margot. "Significado de la vida y obra de don Miguel Meléndez Muñoz." *RICP* 34 (1967).
Díaz Alfaro, Abelardo. "Don Miguel Meléndez Muñoz, cedro de la cultura criolla." *RICP* 34 (1967).
Duca, Robert. "The Puerto Rican National Identity in the Essays of Miguel Meléndez Muñoz." Ph.D. diss., Pennsylvania State University, 1976.
Laguerre, Enrique. "En torno a la obra de don Miguel Meléndez Muñoz." *RICP* 34 (1967).
Lube de Droz, Josefina. "La obra literaria de Miguel Meléndez Muñoz." *RICP* 34 (1967).
Montañez, Rafael. "Una nueva obra de Meléndez Muñoz." *Puerto Rico Ilustrado,* April 26, 1941.
Zeno Gandía, Manuel. "Los 'Cuentos del Cedro' de don Miguel Meléndez Muñoz." *Puerto Rico Ilustrado,* April 26, 1941.

Inside the Hut

This hut is a bit withdrawn from the lane that runs into the highway.

It is typical. It has a roof of royal palm fronds lashed simply and securely to a frame of uprights with *bejuco* vines. The floor is of planks cut from *capa* and *tabonuco* trees, the walls of straw.

Some trees surround the hut: a *guamá* with very green leaves and new shoots, two *achiote* bushes covered with reddish acorns, a leafy mango that shades one part of the house. And in a little orchard—garden-yard, as our campesinos say—there are medicinal flowers and plants: a rachitic rosebush dying of thirst, a few carnations, and mint, *yerba-luisa,* elderberry, mallow—cures for "many ills" endemic in our countryside: headaches, toothaches, coughs, colds, malarial fevers, in simple and humble infusions that sustain the patient pending arrival of the doctor's prescription or of death.

Back of the orchard-garden there are some bananas, and beneath them many white and Martinican *yautía* plants.

The hut has a portable door which is leaned up against a wall by day, at night set in place and fastened with *bejuco* vines, rope, or whatever is handy. This is designed to keep out drafts, rain, and the cold night winds of winter, but they sneak in clandestinely through the gaps in the walls, the holes that rain makes in the roof, and the cracks between the badly joined floor planks.

The hut's interior dimensions would have little concerned its builder, a humble architect who improvised an oblong topped by a roof to shelter him from wind, sun, and rain: a man unschooled, devoid of standards in the art of construction.

The hut has a living room as you enter, and a room at the back comprises the rest of it. This is bedroom, dressing room, wardrobe, pantry, and also the only place to put up a relative or friend staying the night or longer. At times this room also serves to store the harvest of lesser crops—corn, green beans, rice—which the employers will later sell.

Suspended from the living room ceiling by long strips of *emajagua* is an infinity of kitchen and eating utensils, ready for use at any moment.

On the walls are some oleographs representing saints, virgins, and scenes from the Passion and Death of Our Lord Jesus Christ. Smoke from cooking has covered these and all the walls with soot as it blew through the living room in search of an outlet. The blue of the virgins' eyes and bright crimson of their cheeks and flashy lips have paled and yellowed to an old-ivory shade. Yellow, too, are the once florid beards of the saints who gaze heavenward or wear grimaces of pain, of superiority or scorn toward man's squalid passions. The smoke has given them a special hue of age and neglect.

On the door giving into the all-purpose bedroom is a wooden cross, with a nail protruding at the top on which should hang the inscription INRI. From this nail droops a sprig of withered flowers and a "blessed" palm frond which some inhabitant of the hut brought from the village after the last religious festival of Palm Sunday.

The "blessed palm," which for an enlightened and tolerant Christian is a commemorative symbol of the Divine Master's entry into Jerusalem, represents for the hut's inhabitants a symbolic relic, an amulet, and a medicinal aid, according to cases.

From time to time an "evil" spirit, as the *jíbaro*'s hysterical demonology identifies it, "takes possession" of a young girl's body. When the girl is "possessed" she succumbs to melancholy, lack of appetite, and acute nervous crises. Some old wise woman, expert in the rural pharmacopeia and versed in the pranks of the "evil enemy," brushes the face of the "possessed" with some twigs and fastens the blessed palm frond around her neck like a collar. The "enemy" then "dispossesses" the simple soul of this poor victim of hysteria or neurosis.

If one of these crones skilled in secret mysteries and dark formulas fails to calm the girl's nerves or allay her paroxysms with the blessed frond, she burns the frond and administers a potion made from the ashes. Thus if the "evil spirit" does not surrender to a superior supernatural force, the patient violently expels it by the emetic action of the potion.

The hut without a blessed frond is rare. If throughout a year it has not been used for one of the aforementioned purposes, a fresh frond is placed on top of or beside it, likewise blessed by the priest on the classical and traditional Palm Sunday.

Also hanging from the beams of the hut are some corn cobs, green beans, empty sacks, and ironed clothing. In a corner of the living room there are a spade handle, a machete, and stones for grinding corn. And close by these rude implements the children of the house play. There are three of them. They are naked, with dirty faces showing remnants of their last meal. The protruding stomach of one of them paralyzes his movements. This child is very pale. His hair falls in long lank strands over his narrow forehead. He doesn't play like the others and gazes at them with indifference. When one of his brothers annoys him with his play, or says something to him, he lifts his arms and breaks into shrill inarticulate cries. Then he falls back into his habitual stupor. As if his brothers' natural games were foreign to his age, he stays in the same attitude while the others play and jump, burning up their childish energies with their quick movements.

The healthiness, charming ingenuousness, and agility of the other children are in sharp contrast to this sickly offspring of the hut family. Passing in front of the hut, I ask them:

"Why doesn't your little brother play with you?"

"He doesn't know how," one of them answers.

"So he can't play? I think kids don't learn to play. Who taught you what you were doing when I came here?"

"No one."

"Really no one? Then your little brother ought to do the same—jump, throw himself on the ground, get up, run, oughtn't he?"

"Yes . . . ," said one, "but he . . . he's all swelled up, always had a bad stomach, can't move properly."

"Who told you that?"

"Doña Tina said so, the *curandera*."

"And why do you go naked? Don't you have clothes?"

"Well . . . yes, we have."

"Why don't you wear them? You're a bit old to be going around like that."

"It's a nuisance . . . we put clothes on when we go to school or they take us to the village. Mama says they last longer that way."

The sick kid had dragged himself to the door where I was talking to the others.

He stared at me with his sad eyes and, trying to produce a smile that looked more like a grimace, let out an unfathomable cry.

I wanted to caress him then, but he violently repulsed me and hid in the shadow of the door frame.

"Don't pay him any mind," said one of his brothers. "He's scared of people, that one is. He's very *jíbaro,* and funk and the fever just freeze him up."

Lecturas puertorriqueñas, 1919

Manuel Zeno Gandía (1855–1930)

Born in Arecibo, studied medicine in Madrid. Wrote poetry, essays, and stories but distinguished himself as a novelist. Figured in island politics as defender of freedom for Puerto Rico; held legislative office. His first fiction ventures were two sketches for novels, *Rosa de mármol* (1889) and *Piccola* (1890), published in *La revista de Puerto Rico*. His best known works are collected under the general title *Crónicas de un mundo enfermo*. They reflect the poverty of colonial Puerto Rico, both rural (*La charca*, Madrid, 1894; *Garduña*, Ponce, 1896) and urban (*El negocio*, New York, 1922; *Redentores*, 1925). The latter, originally published in the daily press, did not appear as a book in the author's lifetime, although he seems to have virtually completed it by 1916. Most of his essays remain unpublished.

Selected Bibliography

Zeno Gandía, Manuel. *Obras completas.* Río Piedras: Instituto de Literatura Puertorriqueña, 1894; San Juan, 1955.

————. *La charca.* ICP, 1966.

————. *Redentores.* Club del Libro de Puerto Rico, 1960.

————. *Cuentos.* New York: Las Américas Publishing Co., 1958.

————. *Abismos.* Ponce: El Vapor, 1885.

Arce de Vázquez, Margot. "Bibliografía de Manuel Zeno Gandía." *Asomante* 11 (1955): 72-74.

Barrera, Héctor. "La Charca." *Asomante* 11 (1955): 59-71.

Cabrera, Francisco Manrique. "Manuel Zeno Gandía, poeta del novelar isleño." *Asomante* 11 (1955): 19-47.

————. "Notas sobre la novela puertorriqueña en los últimos 25 años." *Asomante* 11 (1955): 20-38.

Cano, Lamberto A. "La montaña, génesis del cromatismo lírico en *La Charca.*" *RICP* 4 (1966).

Colón, José M. "La naturaleza en *La Charca.*" *Asomante* 5 (1949).

————. "La naturaleza en Manuel Zeno Gandía y Enrique Laguerre." Ph.D. diss., University of Puerto Rico, 1949.

Gardón Franceschi, M. *Manuel Zeno Gandía. Vida y poesía.* San Juan: Editorial Coquí, 1969.

Guzmán, Julia María. *Realismo y naturalismo en Puerto Rico.* San Juan: ICP, 1960.

Matos Bernier, Félix. "La novela en Puerto Rico." In *Isla de arte.* San Juan, 1894.

Quiñones, Samuel R. "Manuel Zeno Gandía y la novela en Puerto Rico." In *Temas y letras.* San Juan: Biblioteca de Autores Puertorriqueños, 1955.

Soto, Venus Lidia. *Disertación sobre el arte de novelar en Garduña de Manuel Zeno Gandía.* San Juan: DIP, 1967.

What Are We, How Are We?

The best definition of a nation that I know is this: a body of people coexisting in a finite area, disposed and resolved to achieve many positive things together for the betterment of life.

On this basis, can it be denied that Puerto Rico is a nation?

Perhaps the usual outcry will be raised. No, Puerto Rico isn't a nation because it lacks the necessary conditions to be one. So if it had these conditions, it would be a nation, right?

In any case, who invented the conditions? A conventional technique, a downpour of conventionalisms: an ensemble of sorceries dreamed up by people whom it doesn't suit that Puerto Rico should be a nation.

If we keep insisting that there are white houseflies, we will surely end up convincing ourselves of it. Isn't Puerto Rico a nation? All right, Puerto Rico is a nation.

An English philosopher said that trying in the name of reason to destroy the idea of motherland and nationality, and to put internationalism and universal brotherhood in its place, is like trying to suppress love of one's own mother for the sake of loving one's neighbor's mother.

Let us imagine a woman abundantly and richly bedecked. Is she a woman? Yes. Suppose she is stripped of all this finery and appears before us totally nude. Is she a woman? I would say she still is.

Now let us imagine a country with people, industries, wealth, government, much finery and luxury, very happy. That is a nation.

And let us imagine an area of the earth with people inhabiting it for centuries who are poor, desperate, scorned, misunderstood, reviled, prostituted, etc. Well, before God and truth that would be a nude nation.

But a nation. That is unquestionably the case of Puerto Rico. What matters here as in all things is to seek out the true truth, to ask oneself from time to time *combien de sots faut-il pour faire un public?**

The definition of Puerto Rico, as I see it, is this: a nation of hostages.

The second question is: "Is there a way of being that is unmistakably and genuinely Puerto Rican?"

Puerto Ricans are part of humanity. I don't think there is any discrepancy here, so I affirm that natural laws act upon them.

One of those laws says, "The soil is the man." If this country is soil, how could its man not relate himself to the surface he lives on and the air he breathes?

This is an island, and as in all islands, topographic conditions influence the character of its generations.

Individually the Puerto Rican is courageous, but his collective personality is timid, uncertain, resigned. When Saint Lorenzo was burned on one side, such was his pious resignation that he asked contritely to be burned on the other. That's how the Puerto Rican is.

At the same time he is a man of peace: wealth makes him soft; he is strong as steel in his resistance to indifference and hunger.

Those characteristics cannot be ignored nor confused, and neither can this one: the individual Puerto Rican is born with a deep innate sense of rhythm. A good ear and much aptitude for the collective march; popular music and song of irreproachable cadence, stanzas of fresh spontaneity and admirable rhythm. So much so that we would have a myriad of poets and musicians—we have many as it is—if we capitalized on that instead of looking with awe on the foreign product and down our noses at our own.

The Puerto Rican is an idealist. He positively does not live by bread alone. His woman is delicious, the best in the world. Our Creole is furthermore adaptable to all climates. He emigrates and is happy in the new land. He resents insult and injury. He often uses his machete to settle a score and, in the country, groups of people walk in Indian file.

---

* How many fools does it take to make a public?

He never or rarely laughs. That is the natural consequence of his woes. Breaking into a loud guffaw isn't a very Puerto Rican habit. The sun and the moon rise, stars shine, and flowers perfume the air for happiness. God made none of this to bring people pain; but this Antillean, perhaps by aboriginal atavism, is sometimes shy and almost always taciturn. And it is known that to be happy one must laugh.

Yes, there is an unmistakable Puerto Rican way of being. That's how he is, anxiously awaiting the happy moment to develop the broad physical and moral faculties that it pleased God to give him; waiting for his antidote, for the only sovereign remedy— freedom.

The third question is: "What are the indicators defining our collective character?"

We were better once than we are now. There is depression in our country. A misunderstood positivism seems to want to kill the legitimate aspirations that our people always had. One might think we were being corrupted by the clouded prisms through which we look at life.

Generations of bright and proud youth seem dedicated to the cult of the god Pleasure—a materialist, sterile kind of pleasure. The kind of fleeting pleasure you can get from a burst of fireworks.

But there is some reaction. At times a latent fire flares up, efforts in the right direction are made—flutterings that could perhaps lead our mother island to a better future.

Fellow countrymen, with these lines I wish you the fulfillment you wish for yourselves.

Indice, whose first number I have read, is a good step toward that.

I remain your humble servant.

Revista Indice, July 7, 1929

Luis Llorens Torres (1878–1944)

Born in Juana Díaz, studied letters in Barcelona and Granada. Returned to Puerto Rico in 1901 and became active in the Unionist Party. Distinguished especially as a poet but also wrote plays, short stories, and essays. An initiator of the vanguard movement in Puerto Rico and among the first modernist writers. In 1913, with some other younger poets, he broke with his original verse style and founded the *Revista de las Antillas,* around which gathered various vanguard groups. In that journal he published his poetic series "Visiones de mi musa," preceded by his esthetic theories of *pancalismo* (all is beautiful) and *panedismo* (all is poetry). Later he amplified these in the prologue to *Sonetos sinfónicos* (1914).

Few did as much as he, through his articles and essays on esthetic theory, for Puerto Rico's literary and cultural renewal. Many of these works are still uncollected.

Selected Bibliography

Llorens Torres, Luis. *Obras completas.* San Juan: ICP, 1966.
————. *América.* 1898; Madrid: Editorial Cordillera, 1967.
————. *Al pie de la Alhambra.* 1899; Madrid: Editorial Cordillera, 1968.
————. *Sonetos Sinfónicos.* 1914.
————. *El Grito de Lares.* 1927; Madrid: Editorial Cordillera, 1967.
————. *La canción de las Antillas y otros poemas.* 1929.
————. *Voces de la campana mayor.* 1935.
————. *Alturas de América.* 1940.
Babín, María Teresa. *La obra en prosa de Llorens Torres.* Barcelona: Ediciones Rumbos, 1969.
Hernández Aquino, Luis. *Nuestra aventura literaria.* Río Piedras: UPR, 1966.
————. "Rubén Darío y Puerto Rico: apuntes para nuestra historia literaria." *RICP* 9 (1960).
————. *El modernismo en Puerto Rico. Poesía y prosa.* Río Piedras: UPR, 1967.
Laguerre, Enrique. *La poesía modernista en Puerto Rico.* San Juan: Editorial Coquí, 1969.
Marrero, Carmen. *Luis Llorens Torres, vida y obra.* San Juan: Editorial Cordillera, 1968.
Martínez Masdeu, Edgard. *La crítica puertorriqueña y el modernismo en Puerto Rico.* San Juan: ICP, 1977.
Ortiz García, Nilda S. *Vida y obra de Luis Llorens Torres.* San Juan: ICP, 1977.
Ramos Mimoso, Adriana. *El modernismo en la lírica puertorriqueña.* San Juan: ICP, 1960.

The Unknown Island

It is a sad thing that Vasconcelos* has said to us with stout sincerity: our island of Puerto Rico is unknown in America; those twenty Spanish American peoples out there know nothing of our culture, our struggles, our sorrows and ideals.

Is it true? It must be when we hear it from a man of moral and intellectual seriousness who is visiting those brother countries of ours.

Are we Puerto Ricans to blame for their ignorance of us? Or should we blame Spanish America for its apathy in looking our way?

Such apathy is deplorable, for it means that people who think about the future of our race in America do so with one factor missing.

While they fail to consider Puerto Rico with due intensity, the Latin American nations cannot properly appreciate their greatness and the enormous spiritual forces with which they are endowed. And without that appreciation their study of the great problem ahead of us will be superficial.

Two great human nuclei confront one another in America: the Latin nucleus below with its 100 million inhabitants, occupying the earth's loveliest and richest lands, and the Yanqui or Anglo-Saxon one above, with another 100 million also occupying huge and rich territories.

But in America there is an island, our unknown island of Puerto Rico, where a million Puerto Ricans (Spanish Americans) have lived for the past twenty-five years under the dominion of the Yanqui nucleus.

* José Vasconcelos (1881–1959) was an essayist and secretary of education in Mexico who reformed the educational system. His most influential works were *La raza cosmica* (1925) and *Indología* (1929).

165

This means that America's two great nuclei have been in conflict for those twenty-five years. For the million Puerto Ricans, in their titanic twenty-five-year struggle against the whole Anglo-Saxon nucleus, have stood out as a vanguard of the Latin nucleus's 100 millions.

Doesn't it care to know whether we have overcome or been overcome?

No one forgets how the powerful Yanqui squadron destroyed the disordered Spanish ships in a few hours at Cavite and Santiago de Cuba. And everyone knows that their armies could blow the Puerto Rican people away with a single puff. But the fight in Puerto Rico isn't one of ships or armies. It is a struggle of two races, two cultures, two civilizations. The Yanqui eagle, hovering over our people, bringing over here his millions, his machines, his language, his laws, and all the resources of his undeniable power; and the Puerto Rican people struggling and striving to save their race, their language, their religion, their spiritual character.

Twenty-five years of struggle! The Yanqui has imposed his code of laws upon us. The English language is obligatory in our public schools. Yanqui money has taken possession of part of our lands and industries. We suffer the tyranny of a Court of Justice where lawyers must speak English and witnesses testify through interpreters. And yet our people are as Spanish now as they were before. The campesino is the same as he was twenty-five years ago. Spanish is spoken and cultivated more ardently than ever. In no way have our people changed their racial characteristics. And our soul, our Spanish racial spirit, remains unbreakable, indestructible.

If 100 million Yanquis have been unable in twenty-five years to break the spirit of these million Puerto Ricans, doesn't this demonstration of the firmness of their race interest Latin America? Aren't they proud to know that Yanqui culture has been beaten and repulsed in Puerto Rico by the culture of our race?

For thinking people, for bearers of the Latin ideal, Puerto Rico should be the most interesting scene in Spanish America. Because this is where the test is being made as to which of the two races peopling the American continent is superior.

Puerto Rico is a titan withstanding the weight on its chest of a titan 100 times bigger. This effort, showing just what power of resistance Latin America has, should be a source of pride for Latin America.

It is true that some Puerto Ricans betray the ideal as annexationists and *pitiyanquis;** but these do not detract from our glory, nor do those hack journalists who describe as traitors the patriots fighting most doggedly for our country's redemption. They are ulcers we cannot remove because they are living flesh. Painful ulcers which it is our lot to suffer, wounds we have to lick, as a dog suffers and licks his own wounds and worms.

Our ideal is the independence of our motherland. We claim it with its rich nimbus of popular liberties. But we will accept it and bless it even if it comes clad in the rags of poverty.

If absorption were necessary, if the extinction of our Hispanic personality were necessary to make our island an emporium of wealth, Puerto Rican patriots would prefer hunger and poverty rather than buy happiness so dearly. What does poverty matter? What debases is slavery. Poor or rich, motherland is motherland as mother is mother, the same in beggar's raiment as in courtier's robe. To deny the race, or deny the motherland, is to deny the mother. And to deny the mother is to be less than a sucking pig or calf; it is to renounce the purest and most sacred of altars.

When Latin America loses all concern for us, when the great legions of that America take no interest in this formidable struggle we wage for the whole race's honor and prestige—then it will be time for us Puerto Ricans to kneel and pray God to divide the waters and bury us beneath the waves.

La Correspondencia de Puerto Rico, May 25, 1926

* From *petit yanqui,* servile imitator of the Americans.

III
Under the Sign of Imperialism

Pedro Albizu Campos (1891–1965)

Born in Ponce, studied at University of Vermont and at Harvard where he received his law doctorate. Traveled widely through Spanish America, especially the Caribbean. On his return was elected president of the Nationalist Party in 1931, and fought hard from that position for the Island's independence. Imprisoned several times (1936–1943). In 1943 had to leave as an exile, and did not return to Puerto Rico until 1947. Imprisoned again in 1950–1953 and in 1954. Transferred to a hospital in 1956 and died shortly thereafter.

No complete collection of his articles and speeches exists. Only in recent years have some disparate works begun to be republished.

Selected Bibliography

Albizu Campos, Pedro. *Independencia económica*. Río Piedras: Federación de Organizaciones Estudiantiles de la UPR, 1970.
————. *Así habló el maestro*. New York: Editorial Resistencia Puertorriqueña, 1970.
————. *República de Puerto Rico*. Montevideo: El Siglo Ilustrado, 1972.
————. *La conciencia nacional puertorriqueña*. M. Maldonado Denis, ed. Mexico: Siglo XXI, 1972.
————. *Obras Escogidas: 1923-1936*. J. B. Torres, ed. Vol. I. San Juan: Editorial Jelofe, 1975.
Albizu Campos, Laura de. *Albizu Campos y la independencia de Puerto Rico*. New York, 1961.
Corretjer, Juan Antonio. *Albizu Campos and the Ponce Massacre*. New York: World View Publishers, 1965.
————. *Albizu Campos*. Monetevideo, 1969.
González, Josemilio. "Recuerdos de don Pedro." *Mester* 2 (1969).
Maldonado Denis, Manuel. "Pedro Albizu Campos (1891-1965): revolucionario puertorriqueño." In *Puerto Rico: mito y realidad*. Barcelona, 1969, pp. 139-189.
————. "Martí y Albizu Campos." *Ibid.*, pp. 191-203.
————. "Albizu Campos y el desarrollo de la conciencia nacional puertorriqueña en el siglo XX." *Cuadernos Americanos* 24 (1970).
————. *Semblanza de cuatro revolucionarios: Albizu, Martí, Che Guevara, y Camilo Torres*. San Juan: Ediciones Puerto, 1973.
Medina Ramírez, Ramón. *El movimiento libertador en la historia de Puerto Rico*. 1954; San Juan, 1970.
Ribas Tovar, F. *Albizu Campos. Puerto Rican Revolutionary*. New York: Plus Ultra Educational Publishers, 1971.
Rivera Correa, R. R. *The Shadow of Don Pedro*. New York: Vantage, 1970.
————. *The Pariahs*. New York: Carlton Press, 1967.
Silén, Juan Angel. *Pedro Albizu Campos*. Río Piedras: Editorial Antillana, 1976.
The Nationalist Party of Puerto Rico. Washington, D.C.: U.S. Government Printing Office, 1951.

Observations on the
Brookings Institution Report*

Christian civilization has imposed the rule of law in the internal life and external relations of nations. There have been violent attacks on this rule but, under pain of relapsing into barbarism, it is undeniably respected.

Wars of plunder themselves require justification. The aggressor country must mobilize its masses on the basis of respect for rules of a higher order. If it wants to create armed institutions capable of heroism up to the point of personal sacrifice, it cannot appeal to sordid and selfish feelings.

When a neighbor is attacked, the world must be offered explanations. Outside intervention in the struggle is a danger always taken into account, since it is to the interest of all nations to maintain an equilibrium permitting each to develop within full sovereignty.

Although the United States always planned to become master of the Antilles—to make the Caribbean a Yanqui lake and thus bring strategic influence to bear on Mexico and Central and South America—it could not disclose the real aims of conquest to the North American people; so it talked to them of making war for humanitarian reasons. Before world opinion it portrayed the case of Cuba and Puerto Rico under Spanish rule as something so intolerable to the light of civilization that a peace-loving nation was compelled to intervene so that our right to freedom should be respected.

With North American patriotism thus exalted, the concern of

* Referring to the study sponsored by the Brookings Institution, by Victor S. Clark, *Porto Rico and Its Problems* (Washington, D.C., 1930). To counter the social crisis, the North American team proposed to improve governmental and administrative measures with more federal aid and industrialization. With Franklin D. Roosevelt's accession to power, the New Deal was broadly applied to Puerto Rico.

173

other powers lulled, and Antillean hopes falsely raised, war was declared.

According to the Yanquis' propaganda, their invasion of Puerto Rico in 1898 meant an end to Spanish obscurantism and oppression and the dawn of a regime of liberty, equality, fraternity, and material prosperity. All this felicity was to be ours, generously imposed by North American philanthropy and humane sentiment.

The invaders imposed the Treaty of Paris on Spain. They did not consult us in drawing it up, nor ask our approval. They forced Spain to yield Puerto Rico as war indemnity.

All of this blew the Yanquis' famous humanity into fragments, but their propaganda soothed Puerto Rican worries and international suspicions.

Puerto Ricans, irrespective of party, prepared to cooperate in this supposed dawn of liberty.

No one believed that the invaders had set themselves to profane the most sacred of human rights.

They implanted an absolutist regime enabling them to enjoy all immunities and to transfer all the wealth from native to invader hands. Thus agriculture, industry, trade, and communications became virtually theirs.

Today barely 20 percent of it remains in native hands.

Cries of alarm and of patriotism were heard, curses upon the invader. But Yanqui propaganda again put the Puerto Rican conscience to sleep. Our suspicions duly stilled, we were presented before our own and foreign eyes as a land enjoying extraordinary prosperity, due exclusively to the presence of North America's magical flag.

Workers came to believe that their good wages depended on the Yanqui government. Many intellectuals pinned their dearest hopes on occupying a high post in the North American government, especially in the diplomatic and consular services. Farmers were warned of possible labor demagogy. Businessmen were lured by the supposed advantages of free commerce between Puerto Rico and the United States. Persons of property were convinced that they must deposit their money in the invader's banks, because Yanqui propaganda hinted that we were all dishonest. The teaching profession convinced itself that everything must be taught in English. In short, the nation consented to its material and moral dismemberment, anesthetized by the vaunted good intentions.

The patriotism of a few natives went for nothing.

The workers could not believe that the Yanqui government was the fomenter of latifundism and absentee-landlordism and of the destruction of all native industry, resulting in a great rise in unemployment and cheap labor, to the enormous profit of Yanqui corporations.

Businessmen lost all sense of sane bookkeeping. They were unable to see that the free commerce under which we must sell to the Yanqui at the price he was pleased to fix, and buy from him at the price he deigned to stipulate, meant certain bankruptcy and liquidation for them.

Under the foreign propaganda spell, the ingenuous man of property believed that the branches of foreign banks were backed by mountainous millions of dollars. The money he deposited in them was used by the invader to modernize his own enterprises, withdrawing it from the market so that the interest rate rose and rehabilitation of native enterprises was impossible.

The farmer enslaved himself to the exploiting enterprises and sooner or later had to give up his farm—which for tax purposes the government appraised at the highest possible price—to the hounding creditor. At the same time invader interests were—and still are—allowed to conceal all kinds of holdings, and what they did declare was valued at a low figure; and nonpayment of those taxes that were assessed was and is tolerated, exempting them from compulsory sale of property by public auction in case of default. Meanwhile the auctioning off of Puerto Ricans' farms— often for sums not exceeding two dollars—continued year after year in the most systematic fashion.

With the excuse of teaching English, and at a cost of over $4 million a year, a public education system was maintained, using the invader's language as the only instructional medium. In fact, English was not taught, and the effect of making young people study science and Latin and other languages in English has been rather to benumb their faculties.

The invader reached the point where he no longer had to justify himself, for natives paid to do the job for him had emerged. Thus we have conspicuous "pedagogues" in the Department of Instruction approving the above barbarities.

There are plenty of lawyers to defend the invaders' interests.

A group of intellectuals has had the audacity to preach the hatching of a hybrid type, a half-Yanqui, half-Puerto Rican monster.

North American propaganda had triumphed. In spite of all this it was insisted that we had real and effective prosperity and the most advanced civilization as a special prize.

To the outside world we were portrayed as a prosperous, happy, and completely submissive people enjoying such well-being that others should follow our example.

A nationalist movement arose which did not confine itself to the colony. It sought international cooperation. It exposed the lie of North America's beneficence in Puerto Rico. Sad to tell, even abroad there were Puerto Ricans who took on the government's chore of maintaining that lie.

With Puerto Rican opinion inclining toward the nations of our own race, the colonial legislature gathered the courage to send a cable to the sixth American conference in Havana.

Everyone knows the fury this evoked in the despot Coolidge.

While maintaining the myth that Puerto Rico owed all its progress to North American management, his reply sketched the new-model propaganda of poverty. When Puerto Rico was supposed to be prosperous and happy under the U.S. flag, there was no reason to lower that flag. Now that the Puerto Ricans were admittedly poor and hungry, there was still no reason to lower it: the flag was necessary to help them.

Having played out the propaganda of prosperity, they began the propaganda of poverty.

Came the San Felipe hurricane, and with it the colonial governor Roosevelt* to justify the propaganda.

This man with the style of a populist ward politico made him-

---

* Theodore Roosevelt, Jr., governor of Puerto Rico 1929–1932.

self out to be our great friend, and sallied forth into our hills to take photos of our nakedness and hunger. The propaganda in the United States pleaded for public and private charity, stating that we had no resources to attend to our own needs.

The unwary fell for it fast. The sycophants, as always, responded emotionally to the voice of the master. Others feared to oppose him. Everybody applauded.

The Nationalist Party raised its voice in protest against this perverse propaganda which trampled our credit and prestige underfoot.

The protest rang out in the colonial legislature itself. It said that there was no charity, public or private, for Puerto Rico in the United States. It proudly affirmed that even if there were any, we didn't want it. We only wanted justice for our nation.

The colonial governor sought special powers from the legislature to resolve the alleged crisis. He appeared in the capitol itself to give orders. No one dared protest his presence.

He wanted the whole municipal administration—which was all that remained partially in Puerto Rican hands—to submit to his absolute will. The legislature was suspicious; it wouldn't agree.

It did agree, however, to set up various agencies to function under his direct orders. They were so important that he couldn't let them come under any department.

He spoke of industrializing the country. Everyone was stunned by this delightful prospect.

He introduced the party leaders in the legislature to Davidson Bros.—as our saviors. These newcomers would, according to Roosevelt, build a great refrigeration plant for our country's crops. They had millions of dollars and could scatter many millions among us.

But they needed from the legislature a gift of 6,000 square meters of land with ocean frontage in our country's chief port, San Juan, to build piers of a size to accommodate big ships. Someone investigated the financial standing of Davidson Bros. They turned out to be incorporated in Florida with a capital of *twenty-five thousand dollars.*

Now they tell us that these gentlemen are mere agents of the fearsome Yanqui octopus, the United Fruit Company. And now we understand the presence in San Juan of a United Fruit representative.*

We let them know that we wouldn't allow our poverty to serve as excuse for plundering our last penny. A bad start for industrialization.

Now Roosevelt wants us to believe that Puerto Rico's salvation depends on a $3 million donation from the U.S. Congress, a body notoriously reluctant to part with a cent.

And here the manifest imperial destiny triumphs. They don't need to spend money for their propaganda. We do the job and pay for it with pleasure.

Three million! What are three million to resolve a country's crisis? Enough of this farce.

Let us demand respect for our opinion.

Neither Roosevelt, nor his stand-in Beverly,† nor his subaltern Domenech, dares lay a finger on the great North American interests that owe many millions to the exchequer.

At the same time they ignore the law that was supposed to ease tax payments for small proprietors.

In a word, poverty must be intensified under the guise of alleviating it.

And now we get the Brookings Institution report. Its publication coincides with Roosevelt's presence in the United States.

This is no surprise to those who know something of the Yanqui propaganda system.

The "experts" paint a gloomy picture. They recommend drastic measures to resolve the crisis. Let us look at some of them: that the colonial senate should disappear, for example.

In practice this body has still not come into existence. It has always submitted to the colonial governor's will. To keep it short, let us examine the case of the present treasurer, Domenech. His party opposed his nomination. No one wanted him in that job.

Yet his nomination was confirmed unanimously!

Since the colonial legislature is a comedy—a recognized fact up

---

* On the United Fruit Company, see the already classic work by Charles D. Kepner, *The Banana Empire* (1935; New York: Russell, 1967).
† Jones Rumsey Beverly, governor 1932–1933.

to now, according to the Institution—its acceptance of naked despotism would be nothing strange.

It is dangerous to keep a comedy running which gives serious actors the opportunity to turn it into a tragedy.

In the opinion of these "experts," the restriction of municipal power and the extension of direct centralizing power from Washington, etc., are necessary for our salvation.

The important thing is that the big-estate system should be legalized. Let the 500-acre restriction disappear, because it never existed. The colonial legislators never put it into force.

Let Puerto Rico become a factory. Cheap day-laborers, foremen, and police are needed. A factory needs no legislators nor political power.

It is necessary to economize. Suppress superfluous agencies. When all of Puerto Rico's wealth shall have passed to the invaders, they will for the first time have to bear the weight of the budget. No natives will be available to cover their business deals.

The public power will frankly be a department of the factory administration.

Puerto Rico will be another Hawaii. We Puerto Ricans will be day-laborers, foremen, and policemen to guarantee to investors, against any opposition on our part that may arise, the enjoyment of our wealth.

Yet there are still those with the gall to plead tolerance for the invader. The time has come to apply sanctions to those who cooperate with him here.

There is poverty but not for lack of resources.

We must put an end to the robbery of these resources. We must distribute them among our people. The legion of small proprietors that we had in 1898 must be reborn.

For the Nationalist Party the recommendations of the Brookings Institution come as no surprise. We know the machinations of Yanqui propaganda.

We owe thanks to these "experts" for having filled the cup to the brim for many who till now have supported the invader.

We warn politicians not in our party that the Puerto Rican nation demands immediate suppression of this regime; that it will not let itself be diverted from its effort to have done with this situation.

We do not tolerate pretenses of rebellion. Is the opposition to this tremendous collective tragedy sincere, as we must hope it is? Then why not summon immediately the general assemblies of each party, and there resolve to demand recognition of our right to constitute ourselves as a free and independent country? The Puerto Rican nation demands definitive action by those who claim to represent it.

El Mundo, May 29, 1930

Concept of the Race

When President Hipólito Irigoyen of the Republic of Argentina instituted the Day of the Race, *la Raza*, what race was the great Argentine statesman talking about? Was it a narrow concept blotting out the rest of America's great ethnic mosaic? No, he was referring to the Ibero-American race.

For us *la Raza* has nothing to do with biology. Neither moon-colored complexion nor fuzzy hair nor the slant of the eyes. Race is a perpetuity of characteristic virtues and institutions. We are distinguished by our culture, our daring, our chivalry, our catholic sense of civilization. When ebullient Spain had united the kingdoms of Aragón and Castile, and won her independence with the expulsion of the Moors, she threw herself into the Discovery, the greatest epic of the period. The Discovery is humanity's discovery of itself, the discovery of man by man. God knows what moral cataclysms made possible the separation of humanity to the point where it was ignorant of itself! But with the Discovery, Spain conquered human unity, gave the world its geographic wholeness, made it a globe. Man didn't know where he lived. The map of his residence was conjectural. Spain gave him the security of stability, and man, feeling himself on solid ground, started moving again. The Discovery opened the road for all contemporary investigation in the philosophical and natural sciences. It not only systematized the science of ocean navigation, but gave man a consciousness of the cosmos, sending him on voyages through infinite space in an infinite multitude of constellations. Was the cosmos infinite in the eternal perspective of that infinite space, or was it destined for perpetual increase in the miracle of creation?

The Spanish race's primacy in Europe showed the potential benefit to the world of an equilibrium of daring and dedication. There is a historical experience that destines us to search for

181

ourselves to restore equilibrium to the world. Today the sense of race triumphantly reappears. Yellow peoples join together in the East to save themselves. Japan feels herself destined by Providence to restore yellow unity in Asia. The black races feel the same way in Africa. Anglo-Saxons unite rapidly in confrontation with the Latins. It is the secret law of North American policy to follow the inertia of the policies of their mother country, Great Britain. All get their spiritual weapons from us, because it was we who with fire and sword—the cross of the sword and the sword of the cross—gave old Europe and virgin America the tradition of virtue, of courage, of honor, of sacrifice, of scorn for death and material goods: everything that makes our race the hope of the world today.

In this hour, when Europe shivers at the prospect of catastrophic war, the peace of the Universe rests in the hands of our race. With full confidence in our race's values, the world has put its fate in the hands of two of our people. Salvador de Madariaga of Spain and Linares of Argentina are coolly, serenely, and responsibly confronting the problem of peace—the ideal of our race, emblazoned on the Christian banner with which our friars brought civilization to half the planet and our heroes turned the world upside down.

What if there are dangers? For our race, danger never existed.

La Palabra, October 19, 1935

Gilberto Concepción de Gracia (1909–1967)

Born in Vega Alta, studied law at the University of Puerto Rico and at George Washington University, where he obtained his law doctorate. Wrote articles on legal and political themes for Puerto Rican magazines and newspapers. President of the Puerto Rican Independence Party from its foundation in 1946. Traveled through many Latin American countries and the United States as delegate of that party. His articles and lectures remain scattered in various journals and newspapers.

Selected Bibliography

Anderson, Robert W. *Party Politics in Puerto Rico*. Stanford, Ca.: Stanford University Press, 1965. Rpt. Editorial Tecnos, Madrid, 1970. Traducción de Cecilio Sánchez Gil.

González, Antonio J. *Economía política de Puerto Rico*. San Juan: Editorial Cordillera, 1967.

Lewis, Gordon K. *Freedom and Power in the Caribbean*. New York, 1963. Rpt. abridged, Harper Torchbooks, N.Y., 1968.

Matthews, Thomas G. *Puerto Rican Politics and the New Deal*. University of Florida Press, 1960. Rpt. UPR, 1970.

Medina Ramírez, Ramón. *El movimiento libertador en la historia de Puerto Rico*. San Juan: Imp. Borinquen, 1956. Rpt. San Juan, 1970.

Pabón, M., R. W. Anderson, J. R. Rivera. *Los derechos y los partidos políticos en la sociedad puertorriqueña*. Río Piedras: Ediciones Edil, 1968.

The Revolution of 1950

On October 30 a revolution broke out in our country, organized by members and leaders of the Nationalist Party of Puerto Rico (PNP).* The revolutionary movement extended to various towns in the Island, with the usual results of any armed revolt. That movement has deeply shaken the Puerto Rican conscience.

I come before the public opinion of my country as president of the Independentist Party (PIP) to state the position of our group and of its executive committee on these events. For better understanding of the PIP's position it is necessary to state the following:

The October 30 revolution was organized by men and women who maintain that armed revolution is the road to our independence. As against the movement that has for many years defended this thesis before the public conscience, there has existed in our country since October 12, 1946, the PIP, over which I have the honor to preside: a political organization of democratic struggle founded to win our people's independence through all legal and peaceful means at our disposal, in peace and harmony with all the world's people and all men of good will.

While the PNP advocates permanent electoral abstention under all circumstances, the PIP went to the polls in 1948. It obtained 66,141 votes and occupies the third position among our country's parties, thus displacing the historic Socialist and Reformist parties. It opened its electoral campaign for 1952 on the day after the 1948 elections, and actively pursues that campaign with the enthusiasm which has sustained it until today.

---

* He is referring to, and criticizing, the nationalist insurrection of October 30 when Muñoz Marín's residence was attacked. There were outbreaks in Arecibo, Jayuya, Utuado, Adjuntas, Ponce, Naranjito, and Mayagüez. On November 1 the Nationalists Oscar Collazo and Girselio Torresola attacked Blair House in an attempt on the life of President Harry S. Truman.

185

While the PNP defends before the people positions and slogans in accordance with its program, doctrine, and political philosophy, the PIP used the written and spoken word, the press and radio, to convince the Puerto Rican electorate that it should swell our ranks; and it organizes the Independentist masses of the country in wards, villages, towns, and cities for the defense of their rights and for the electoral struggle in 1952.

While the PNP concentrates on putting Puerto Rico's case in international forums, the PIP, without forgetting that task, concentrates its daily work on developing in Puerto Rico a force opposing and criticizing the government party. A force able to serve as counterweight to the government party and fully prepared to defend the people's interests—the rights of Puerto Ricans and the physical patrimony of all sons of this land.

In the fight for our independence these two parties, then, have represented the two methods historically used throughout the world to win the peoples' independence. The task of winning independence by the first method has belonged historically to select minorities with the vocation of martyrdom. The task of winning it by the second method has belonged to majorities: not debased majorities paddling in the mud of momentary personal advantage, but majorities of superior civic caliber—awakened, educated minorities responsible to their people and to history.

The method defended by the PNP is the one used by the United States to gain its freedom, by all countries of our America except Brazil, and by nearly all nations of the world. The method actuated by the PIP is the one used by the Philippines in its now victorious struggle for emancipation.

Thus the PIP's program puts forward its political goal and the procedure to win independence for Puerto Rico. And it does so with these words which I take from our program:

> FIRST: *Political goal.* The PIP is organized with the basic aim of working peacefully to constitute the people of Puerto Rico as an independent, sovereign, and democratic republic. This goal cannot be changed without the party losing the essential motive of its existence; and those who seek to hold back, postpone, or slow down its realization will be automatically excluded from the party. The governmental work to be done before the constitution of the Re-

public will be directed toward maintaining necessary services; toward improvement of living standards and introduction of such reforms as will contribute to the fastest and firmest establishment of the Republic, under a regime of order and justice whose authority emanates from the people.

SECOND: *Procedure for winning independence.* The PIP will use the elections as a means to obtain a people's mandate for the independence of Puerto Rico. Once this party obtains a majority in both houses of the legislative assembly, its first official action will be approval of a resolution demanding from the United States government immediate recognition of Puerto Rican independence. As part of this action a commission will be appointed to negotiate implementation of the resolution, and to work out in conformity with this program the basis of future relations between the two peoples. No negotiation will be undertaken on the basis of any curtailment of the integrity of our territory or limitations on the Puerto Rican people's full sovereignty. In order that they shall be effective, all negotiations must be finally approved by the people of Puerto Rico. The commission will make periodic reports to the legislative assembly, which in turn must inform the executive committee of the party. Within six months of the appointment of the commission, the party's general assembly will meet to hear the commission's detailed report on the result of negotiations with the United States government. The assembly will approve such measures as it considers adequate to shape the action of the party to the needs of the independence struggle.

Such are the clear and unambiguous words of our political program.

The PIP has accepted and accepts the electoral struggle in full awareness of the vices inherent in the system. We have accepted it knowing that those vices are aggravated in a colony; the more so when the ballot box must be used as a liberating weapon, in conflict with the representatives of a system that keeps our people in a state of submission, inferiority, and servitude.

We have accepted it because the men and women of our party have total confidence in the intelligence, civic sense, and courage of our people, and full faith in their creative capacity. Furthermore because these men and women firmly believe that the ballot box is the fastest and most direct road to win our independence, and the only one that can guarantee economic stability for the future Puerto Rican Republic. Having this firm and unshakeable conviction, the women and men of the PIP reject the road of armed revolution and dedicate themselves sedulously, religiously, in body and soul, to building a great party ready and able to win the elections of 1952 and to make our country independent.

The Referendum Law is a colonial measure with the sinister aim of confirming (with the Puerto Ricans' vote) the unjust political, economic, and social relations now prevailing between Puerto Rico and the United States. This measure, a fraud and swindle, seeks to pervert the sacred concepts of our struggles for liberty; to mystify the meaning of those concepts, such as the constitution and constituent assembly, and to deceive the Puerto Rican people and world opinion. It constitutes a moral crime and the greatest affront to a good and worthy people who have fought a hundred battles for their freedom and the freedom of other peoples. It is the final insult to ask this people to tell the world that Puerto Ricans spontaneously want to continue as a colony! A horrendous moral crime to seek to install in Puerto Rico the colony by consent!

Historical truth demands that the world be told that the government has tried to impose this shameful measure on Puerto Rico, using every coercive means at its disposal: monopolizing all the propaganda media and agencies of government (including the public schools), and putting at the disposal of those defending the monstrous "Law of Colony by Consent" all of the state's infinite resources and all the terrible power of its officials. The government furthermore rushed the registrations and elections provided for in the spurious statute, to prevent opponents of this disgraceful legislation—undoubtedly the majority of the Puerto Rican people, but lacking economic resources to confront the government's corrupt machine—from organizing adequately. All this the government has done against the strongest protest of the PIP, which is the ONLY voice of opposition to that government.

In face of the Nationalist revolution, and having in view all the above considerations and many others we lack time to discuss here, the executive committee of our party meeting in Aguadilla on the night of November 1, 1950, approved a statement appraising the events that had occurred in Puerto Rico. Here is the text:

> The executive committee of the PIP, convening in extraordinary session in the city of Aguadilla on the night of November 1, 1950, to consider the prevailing revolutionary situation in Puerto Rico, unanimously agreed on the following decisions: "First: To ratify the principles of the PIP set forth in these words in our program: 'The PIP is organized with the basic aim of working peacefully to constitute the people of Puerto Rico as an independent, sovereign, and democratic republic.'
>
> "Second: To hold the present government of Puerto Rico responsible for having sought to impose on the Puerto Rican people a political measure, under the name of a constitution, which is a fraud upon this people's legitimate rights and which tends to confirm the colonial system in our country. We declare that this outrage to the Puerto Rican people's dignity has led one of the world's most peaceful people into a state of intranquility and protest, which has culminated in the present revolutionary movement.
>
> "We also hold the present government of Puerto Rico responsible because, having made no formal declaration of martial law (with the clear intention of belittling the importance of the Puerto Rican revolutionary movement before the world), it has committed a long series of violations of citizens' rights, thus illegally establishing de facto martial law. We therefore demand an end to these violations of rights and to the government's vicious persecutions. We also demand complete legal guarantees for all Puerto Ricans involved in the revolutionary movement.
>
> "Third: To hold the government of the United States of America responsible for the historic fact that, throughout the half-century of its domination of Puerto Rico, it has denied the right of our people to enjoy its sovereignty. And at the end of that half-century it seeks (in combination with the actual colonialist bosses on the island) to unload its responsibility upon Puerto Rico through the deception of a false constitution.
>
> "Fourth: To express the deepest respect of the PIP for those compatriots who have offered and are offering their lives for the cause of Puerto Rico's independence."

This resolution does not constitute an act of solidarity with the revolution, as the governor and president of the Popular Democratic Party, señor Luis Muñoz Marín, and his collaborators maliciously said in commenting on our statement. Far from it.

Our party pursues and must pursue, actively and firmly, the peaceful road of the ballot box, to obtain a majority mandate from the people of Puerto Rico for achieving our independence.

If we supported the Nationalist revolution and were in solidarity with it, we would not be here serenely defending our party's position in the field of ideas. We would certainly be somewhere else!

This being so, our party must plainly fix responsibility for the events where it belongs. And it has done so. We have fixed it on those in Washington who stubbornly maintain the colony of Puerto Rico. We have fixed it on those who have tried to impose the fraud of the misnamed constitution upon our people.

Even though we don't believe in the method used by the PNP to win independence, we attest our highest respect for those who gave their lives for the cause that is our own polestar. The cause that nourishes all our dreams: independence for Puerto Rico.

This does not mean that we have departed one iota from our party's political program. It does not mean that we have to abandon for one moment the paths we have followed in the struggle for freedom. It does not imply the smallest variation in our form of propaganda, the smallest change in our peaceful pursuit of independence, nor in our respectful deference to law.

Up to October 30, 1950, the PIP differed in its tactics from the PNP. After that date our party continued—and it will so continue—to differ in tactics from the PNP. And so it will be until our party wins at the polls the mandate from the majority of our people to establish here a democratic republic truly "of all and for the good of all." A republic where we can all live in peace, and where all citizens' rights are guaranteed, poor and rich, black and white; where the campesino, the worker, the man and woman of middle class may attain true social justice, something they could not and never can attain in the colony.

Taking advantage of the situation created in our country, the government of Puerto Rico conceived a diabolical plan to try to destroy the PIP, knowing perfectly well the historical reality faced by our people. Let us mention a few manifestations of this devilish plan.

While the governor of Puerto Rico told international press

correspondents that the PIP worked with full legality for independence and to win a majority in Puerto Rico, lists of Independentist leaders were being compiled in La Fortalez so that they could be arrested throughout the country whenever such arrests might better serve the government party's Machiavellian electoral plans. At the same time they were working on other lists of our leaders to be arrested in every community across the Island. And these lists were drawn up with the chief of government's approval by mayors of the government party, legislators of the government party, and community police chiefs addicted to the government party—the Popular Party, heretically proclaimed *democratic*.

The obvious scheme was to crush the PIP in the November 4-5 voter registrations. To this end, the petition to postpone the registrations, jointly formulated on November 1 by our party's official representative in the Electoral Commission and by the president of the party, was not even considered. While we were conferring with the General Superintendent of Elections, explaining to him the impossibility of holding voter registrations under an undeclared state of martial law, on that very day orders for the arrest of our party leadership were being issued, disguised as "citations to testify in an investigation." Those illegal arrest orders were issued, and those lists prepared, *before* our party's executive committee met in Aguadilla, and thus before the committee issued its historic and momentous statement.

But we must go into more detail about the demagogic official procedure used in the arrest of our Independentist leaders. Their homes were raided without judicial warrants. They were denied any kind of bail. They were taken to barracks and jails under heavy custody, a ridiculous thing in view of our arrested leaders' civic records. They were photographed from every angle with numbers on their chests, like common criminals. In some contemptible cases these patriots were taken *handcuffed* to barracks and jails!

They were submitted to every sort of scurrility. They were fingerprinted and held at the point of rifles, revolvers, and bayonets by police and national guards, as if they were the most hardened and dangerous of criminals.

Five members of our party's executive committee were arrested
on their way to the executive meeting in Aguadilla. And all this
abusively carried out, without the remotest justification for arrest. And at this moment one member of our executive is still in
jail for no reason whatever.

Our party's various committee leaders and members were arrested all over Puerto Rico under the government's preconceived
plan. Many members of our committees were arrested in communities where not a single Nationalist is known, where such
members are of Socialist, Statist, Liberal, and Popular formation.

It was obvious that in those conditions, with undeclared martial
law in Puerto Rico and with our members and leaders being
maliciously and unjustifiably hounded, we could not participate
in the registrations. Yet the PIP was ready to participate in them
and *to win* them. We had provided the Island Electoral Commission with the names of local registration commission members
island-wide, as may easily be checked from the Island Electoral
Commission records.

We asked that the registrations be postponed because we honestly *wanted* to participate in them. Furthermore because we had
worked to win them, and we were—and remain—confident of
the support of new voters.

The government preferred to go ahead on its own. And the
registrations were a colossal fiasco for the government. The government went to the registrations *alone*. Without opposition, ignoring the most elementary principle of the democratic system.

The fiasco for the government of these registrations is plain to
see. Instead of registering the number of new voters as calculated
by the Island Electoral Commission, amounting to some *four
hundred thousand,* only *one hundred and fifty-six thousand* were registered. And instead of accepting this great fiasco the government
panegyrists undertook a further swindle of the people, in bad
faith comparing the latest registrations with those of 1948; the
truth being that registered voters who didn't vote in the 1944
elections had been incorporated by law in the electoral lists. The
honest comparison would have been with the registrations in
1944 (six years ago) when the situation was the same as in the
latest registrations: that is, qualified voters who didn't vote in

1940 had been *eliminated* from the electoral lists, and *had to register again.*

Everyone knows that the Puerto Rican legislature had eliminated from the lists qualified voters who didn't vote in 1948, amounting to *two hundred and thirty-two thousand.* We know it and the government knows it.

Thus the fiasco of the latest registrations has shown the overwhelming strength of the PIP. The government knows from its recent electoral census throughout Puerto Rico—and knew—what an enormous number of new voters had declared themselves for the PIP.

Conscious of our deep roots in public opinion and the strength of our electorate, we have continued our electoral work and are now selecting the officials to represent our party in all the electoral colleges, in all Puerto Rico, for the referendum elections due on June 4, 1951. And we are strengthening our forces for the electoral struggle in 1952, completely confident that in those elections we will decisively defeat the forces of reaction and colonialism represented by the present government party in Puerto Rico.

For the 1952 elections we will register all who have not registered in the past. This has nothing to do with the general registrations of new voters which *by law* must be held for the next general elections.

We are in the fight. We are moving firmly toward victory by the road of legality and democracy.

We are not scared by the reprisal threats that already seem to be incubating in the marrow of small-time opportunist politicos. Fearing the defeat that awaits them, these people seek to frighten the permanent public officials who, with every right and protected by the Personnel Law, hold positions in the government and are members of the PIP. Those employees and officials cannot be ousted from their posts; and if anyone were to try it, we would obtain from the courts the binding protection of their rights.

Our party is a party of struggle. Of tireless struggle for our people's freedom and the happiness of all Puerto Ricans, following the clear principles of our program.

So will always be the PIP! So must we always be till the end of our days! Without weakening or straying, without fear of the powerful, our lives will ever be dedicated to democracy until our souls enter the mystery of eternity: to democracy, to peace, to independence for Puerto Rico, to genuine social justice, to the brotherhood of all Puerto Ricans.

Many thanks, and—on to the struggle and to victory!

San Juan, P.R., November 1950

Speech delivered on November 10, 1950

Juan Mari Bras (1926–)

Lawyer; general secretary of the Pro-Independence Movement (since 1971, Puerto Rican Socialist Party), most radical of Puerto Rico's independentist groups. Editor of the weekly *Claridad*. An extensive traveler in the United States, Spanish America, and Europe, giving lectures on the Puerto Rican case. His works have never been collected.

Selected Bibliography

Mari Bras, Juan. *Betances. Santo y seña de la revolución puertorriqueña.* New York: MPI, 1970.
————. *El gran fraude.* San Juan: Editorial Claridad, 1967.
————. *Presente y futuro de Puerto Rico. La doctrina de la nueva lucha de independencia.* Río Piedras, 1969.
————. *Tesis política del MPI.* San Juan, 1963.

Albizu Campos: His Historical Significance

At this juncture no great theoretical complexities are required to place the figure of Pedro Albizu Campos in the history of our motherland. A glance at the course of that history fixed him unquestionably as one of the two greatest of our nation's great men.

As Marxists we have the classical view of history. We see it as an interconnected series of social conflicts powered by the class struggle between oppressors and oppressed in each epoch.

In the specific conformation which is our Puerto Rican motherland, the class struggle is intimately related to the struggle for independence, ever since Puerto Ricans became fully aware, in the nineteenth century, of the existence of a motherland in their island.

We accept the theory of Ho Chi Minh that the chief function of communists in any colonial country is to fight for their people's independence. With him we see the contradiction between imperialism and colonized people as the most profound expression of the class struggle in a colonial setup, regardless of its geographical location or its historical period. When we speak of Albizu Campos, we do so from our Marxist-Leninist perspective, using the analytical methods of scientific socialism.

Throughout the nineteenth century and during most of the twentieth, the struggle for our independence was led by the most enlightened sectors of our country's Creole bourgeoisie. The revolution for independence that exploded in Lares on September 23, 1868, is the supreme expression of the flowering of national and class consciousness in those sectors, including the nineteenth-century professionals.

Betances, "Father of the Nation" and outstanding figure of the nineteenth-century independence struggles, represents the lofiiest voice and most advanced thinking among the bourgeoisie of his time. And the Betances tradition represents the most advanced contribution of bourgeois democratic-liberal thought to civilization and human history. Nationalism, its direct connection and continuation in the twentieth century, made a faltering debut with José de Diego's message in the century's second decade, the founding of the José de Diego Institute, the campaigns to affirm Puerto Rican identity and vernacular and historical values, and the founding of the Nationalist Party in 1922 by a group of Puerto Rican intellectuals. And it achieved maximum expression in the radical revolutionary nationalism of the Thirties under Albizu Campos's leadership. It is in this perspective that the figure of Albizu must be viewed in our history. This has been recognized by great communist intellectuals of Puerto Rico and of other countries who have appraised that towering figure of our motherland and our America.

Juan Marinello, president of the Cuban Communist Party, who championed Puerto Rican independence through his half-century of fertile revolutionary life, often expressed admiration for the Puerto Rican nationalist leader. He wrote this in *Pueblos hispanos* on March 20, 1943:

> In Cuba, Santo Domingo, Haiti, and Puerto Rico we have a surfeit of weak-kneed, compromising folk, of skeptics and cowardly capitulators. But when a land—and the Antilles are one land—produces a man like Albizu Campos, who embraces a faith and knows how to die for it, we can justly say that in the blood that makes such a man there is material to make us great.

Later, paying homage to the Puerto Rican Nationalist leader after Albizu died in 1965, Marinello said:

> As in Maceo and in Mella, the formative bloodstreams of Antilleanism flowed together in Albizu Campos. We had differences with him in specific situations but we felt him to be very much in our lineage and vigor, in the root and in the flower. He was a truly rare coincidence of our essential virtues, a superior but organic exaltation of the profile of our lands. He was born to stand in erect and radical confrontation with destiny in one of America's most decisive challenges, liberation from imperialism.

Juan Antonio Corretjer, who was his disciple, comrade, and friend in struggle and in prison, and who in the course of his Nationalist activity developed ideologically to become a communist, is one of the Puerto Ricans who have most insistently exalted Albizu's historical stature in various lectures and studies, some of which were published in books and pamphlets.

"The mystery of his existence is so transparent," said Corretjer,

> that it stares us in the face in his astonishing versatility of leadership. No previous leader combined and vindicated so many forms of struggle. He wielded the magic of the spoken and written word in almost all their most effective forms: philosophical discourse, juridical exposition, religious, political and inflammatory oratory, pamphlets and articles and private correspondence; discreet intervention with friends and sympathizers in the opposing camp; street campaigning as an avenue of political organization and diffusion of doctrine; boycotting elections as a revolutionary resistance technique; the workers' and students' strike; diplomacy and international work: contacts with foreign governments and institutions, with Puerto Ricans abroad, mainly in New York—whom he inspired to become a voting force, putting a champion of Puerto Rican independence into the U.S. Congress, the great Vito Marcantonio whose parliamentary skill made his Puerto Rican base numerically significant in congressional votes; in conspiracy, in direct action, in street struggles, in insurrection. To sum up, in the mobilization of every factor with fascinating effectiveness, with a political imagination which, unmatched in the annals of our creativity and backed by a total disregard for personal convenience, made him a great poet of life.

A marvelous synthesis of a communist intellectual's historical assessment of this Puerto Rican nationalist leader.

Certainly Albizu cannot be judged as a strategist of the Puerto Rican socialist revolution, because he never claimed to be a socialist nor a Marxist. He was above all a man imbued with a highly idealist philosophy combining, as major influences, the main currents not only of Christianity but of other religions such as the Hindu, which also contributed to the total development of his personality. It is from this perspective, on the basis of his own position, that any judgment must be made.

We communists do not pretend that history, either in the

universal or the national dimension, began with us. We do not ignore history prior to the development of scientific socialism. When the founders of that science such as Marx and Engels were maturing their philosophical, economic, and political principles, they did so by taking different strands of philosophy, economics, and political science from before the discovery of scientific socialism.

So it is, too, on the Puerto Rican national level. As a young nationality which has still not won independence in the last quarter of the twentieth century, the century of decolonization, we are much less able to make history and interpret our people's destiny in disregard of the extraordinary contributions that have been made to it and to socialism in the past.

Albizu and the nationalism of the thirties unquestionably constitute the vanguard of the Puerto Rican people.

It is true that Puerto Rico's first communist party was founded in that same decade. And that that party gathered up the best of the Puerto Rican working class's tradition of struggle forged in strikes, in fighting movements led by the old Socialist Party during the century's first decades. And that the theoretical cleansing of that tradition and experience led the most enlightened militants of the labor movement to found the Communist Party in 1934. But it is also true that that party was born with a deformation which greatly constricted its potential for fulfilling the vanguard mission of communists everywhere and especially in colonial territory.

It was born and developed under the Stalinist deformation. This acquired most seriously negative dimensions in the Communist Party of the United States, which was the base for creation of the party here. It was the CPUSA that directed and in every sense served as example and image for the ideological and practical activity of Puerto Rico's communists in the thirties. And it was that same party that later produced the Browderite deformation—the tendency to liquidate the party in countries with bourgeois governments claiming to be liberal or progressive. Accepting this claim by Franklin Roosevelt's New Deal and the Democratic Party led by him at the time, the U.S. communists dissolved their party and constituted themselves as a pressure group within the Democratic administration. The Puerto Rican communists followed suit, dissolving their party in the same month. These deformations, marking the birth and first development of communism in Puerto Rico, prevented the communists from playing the vanguard role which Ho Chi Minh allotted to them in every colonial territory.

Corretjer himself made this analysis—in our view a very correct one—in one of his works on Albizu Campos and the Ponce massacre.* Referring to that period in our history, from 1930 to 1937, Corretjer wrote:

> In this extremely difficult situation his party and leadership were additionally affected by the absence of a fully developed Marxist movement in Puerto Rico. It was very late in Puerto Rican history for the national bourgeoisie to take leadership, since it was in the main compromised through its collaboration with the foreign oppressor, and the absence of a Marxist leadership accentuated the weakness of the petty bourgeoisie. Albizu Campos himself, with all his talents, was a bourgeois leader with no bourgeoisie to lead.

And concerning the sugar workers' strike which Albizu then led at the behest of the workers, Corretjer commented: "It was at this decisive moment that the petty-bourgeois character of the whole independentist camp cried aloud for a Marxist ally, consisting of a cadre team that could transform Albizu's enormous attractiveness and popularity into a single revolutionary labor organization."

There have been attempts to blame Albizu and the nationalism of the thirties for inability to translate into a revolutionary organization the massive awakening that was evident in the 1935 sugar strike. It has been rightly noted that the workers, having been betrayed by the Free Federation of Labor leaders of the old Socialist Party who were already allied with the Republican Party in the coalition government, sought in Albizu the leadership they needed to push ahead the strike and its demands.

In that moment the figure of Albizu indeed filled the void of a proletarian leadership responsive to the needs of the Puerto

* See Juan Antonio Corretjer, *Albizu Campos* (Montevideo: El Siglo Illustrado, 1969).

Rican working class. The vast majority of labor leaders in this
country had surrendered to the sugar interests. And those not
involved in the surrender could not get off the ground a labor
organization capable of becoming a proletarian vanguard in such
a vital situation.

Nothing more natural than that the striking sugar workers in
their mood of proletarian militancy should call out to the figure
who represented what was most radical in the Puerto Rico of the
day: the man who had confronted face to face the most powerful
enemy, United States imperialism, dedicating his life and brilliant
talent to the people's cause with no thought for his personal
problems; who had set an example of courage, of heroic capacity,
of standing at the head of his people in the demand for their
rights; in sum, the emergent figure already then synthesizing the
highest Puerto Rican values.

As with every charge that his people entrusted to him, as with
every task he undertook in his long march, Albizu fulfilled this
one to the hilt. He assumed leadership of the sugar strike and
went through cane fields and public squares explaining the development of strike strategy to the workers. He dug deep into
many aspects of the workers' demands to bring out the basic
causes of the injustices their demands denounced. He fought and
led in full and fervent identification with the workers' cause—like
a real proletarian leader without in fact being one. Witness the
extensive newspaper analyses of the sugar-strike period of
Albizu's journey. Witness the primary-source writings that attest
to the nationalist leader's glorious participation in this proletarian
epic.

It is impossible to impute either to him or to the nationalism of
the thirties the failure to give the sugar workers' strike continuity,
in terms of deepening it into a proletarian organization that could
have begun posing greater objectives than some immediate demands. Such a thing was not on the nationalist agenda. Nationalism was not an organization based on socialist ideology. Yet we
must stress that the anti-imperialist nature of nationalism placed
it objectively in alliance with the working class in its most critical
experience. He did become the chief spokesman of that class in

the sugar-strike crisis, filling the gap created by lack of a communist party which could fulfill its vanguard function.

The history of the national liberation movement has increasingly demonstrated the objective alliance that exists between all the forces fighting imperialism, colonialism, and neocolonialism on the one hand, and socialism as the definitive cause for liberation of the human species. Independently of one's estimate of a leader or of a generation in the long process of struggle for national liberation, history shows that objectively their contributions fertilize and develop the socialist cause.

Just today *El Nuevo Día* published an article by the journalist Rafael López Rosa in defense of Albizu Campos. Rafael cites a statement by Lenin that a Moslem nationalist leader fighting for Islamic independence made more socialist revolution than a British socialist having his tea in a London café. And that is the heart of the matter. We cannot appraise Albizu Campos and his role in our history outside the context of his revolutionary practice, of the practice of his life, of what Albizu Campos did.

It was Albizu's destiny to take up the banner of Betances at a time of mounting demoralization among the disoriented Creole petty bourgeoisie and bourgeoisie, following the death of de Diego and the negotiations, coalitions, and dirty tricks in which the parties indulged in the twenties. Came Albizu like a great thundering on the door to rouse the consciousness of his people in the name of millenary human virtues which he saw from his idealistic perspective and deep religious convictions—but which fully coincided with the virtues fomented by socialist revolution as essential for any revolutionary transformation and for the definitive transformation of humanity.

Albizu's theory about heroism is a key to this: "The most lasting value in man is heroism," he said. "Heroism in the individual is the supreme good." "Only heroism permits a man to stroll firmly and serenely in the face of death, and when a man passes serenely over the shadows of death he enters into immortality."* "The motherland is founded on the emulation of heroism."

* In this sense, Albizu's ideas are close to those of the Generation of '98 in Spain. Unamuno, for example, stresses heroism.

Exaltation of heroism as the supreme virtue of the species is confused with fascist attitudes by those whose skin is barely scratched by Marxism. They lose sight of the fact that for Marxists, any historical personality or movement must be seen in the context of the given situation. When Hitler and Mussolini were needling their bourgeoisie into taking over Europe, communists censured and criticized not the exaltation of heroism in itself—since it was not a valid heroism, not an indispensable virtue—but the demagogic use of that essential human virtue for the purpose of aggression and domination, to put an exploiting class in the slavedriver's seat over Europe's exploited masses. Some seek to confuse this with the totally false notion that the exaltation of heroism is alien to the proletarian revolution. This would completely contradict the essence of Marxism-Leninism which proclaims that the taking of power by the working class must be through a revolutionary process, especially an armed one; and that it requires full deployment of the most heroic qualities of all who fight in the socialist revolution.

Albizu Campos gathered up in our land the best of our people's fighting tradition, exalted it, and put it in its proper perspective. Thus it was he who disinterred Betances from anonymity and rose in defense of the "Father of the Nation" at his centenary. Thus it was also Albizu who rescued Lares from semianonymity. Furthermore, he gave its true dimension to this historic pinnacle of our people in their nineteenth-century struggle for liberty, and set the tradition of paying homage to our heroes and martyrs who gave their lives for our motherland's independence. Thus on every occasion throughout his days he affirmed the heroism of the nationalists, and thus he assumed leadership in a period of glory paid for with great sacrifices, which led to his imprisonment for half of his active life and his mortal illness.

It was precisely for lack of a communist party, of an organization based on Marxism-Leninism which from the working-class standpoint could unite all classes concerned with our motherland's liberation and independence, that nationalism had to make the first effort in this direction. And it made them, as Corretjer

* The *Grito de Lares* in 1868.

brings out in his inventory of the forms of struggle undertaken by Albizu. If we examine the forms and concrete manifestations of struggle in today's Puerto Rico, we see that all of them were anticipated in practice by Albizu. In the last analysis, what we who now fight for Puerto Rico's liberation have to do is to enrich and develop Albizu's example. For Albizu set the basic strategic model for our fight for independence.

From this we cannot jump to the conclusion that we who now carry on the fight are tied to the tactical or strategic conceptions of Albizu's nationalism. Each generation in the struggle is independent of previous ones in putting into practice the strategy and tactics arising from better understanding of present reality. But that understanding of today's reality is rounded out by full understanding of our country's history, of the developments in a people's levels of struggle that history marks out for us. Thus we have recognized in this stage of our fight for independence that its leadership must be definitely shifted from the petty bourgeoisie and the Creole bourgeoisie to the proletariat. Only to the extent that this is fully done, and that our young proletariat can incorporate in the fight for its own demands the anti-imperialist, combative, and revolutionary substance of Puerto Rican nationalism, can the working class muster the orientation and strength to preside victoriously over our national liberation struggle.

We cannot make history at the whim of our desires. We cannot avoid the realities that have formed the history of our land. The struggle for liberation has presided over the history of Puerto Rico, and it is the more enlightened sectors of the creole bourgeoisie, the petty bourgeoisie, and in particular its intellectuals and professionals, who have presided over that struggle.

No communist, no Marxist-Leninist, need lose sleep over this. It is the reality of all human history. In the process of assuming its protagonist role in any historical stage, each class has to take a whole legacy of contributions from opposing classes. That is why history is a continuity and chaos does not prevail when great revolutionary changes are made. And that is why a healthy sediment persists into each stage of human development, a progress that, even within the great antagonistic contradictions produced by the class struggle, has permitted humanity to emerge from caves into the civilization of today. These fragmentary visions, that would deny validity to representatives of progressive positions in a given epoch, are schematic, antidialectical, and anti-communist.

We are well aware that both enemies and friends will continue aiming diatribes at the figure of Albizu Campos. Some because they know that the inspiration of Albizu in Puerto Rico's future life must take on ever greater importance, and hence they want to demolish it. A vain illusion on their part, since the towering figures of the history of the people resist all blows they may receive. Others are moved by a false interpretation of what the class struggle is and what adherence to an ideology is; by a historical myopia and inability to internalize the essentials of dialectics and of historical materialism. These would reduce Albizu to an interpretation placing him in his country's spectrum of classes, without reference to what Albizu achieved in practice in his historical context.

The Chinese Revolution, with all its convulsions, has always kept on the highest pinnacle the figure of Sun Yat-sen, founder of the Chinese Republic. The Cuban Revolution—defined as Marxist-Leninist, and maturing in the glorious role of the American hemisphere's first socialist state—has seen nothing incompatible in the search for its ideological foundations not only in Marxist-Leninist thought but in the thought of Martí and the great theoretical and practical figures of its revolution for independence. In the same way, the Puerto Rican revolution must base itself in the combined inheritance and experience transmitted to us by humanity and by the international working class, which includes the whole theoretical structure of Marxism-Leninism and the legacy of our own history—of our national struggle through the centuries in which Puerto Rico has taken shape as a nation.

We endorse the view of the Cuban Revolution's commander-in-chief when he said at the centenary of Yara,* referring to Carlos Manuel Céspedes and those who raised the Cry of La

* The *Grito de Yara* in October 1868 initiated the first war for independence, which lasted ten years.

Demajagua: "If they had happened to live in our time they would be like us. If we had happened to live in their time we would be like them." In this apt statement Fidel Castro demonstrates the practical application and flexibility that the dialectical method applies to the analysis of history. In our own case—the Puerto Rican revolution which must be increasingly independentist, socialist, and revolutionary—we submit that it should be equally enriched by the whole pyramid of sources that have accumulated experience of struggle in the world and in our motherland.

We must take inspiration in revolutionary practice from Marx and Lenin, from Ho Chi Minh, and from Che Guevara, but also from Betances and Albizu Campos and the Puerto Rican Nationalist heroes and martyrs who raised our struggle to a heroic level when the national will of our people looked as if it was collapsing. We must emulate the courage, the readiness for sacrifice, and the dedication of Pedro Albizu Campos. Emulate his dedication to his country's cause, his renunciation of all material ambition, his capacity for suffering in face of adversity, his genius for transmitting indignation so that his people might steel their consciences and assume the liberating role history has assigned to them.

On this anniversary of Albizu's birth we pay tribute to the memory of this great Puerto Rican in the name of Puerto Rican socialists, of the men and women who are daily carrying forward here the independentist, socialist, Marxist-Leninist revolution. We invite the youth of Puerto Rico to continue studying and emulating the splendid life of this illustrious son of Ponce, of Puerto Rico, and of America, whose moral and revolutionary eminence has been matched by no other Puerto Rican in this century.

Speech at the University of Puerto Rico, Río Piedras, September 12, 1977

César Andreu Iglesias (1915–1976)

Journalist, short-story writer, and novelist. For many years contributed a fighting column to the newspaper *El Imparcial*. Was a labor leader and one of the founders of the General Confederation of Workers (CGT) in Puerto Rico and of the Pro-Independence Movement.

His novels and stories have political themes; he analyzes the colonizing process since 1898. *Los derrotados* deals with the Nationalist Party and its extermination. Two plays, *Los astrólogos se equivocan* and *The Rodríguez*, remain unpublished; some of his political essays were published in 1951 under the title *Independencia y socialismo*. One of the most incisive researchers of Puerto Rican history, he wrote important expository works on economics and on the development of the labor movement. For the most part his writings remain scattered in the periodical press.

Selected Bibliography

Andreu Iglesias, César. *Los derrotados.* 1956; Río Piedras: Editorial Cultural, 1964.

————. *Una gota de tiempo.* San Juan: Editorial Puertorriqueña, 1958.

————. *El derrumbe.* Club del Libro de Puerto Rico, 1960.

————. *Independencia y socialismo.* Librería Estrella Roja, 1951.

————. *Luis Muñoz Marín. El hombre acorralado por la historia.* San Juan: Editorial Claridad, 1964.

Fromm, Georg. *César Andreu Iglesias. Approximación a su vida y obra.* Río Piedras: Ediciones Huracán, 1977.

Guevara Castañeira, Josefina. *"Los derrotados,* de César Andreu Iglesias." In *Del Yunque a los Andes.* San Juan, 1959.

Rosa Nieves, Cesáreo. *"Los derrotados:* novela de trasfondo político." *Semana* 4 (1958).

Sánchez-Boudy, José. *Las novelas de César Andreu Iglesias y la problemática puertorriqueña actual.* Barcelona: Casa Editorial Bosch, 1968.

Vargas Boda, Pilar. "El concepto de la libertad en la novela *Los derrotados,* de César Andreu Iglesias." *El Imparcial,* September 30, 1967.

The Labor Movement and the
Independence of Puerto Rico

I

If anything has held back development of the independence struggle in Puerto Rico, it is the breach that has historically kept the independence and labor movements on separate roads. That separation has affected both but the first more than the second, because it has prevented the independence movement from nourishing itself with the ideology of the working class, the most advanced in modern society.

But in recent years there has been an ideological transformation in the independence movement. This has been due to a series of causes, among which the following are probably most important:

1. Recognition that the national bourgeoisie is a creature of imperialism and that this class's essential ideologies prove useless and impotent as sources of orientation for the independence struggle; and

2. Recognition that at this stage of world history the independence struggle forms part of the peoples' national liberation revolution against imperialism, and hence is inexorably linked to humanity's great struggle for socialism.

To a greater or lesser degree, by conscious impulse or simple emotional inclination, the independence movement is evolving in that direction. In addition to its own experience, the reflection of the surrounding world has contributed to this; and in the latter area the Cuban Revolution has been the chief factor.

In order to act in the vanguard of events we must start with a correct appreciation of Puerto Rico. Of course we belong to the great family of Latin American peoples. But our development took a certain direction after the invasion of 1898: a different direction from that of Latin American countries, yet not so different as to set us apart from prerevolutionary Cuba or the present Dominican Republic.

Latin America has been called the backyard of the United States. In the past Britain, France, Germany, and other minor powers competed with the United States for financial domination of the Caribbean basin and South America. With World War II the competitors disappeared and hegemony passed to North America's financial and industrial centers. That economic imperialism rests today on the oligarchies who govern the Latin American countries.

The latifundio did not prevail in Puerto Rico during the Spanish colonial epoch. Nor do we inherit a military tradition. Thus the nondevelopment of an oligarchy in our country is not surprising.

The independence revolution in Latin America did not destroy the base of the latifundio and, on the contrary, created a military caste. Landlords sit with national military hierarchs as the governing class on a great campesino mass. In comparison the middle classes are small or nonexistent. Hence the precariousness or complete failure of the representative system of government in Latin America.

Puerto Rico presents a different picture. In addition to the contrasts already mentioned there is the easy access to U.S. cities. This has enabled young workers to leave in a mass emigration that has acted as a safety valve for social pressures.

The process in whose culminating stage we now live began with the 1898 invasion. Almost overnight Puerto Rico jumped from semifeudal conditions to the relationships prevailing in the world's most advanced capitalist system. The landing of troops was followed by the invasion of capital. Its first areas of concentration were sugar and tobacco. This led to an agricultural capitalism revolving around four great North American corporations, which became the directional basis of the country's economy. Politics was subordinated to these imperatives.

But agricultural development under capitalism is necessarily limited. Hence the concentration on the sugar industry. Its growth finally stopped in the thirties with the world economic crisis. The great-estate, absentee-landlord sugar economy began to collapse. The present closing down of sugar estates merely marks the end of that cycle. But it had already reached its peak before the decade of the forties. Then began the period of reforms with which we are all familiar.

The results of World War II and the emergence of the United States as chief center of world capitalism (with the fall of Germany and decadence of Britain, France, etc.) were decisive factors. The outcome for Puerto Rico was a new period of capital invasion (which is all that the triumphs of the Economic Development Administration amounted to), this time in all-out form, not limited to one or two industries but aiming at total possession of the country. Thus Puerto Rico ceased to be on the threshold or sidelines of the capitalist system and became its complete captive.

The panegyrists of imperialism would have us believe that what has happened in our country is a progressive transformation. They tell us that our economy has evolved from a backward one based on agriculture into an advanced one based on industry. They suggest that the Puerto Rican people have been transformed from a society of a handful of big landlords sitting on a mass of campesinos and agricultural day-laborers into a society of professional entrepreneurs, technicians, and skilled workers. It is further suggested that this road will quickly lead us to the complete abolition of poverty.

The picture is very far from reality. One fact should suffice: in the period of this alleged transformation Puerto Rico has lost a third of its population—the million Puerto Ricans now in the United States. Another may be added: three quarters of a million inhabitants depend on public relief for their subsistence. Finally, a permanent unemployment of 12 to 14 percent of the labor force is officially recognized, and in fact 30 percent of the potential working population is idle.

The key to the transformation that has taken place here cannot be found in the number of industrial enterprises. Nor in the fact that we have today a greater number of professionals, technicians, and workers. One must begin by asking: what are those professionals, technicians, and workers doing? Obviously they are working, but where? In industrial enterprises. Yes, but who owns those industrial enterprises? The key to the changes in Puerto Rico is in the reply to that question.

The fact is that no real transformation from agricultural to

industrial economy has occurred in our country. What we have
had is at best an injected economy, an economic enclave similar to
but not the same as the extraterritorial concessions exploited by
the old imperialist powers in Asia, especially China. Properly said,
the Puerto Rican economy with its traditional agricultural base
has fallen apart without being replaced by a Puerto Rican industrial economy. There was no development from that agricultural
base into a modern industrial economy. All that has been
achieved is to provide a base for a prolongation of the U.S.
economy, injected into our country's flank: tourist hotels,
branches of North American concerns, chain stores, etc. And to
cope with the general dislocation of our population, a permanent
character has been given to measures of emergency economic
aid. . . . This has clearly produced in the country's economy a
broad parasite sector, in which bureaucratic officials pullulate
along with thousands of wretches whose personal pride they
break in exchange for a crust of bread.

The result is beyond no one's comprehension: the injected
economy, the economic enclave established by big U.S. corporations and their Puerto Rican affiliates, constitutes the center
where the most important economic decisions are made; hence it
is there that the weight bears down on our destiny. This is not to
deny, however, that there has been relative industrial development in Puerto Rico.

Certainly agriculture has yielded supremacy to industry, and
this is now the major generator of income. As a consequence the
local market has been extended, resulting in rapid development
of construction, transportation, and trade. Government activities
have expanded by some 100,000-odd employees. At the same
time almost unlimited credit facilities have multiplied the so-
called middle classes. . . . All of which has provided a broader
base for U.S. domination of Puerto Rico.

With some individual exceptions, the national bourgeoisie has
identified with North American interests. Companies with mixed
capital (native and North American), representatives and agents
of North American concerns, plus the professionals and technicians closely linked to them, are the aggregate of interests form-
ing the foundation of the existing colonial system. Around them

is erected the imperialist superstructure served by all the communication media (press, radio, television, school, church, etc.) which provides colonialism in Puerto Rico with a continuous sheen of equity and justice.

II

Imperialism is the highest phase reached by capitalism. Its fundamental characteristics are: concentration of the reproduction of capital in terms of monopoly, fusion of bank and industrial capital, export of capital, formation of international monopolists' associations, and world domination. Puerto Rico has become important as an economic, political, and military base for the imperialism that now rules the earth: Yanqui imperialism, which has that threefold interest in our country. Our present concern is to examine the first, its economic domination, so that we may learn how to fight it successfully on that ground.

According to Planning Commission data, direct U.S. investment as of June 1965 in enterprises operating here amounted to $1,328,000,000. Those investments grow every day. In the petrochemical industry alone, a further billion-dollar investment is planned over the next ten years.

An Economic Development Administration brochure published for circulation in the United States (*Puerto Rico '63: A Report to Industry on Productivity and Profit Potential*) admits that "manufacturers obtain an average 30 percent on their investments" in Puerto Rico. Another similarly aimed brochure (*Advantages of Plant Location in Puerto Rico*) states that labor-movement activity "is concentrated in agriculture, communications, and public services and not strictly in manufacturing industries." Evidently one of the factors favoring corporate profits.

Maintenance of wage differentials between the United States and Puerto Rico (less than half in many cases and generally one third) is the cornerstone of industrial development under imperialism. It is the primary condition without which no colonial industrialization would be possible. It presupposes the absence of collective bargaining and the nonexistence of a labor movement or any workers' organization.

Added to this are tax exemption, technical aid, etc., but without the former these would have no value. The heart of the contradiction therefore springs to the eye: it is in the interest of imperialism to keep wages low and prevent workers from organizing and fighting for economic demands. At the same time it is in the Puerto Rican people's interest in their present and future fight for independence to spur organization and the workers' struggle for higher wages and better work conditions. Even the smallest and most limited economic struggles carry the seed of the great and broad struggle against imperialist enterprises.

According to the 1966 Industrial Census, Puerto Rico has 2,417 industrial establishments employing a total of 119,335 persons. The sector providing the most jobs is the garment industry, with 33,447 workers, mostly women. The next highest in employment is food production with 19,886. The leather and leather-products industry comes third with 9,464 workers, and cigar manufacture fourth with 7,877. And so on in descending numbers with other industries.

Concentration of workers in a single enterprise is not large. Only 9 percent of industrial establishments have more than 150 workers, and the average one employs between twenty and 149. Sixty percent of enterprises have twenty employees or less.

The proportion of women in the industrial proletariat is high: 57,651, almost as many as the 61,684 men. That has more or less been the proportion since 1958—four or five thousand more male than female employees.

The average hourly wage of production workers in the manufacturing industries (October 1966) is $1.31. On the basis of the Consumer Price Index (1957–59 equals 100) this is a real wage of $1.06 an hour.

The contrast between nominal and real wages is even more striking when weekly income is considered. The average weekly wage of $49.01 falls to $39.72 in terms of buying power. . . . That is the average real weekly wage of workers in manufacturing enterprises.

There is a big difference in pay between workers in oil refineries and other industrial workers. The average refinery worker gets $2.76 per hour, highest in all manufacturing enterprises. As can be seen, this is more than double the average of $1.31 for industry in general.

Second highest in wage levels is the chemical-products industry. Its workers get $2.32 per hour. After that come cement-factory workers with an average of $2.21 per hour.

Those are the three best-paid sectors in all industry. They are a small minority among the 119,335 industrial workers. All three combined have only 2,585 workers.

In contrast to this is the garment industry which, with 33,447 workers, provides the most employment. There the average wage is $1.17 per hour, that is, 14 cents less per hour than the average for industry in general.

The difference is even greater in the shoe industry which pays its 4,788 workers, mostly women, an average of $1.11 per hour— 20 cents less than the average for industry in general.

Much greater yet is the difference in the handbag and leather-goods industry, which employs 2,963 women and 582 men at an average wage of $1.01 per hour—30 cents less than the general industrial average.

Another industry employing relatively numerous personnel at wages lower than the general industrial average is tobacco. Apart from the stripping process, the modern cigar-manufacturing industry with 2,945 workers pays an average of $1.24 an hour—7 cents less than the general industrial average.

All these industrial sectors paying below the average share one characteristic: the absence of collective bargaining. Only garment-industry workers have partial organization embracing about half of all in the industry. That is the International Ladies Garment Workers, a union notorious for its leanings toward employers, which as a rule makes its contracts in New York with no participation by men and women workers in Puerto Rican factories.

While agriculture and traditional agriculture-based industries fall off as sources of jobs, absentee-capital industry continues expanding. Oil refineries and the chemical industry plan to grow on an increasing scale in the next six years. In 1967, seven new oil-derivative chemical plants went into operation. Four more are to be built during 1968 and others are in various planning stages. Altogether the new petrochemical enterprises, plus older ones that have been expanded, plan to generate 53,861 additional jobs by 1973.

Clearly imperialism is broadening its base in Puerto Rico. Its growing investments produce an increasing number of factories. And with more production, more sales, and more profits. That is the aim of imperialist investors: to multiply their capital. . . . By the nature of things this is achieved faster in colonies through the abundance of cheap labor.

Up to now the independence movement has fought imperialism in general terms. But imperialism has to be fought in concrete terms: the attack must be launched where it is most felt, at the heart of profit.

The chief profits of imperialism (there are other sources such as bonds, mortgage loans, etc.) come from industrial enterprises. And there is the Achilles heel, for such profit originates from factories which must employ workers to generate it.

Workers individually are victims of the impersonal will of imperialist enterprises. The enterprises dictate wages to be paid and conditions of work. One factor alone can alter this relationship of forces wholly favorable to imperialism, and that is collective action by the workers. The breadth and depth of that action is what tips the balance. Thus the only defense for wage-workers, the hope of a better future, is labor organization. Only through that can higher wages and better conditions be won.

The particular demands of the working class are in harmony with our people's general struggle for independence. Two parallels that meet on the horizon of history. . . . The better this is understood, and the more intensively they act together, the more the independence struggle will be broadened.

III

The history of the Puerto Rican labor movement has yet to be written. Present generations know nothing about the initial struggles toward the end of the nineteenth century: the first ideological discussions, the labor press (*Ensayo Obrero*, the daily *Unión*

Obrera, the weekly *Justicia,* the organs of various tendencies that appeared over the years in San Juan, Byamón, Ponce, Caguas, Mayagüez and other communities); the formation of the Free Federation of Labor (FLT), the tobacco workers' revolutionary role, the fighting strikes in the cane fields, the martyrs gunned down by police; the evolution of the economic into the political struggle, founding of the Socialist Party, repercussions in Puerto Rico of the 1917 Russian Revolution. The history of the working class's struggles is an arsenal of experience which present generations should know for their own ideological enrichment.

The labor movement is not only Santiago Iglesias, Prudencio Rivera Martínez, Eduardo Conde, Epifanio Piz Jiménez, Bolívar Pagán, and the whole constellation of leaders who left their mark on history.* Those men must be judged by what they did. But the development of the working class should be more important for us than the role of individuals. We need to consider the whys and hows of past events and of the outcome.

To help toward quicker understanding, we may divide the early history of the labor movement into three periods:

1. From the turn of the century to the foundation of the Socialist Party.

2. From the rise of the tobacco workers as leaders to the decay of the cigar industry.

3. From the establishment of the Republican-Socialist Coalition to the liquidation of the Socialist Party.

During the first period (1900–1915) the labor movement built its organizational foundations. At the turn of the century the first ideological currents arrived in San Juan from Spain and Havana. As is known, after the split in the First International, the French, Spanish, and Italian sectors—especially the last two—were dominated by Bakuninism. In consequence of the emigration, anarchism provided the original nourishment for Latin America's burgeoning proletariat. The founders of the labor movement in Buenos Aires, Havana, etc., were anarchists. This explains why

---

* These were Socialist leaders in the early twenties. Cf. Igualdad Iglesias de Pagán, *El obrerismo en Puerto Rico* (San Juan: Ediciones Ponce de León, 1973).

the first ideological influences on the nascent Puerto Rican labor movement were anarchosyndicalists.

Here we find the roots of many of the labor movement's later errors. Most serious of these, with the gravest consequences, was the persistent ignoring of the colonial and national problem.

The anarchist concept of a frontierless world, of the non-existence of country in proletarian terms, led to identification with the American Federation of Labor. The traditional anarchistic repudiation of politics and the exaggerated notion of the unions' role as instruments of revolutionary transformation were in paradoxical agreement with the AFL's strictly economistic position and political neutrality. This contiguity of positions apparently so far apart made it possible for Santiago Iglesias, after his expulsion from Havana as an anarchist, to welcome the 1898 invasion and make common cause with the U.S. troops; and, a few years later, as a leader of the FLT, to be appointed AFL organizer in Puerto Rico where the new union organization obtained recognition on an equal level with state federations. This naturally propelled the labor movement down the road already charted by the AFL.

However, the differences of scene, language, culture, etc., and the economic contradictions made notable divergencies. The Puerto Rican labor movement did not develop in at all the same way as the U.S. labor movement. In practice, under our country's particular conditions, it opened up its own channel.

During the first period and the beginning of the second (1916–1932) the tobacco workers, especially in cigar factories, gave the movement its firmest base and outstanding leaders, who took the organization to cane-field workers and sugar factories.

In the course of the twenties the tobacco industry declined, fundamentally for two reasons: the popularity of the North American cigarette and the mechanization of cigar-making. Up to then the labor movement had been on the rise. Its main weekly, *Justicia,* was considering plans to become a daily. The rising Socialist Party vote, and Santiago Iglesias's election to the legislature along with other labor leaders, marked its apogee. From that point the labor movement began to decay.

Its third period (1933–1940) illustrates the total bankruptcy of reformism, opportunism, and colonialism in working-class ranks. Once it had made the coalition pact with the Republican Party, the Socialist Party leadership, which also shared leadership of the FLT, took the road of compromise. There is nothing wrong with a coalition as such. Political alliances between a workers' party and other political parties are not to be ruled out in principle. It is the content of the alliances, their immediate proposals and long-term goals, that make alliances or coalitions acceptable or inadmissable. They have to be judged as such in the context of the historical moment. In the specific case of the Republican-Socialist Coalition, formally established in 1932 but actually put into practice some years earlier, there was nothing to justify it from the standpoint of working-class interests.

The coalition had immediate and fatal consequences for the labor movement. The following may be mentioned:

1. It fixed the labor leadership's attention on electoral contests and on government posts and positions.

2. It deferred the trade-union struggle and development of the FLT, and replaced the formation of leaders through trade unions with the promotion of political agitators through Socialist Party organs.

3. It subordinated the leadership of the labor movement and of the working class in general to the purely colonialist political expediencies of the Republican Party.

These conditions hastened the movement's degeneration both in its political organs and in the unions, and initiated a new stage in labor-movement history which may be divided into two periods:

1. From the decay of the FLT to the founding and development of the General Workers' Confederation (CGT).

2. The split in the CGT, invasion by North American international unions.

IV

The CGT's antecedents are to be found in the formation of communist groups in the early thirties. Not all of the Socialist Party went along patiently with the Republican alliance. The coalition was repudiated by leaders in various areas, especially in

Cabo Rojo where Manuel Cofresí, Julito Camacho, and Martiniano Ayala of the Socialist Section, and others such as Jorge Carbonel and his brother Pablo, later set up a Communist Section. In Ponce the important Socialist leader Dr. José A. Lanauze Rolón condemned the top leadership's action and concluded a historic newspaper polemic by proclaiming himself a communist. The same course was followed by Licenciado Miguel A. Bahamonde who launched a newspaper called *La Gaceta Comunista*. At almost the same time in San Juan, Eugenio Font Suárez, a lawyer of Unionist Party formation and disciple of José de Diego, also declared himself a communist in a press polemic. Around these personalities—to whom another lawyer, Luis Vergne Ortiz, should be added—some worker groups began to gather, and these finally chose delegates to an assembly which met in Ponce on September 23, 1934. There it was decided to form a Communist Party of Puerto Rico and to affiliate with the Communist International. Alberto E. Sánchez was elected general secretary.

This party's development as such is not our concern here. What concerns us is its contribution to the evolution of a new stage in the labor movement.

The first tests of trade-union action took place in the sugar industry. Discontent was growing among the workers. The Socialist leadership of the FLT had succeeded in signing agreements with the Sugar Producers Association, at that time the most influential employer group. On the eve of the 1934 sugar harvest the cane-field workers repudiated these agreements made behind their backs, and a strike movement spontaneously arose and extended from Yabucoa to Guánica. Such was the workers' indignation that they disowned their traditional leaders and called upon the president of the Nationalist Party, Pedro Albizu Campos.

That sugar strike marks the beginning of the decay of the labor movement's old Socialist leadership. But neither Nationalists nor Communists yet had what it took to supplant them.

The Nationalists, for their part, had no notion of giving leadership to the workers as a class. The thinking of Albizu and his circle had no room for temporary measures. For them the national problem overrode all other considerations, and only in complete subordination to that did they note the existence of other problems. Since it was inconceivable to them that there could be any solutions within the colonial framework, they saw anything else as a trap which could only hold up the independence struggle. Hence their inability to lead the workers, whose situation obliged them to seek concrete and immediate outlets.

The Communists had no such ideas but, lacking roots in the working class, they could bring little force to bear against the mass influence of the Socialist leadership. They started out with a completely sectarian trade-union policy. Overestimating the workers' revulsion, they did not confine themselves to opposing the opportunist leadership of Santiago Iglesias but wanted the workers to reject the FLT and remuster in new organizations. Having no ties with organized labor, they concentrated all their effort on organizing parallel unions to those of the FLT. This policy inevitably caused splits and, far from contributing to the development of union consciousness, helped disarm the working class and retard its organization. The feeble forces they managed to organize were powerless to win the minimal immediate victories that were necessary to raise the workers' morale.

Keeping the working class in a state of civil war leads nowhere. On the contrary, it retards and weakens the struggle. To overcome the opportunism rooted in the labor movement, opportunist leaders must of course be unmasked. The essential thing is to destroy them as leaders, but this can only be done when the workers turn their backs on them. Until that is achieved, attacks on the persons of such leaders are worthless; indeed they may sometimes be counterproductive. In trade-union politics properly understood, attacks on leaders are quite secondary. What is fundamental is to fight side by side with the workers, and the rest will be added unto you.

The Communists began to move in that direction at the end of the thirties. Four actions resulted which decisively influenced the new awakening of the labor movement. These were:

1. The militant strike of some 800 workers in the Sunoco (now Villa Palmeras) button factory in 1937.

2. The founding of the Chauffeurs' Association with its First Congress in San Juan in 1937.

3. The organization of sugar workers in the Toa Baja–Dorado–Bayamón district under new militant leadership in 1937.

4. The winning of leadership in the UTM (National Maritime Union)-FLT longshoremen's union, the formation of an alliance with CIO-UTM seamen, and the victory of the forty-two-day general longshore strike in 1938.

Paralleling these events was the birth in the United States of the CIO with its strikes culminating in the organization of big industries. Those were years of militant labor struggles in France, Spain, etc. In France the workers fought great battles using the sitdown method. In Spain the triumph of the Popular Front opened promising avenues to development of the working-class struggle. The latifundists and reactionary autocracy unleashed civil war against the people. Those were years of struggle against Nazism, fascism, and imperialist war.

During this period the Communists fought inside and outside the FLT. Inside, wherever the workers still identified with the old Socialist leadership. And wherever workers remained unorganized, or had been organized but felt deceived by the old leaders, independent unions came into being. In one form or the other, what mattered was to organize the workers for the struggle. If there were those among the old leaders who would go along, they were welcome. If they tried to obstruct or paralyze the struggle, they were unmasked. . . . This was the policy being applied at the dawn of the forties.

On January 29, 1940, the Fifth Congress of the Chauffeurs' Association convened in Coamo under the leadership of lawyers Francisco Colón Gordiany and Alberto E. Sánchez. It approved a document entitled "A Call to the Workers of Puerto Rico," an analysis of the working-class situation bringing out these points among others:

> For almost half a century the wage-workers of Puerto Rico have fought in the FLT for their socioeconomic betterment, higher living standards, and the observance of laws protecting their class. . . . The victories won are advanced trenches from which to carry forward the battle for total emancipation of the working class.
>
> In this critical moment full of social antagonisms and abrupt transitions, the Puerto Rican proletariat must take stock of its

struggles and make an impartial analysis of its history in order to chart new roads. . . .

The Free Federation of Labor created the Socialist Party as the Puerto Rican proletariat's instrument of political struggle. The FLT thoughtlessly detached from the trade unions many of their veteran labor propagandists to put them in the state apparatus. . . . The old guard of the Federation went into the business of leading the workers from government desks. . . .

The FLT policy of class relationships has established a political base of relations with the ruling class. . . . We believe that the Free Federation has completed its historic mission . . . today it is a corpse which is remembered for what it did when it was alive, but which the proletariat can no longer respect. . . . The working class needs a live, young, vigorous, strong instrument which, built on healthy principles of organization and class struggle, will show the workers the healthy and wise course to pursue.

Rather than comment on the document, we have preferred to cite it fairly extensively for the historical significance we attribute to it. Unquestionably it represents a starting point, and subsequent events show it to be such.

The historic call ends with a plea for "creation of a central union organization guided by the FLT's best tradition of struggle, to embrace all workers without distinction of race or political or religious belief." And on March 31, 1940, the General Workers' Confederation was founded at a Constituent Congress in San Juan attended by 112 delegates of forty-two unions. Among its leaders were Francisco Colón Gordiany, Alberto E. Sánchez, Ramón Barreto Pérez, Juan Sáez Corales, Sergio Kuilan Báez, and the present writer.

To give an idea what the CGT was and meant in labor-movement history, here is what General Secretary Juan Sáez Corales said about its origins and first struggles in his report to its Third Congress, on March 22-24, 1945, at the University of Puerto Rico theater in Rio Piedras:

When this chapter of labor-movement history began to be written, the working class felt abandoned. . . . The labor leaders who were in public power purported to lead the whole island's workers from the cabinet of Governor Winship, the offices of the Department of Labor, and the desks of the legislature. The old labor leadership had succumbed to the sinecures of a government dominated by the interests of the bosses. . . .

The general secretary went on to say that in the five years since its founding the CGT had established new practices in the movement. As a result of its efforts, 378 unions were now integrated into the CGT. During the two years before its Third Congress the CGT had led sixty-seven strikes, including "the last general strike of the sugar industry." That strike ended with the signing of a general agreement between the CGT and the Sugar Producers Association, covering both industrial and field activities of all production centers. At the time of the Third Congress the CGT had a total of eighty-three collective labor contracts in operation.

V

The CGT linked itself to the Latin American labor movement as an affiliate of the Latin American Confederation of Labor (CTAL). At the same time it established close ties of solidarity with U.S. workers through the CIO. Francisco Colón Gordiany and Ramón Barreta Pérez represented the CGT as fraternal delegates to the CIO congress. On these international relationships the abovementioned report said:

> As part of its activities to strengthen international relations, the CGT was also represented at the Cuban Labor Confederation's (CTC) Fourth Congress in Havana in mid-December of 1944. . . . In July of last year our organization was visited by the Chilean Labor Confederation's general secretary Salvador Ocampo, as a delegate from his confederation and from the CTAL. . . .

As can be seen, the CGT began breathing a new spirit of proletarian internationalism into Puerto Rican workers. This is shown by the effect in Puerto Rico of the resolution adopted by the CTAL at its congress in Cali, Colombia, calling for a continental work stoppage against the military coups in Latin America. And at that hour of that day, said the general secretary in his report, "all labor activity in the country was paralyzed." He added:

"That stoppage is highly significant because it was the first coordinated protest by the workers of America, and the first stoppage by Puerto Rican workers in solidarity with the labor movements of other countries."

In his Third Congress report the general secretary tackled the problem of working-class unity in these words:

> The majority of workers are now united under the CGT banner, but that is not enough. It is necessary, it is indispensable, that all Puerto Rican workers should constitute a single labor organization. . . . The CGT was organized to unite the workers and has demonstrated this objective in practice. But our ranks still lack a clear orientation on the significance of working-class unity . . . there are some who seek to use the correct slogan of working-class unity for the destruction of the CGT.

Understanding the problem of unity involves knowing how to adjust the role and actions of unions with politics. To clarify this the general secretary quoted the following from the call that gave birth to the CGT:

> The character of the unions as an organization without party banner needs clarifying. The unions are organizations of all workers without distinction of political creed. They participate in all struggles favoring the working class and the people. They fight against all political measures that harm their interests, but they do not carry the banner of any political party, nor do they take sides in any political-party conflict that could break or weaken their unity. The strength of the unions is in their members and they should think as members of an exploited class, as workers, as an integral whole.

Then he made these comments:

> We quote this correct orientation . . . because it is now more than ever necessary to avoid disorientations and false directions in the labor movement. We have always tried in our struggle to concentrate on the basic principle that labor organizations are and should be essentially political. That position has been one factor contributing to the CGT's fast and sturdy growth. That is why the CGT maintains that no problem in Puerto Rico is outside its concern. . . . We workers are concerned about all of Puerto Rico's problems and about the problems of the world. That is why we practice an

essentially political form of cooperation, and why we don't want to be and must not be the tail of any political party. . . .

The big problem that was threatening to destroy the CGT shines through those words. In fact, the problem of the unions' class role and of political-party influence in the union movement dominated the deliberations of the Third Congress, which ended with the organization splitting into two groups. Foreseeing the tragedy that the split would mean for the working class, the general secretary said in his report:

> Two mistaken tendencies have always prevailed in the organized labor movement of Puerto Rico. The first seeks to make our movement a dependency of particular political parties. The second tendency raises a hullabaloo about labor organizations having nothing to do with politics. Both are wrong. The first because the union movement cannot be any kind of tail or passive instrument of any political party if it is to fulfill its mission of organizing workers. The second because, while it is true that the movement should not be any political party's tail, it is no less true that the workers and our organizations must be essentially political: they must be alert and prepared to defend any political measure beneficial to the workers, and to forestall any measure harmful to the workers. Consequently the labor movement must be on guard against politicking and politickers who try to speculate with the power of the workers for ends that are not the workers' ends.
>
> We must repeat again and again: the CGT is not a political-party organization. It is an organization of workers of all parties, with room for all workers regardless of their political views. . . . The organized labor movement is not Popular Democratic, nor Socialist, nor Republican, nor Nationalist, nor of any other party. It is the organization of all workers belonging to all parties, to defend themselves against exploitation.

Another problem in need of clarification, which the general secretary broached on that occasion without evasions, was that of Puerto Rico's political "status." In view of its importance, his words deserve quotation:

> Since we are discussing the political role of labor organizations, we cannot but mention the most serious of the political problems faced by the Puerto Rican people. I refer to our political "status," a

problem the working class cannot and should not avoid, which workers and their organizations should discuss without beating about any bushes. Up to now the Puerto Rican labor movement has taken an attitude of indifference. . . . Labor organizations have done nothing more than some occasional faint stammering in resolutions demanding that our political "status" be resolved. But they have yet to take the position that the fight against colonialism and for national liberation is the labor movement's fundamental duty.

He went on to cite a series of pronouncements by union organizations in various countries, demanding independence for Puerto Rico. He added:

The labor movement has the responsibility to move deeply into the matter. . . . We Puerto Ricans can never expect to mold our own economic, political, and social life while we remain forcibly tied to the U.S. market. That is why the Puerto Rican working class cannot remain indifferent to a problem so vital for our people. We Puerto Ricans cannot talk of economic emancipation without preparing ourselves to win our political freedom. . . . So I propose that the program of the CGT include a clause establishing the struggle for Puerto Rico's independence as one of our basic objectives.

I have quoted CGT General Secretary Sáez Corales at length to help the present generation grasp the problem being debated by the movement at that time. It seems to me that the study of such problems at this historical distance contributes to better understanding the movement's present problems.

No need to extend myself in explaining the causes of the split in the CGT. They can be deduced from this report to the Third Congress, the congress that produced the split. The CGT emerged from it in two groups: one led by Popular Democratic Senator Ramón Barreto Pérez, which came to be known as the "government CGT." Recalling these events years later, in April 1955, Sáez Corales wrote:

The CGT became an organized force of the industrial and agricultural workers. . . . As its general secretary I presided over the Island Strike Committee of sugar workers during the general strike in 1942 of workers in that industry. In that year I was a member representing the workers of the Special Committee of the Mini-

mum Wage Commission, which studied the sugar industry and
recommended minimum wages and conditions for its workers. . . .
After the victory of the 1942 sugar strike I was offered the post of
Subcommissioner of Labor. I didn't accept it. I believed I could
serve the working class better as general secretary of the CGT. I saw
the offer of the subcommissioner job as a bribe. . . .

After the 1942 sugar strike the Popular Democratic Party (PPD)
government began fighting to head off an independent labor
movement. To achieve that, it aimed at control of the CGT, using
two methods: first, naming CGT leaders to public posts; and second, pushing local PPD leaders into top positions in local unions.
The scenario was that anyone wanting to be a mayor, representative, or senator started by brandishing the banner of labor. . . . At
the same time objections against political participation were raised
in the CGT. . . . Thus the CGT fell into an economistic position
pure and simple.

Passing to the subject of the split, he wrote:

In March 1945, to the misfortune of the Puerto Rican working
class, the CGT broke into two. The split was the fruit of the
government's policy of aborting a united labor movement that
would be nonparty and an effective voice of working-class interests. . . . Soon after the split in 1945, my deferment from compulsory military service was withdrawn. . . . I entered the Army. . . .
It was necessary to complete the breakup of the CGT with the
fewest possible obstacles.

Years later, at a congress in San Juan on September 28, 1947,
the General Workers' Union (UGT) was founded under the
leadership of Juan Sáez Corales, now out of the Army. In his
memoirs he analyzed this event and concluded:

I think organizing the UGT was wrong, since it resulted in a
further split in the movement. When it was set up, the U.S. Congress had already passed the disgraceful Taft-Hartley. That law
applied to Puerto Rico. All labor organizations in the country
yielded meekly to it except the UGT, which took a stand against the
application of that enslaving law to Puerto Rico. For three years it
conducted a militant struggle. . . . The struggle culminated in
strikes. . . . The state used all its repressive force to break them.
Strikers were jailed and the labor leadership hounded. . . . After
those strikes the bosses and the National Labor Relations Board got
together to crush the UGT. They went on until they succeeded in

making the UGT bow to the Taft-Hartley law. They compelled some unions to break away from the UGT. They used the anticommunist argument to confuse the workers. . . .

So the UGT ended by fulfilling the requirements of the law. Thus ended the state that the CGT had opened in the history of the labor movement.

VI

The Puerto Rican working class has struggled under a heavy political weight since the mid-forties. As we know, the original conception was that the country would be industrialized under its own steam. The government's direct initiative, including investment of capital, was point one of the program. But conservative forces and imperialist pressure forced a change of tack. The new concept was industrialization on the basis not of Puerto Rican capital but of investments of foreign capital. Practical application of that policy involved limiting, checking, and even destroying the labor movement—the indispensable condition to ensure the flow of investment capital. This explains the policy of controlling the unions, or splitting them where it was hard to dominate them—a method applied through government agencies and the majority party itself.

We all know what the outcome was. After the curtain fell on that stage of the movement with the sowing of division and the disappearance of a national body of leaders, North American international unions began moving in directly and no longer through the AFL. . . . Thus began a new period in labor-movement history.

At the present time the movement consists of some 150,000 organized workers. A considerable number of unions are in decaying sectors of the economy. The sugar industry, for example. At the same time a substantial number of key factories, including some that employ from 400 to 1,000 workers, operate with no collective contract. The same applies to the big chain stores employing thousands of workers. Clearly, the union movement marches in the rearguard of the present transformations in Puerto Rico's economic structure.

In the United States, in 1940, 8,642,000 workers were organized in AFL-CIO and independent unions. This was 25 percent of the labor force at the time, including agricultural workers. If the latter are not included, the organized sector of industrial workers amounted to 27 percent.

By 1948 the United States had 16,000,000 organized workers. This means that some 30 percent of the labor force belonged to the labor movement. In succeeding years until now there has been no appreciable growth in union membership.

U.S. organized workers, even when they are only 30 percent of the country's labor force, represent a power—economic, political, and social—much greater than Puerto Rico's organized workers. Only 18 percent of our country's labor force is organized.

Leaving aside the socialist countries for obvious reasons, the countries where union organizations have the most influence are England, France, Italy, Germany, Belgium, and the Scandinavian nations. In colonial and semicolonial countries, and generally in countries described as underdeveloped, the number of workers in unions is proportionately much smaller than in economically advanced countries.

That is the rule but there are exceptions. One of them was Cuba in the forties. With a labor force of 900,000, the country's sole union federation, CTC, had 557,000 members in 1949. That is, 60 of every 100 Cuban workers belonged to some union—demonstrating a class consciousness that unquestionably contributed to the Cuban Revolution's strong proletarian base.

The total of organized workers in Puerto Rico is no greater, but on the contrary much smaller, than twenty years ago.

How to explain that, with all the (supposedly) advanced labor legislation, and with trade-union rights guaranteed, the labor movement is numerically weaker now than in the past, has less hold in the chief production centers and less influence in society generally?

The reasons are various. Among others, the Taft-Hartley law on worker-employer relations, which the Puerto Rican people had no part in writing and approving nor have any part in applying. A collective bargaining process which even uses a language foreign to the workers, administered from Washington, with officials named by and responsible to Washington and feeling no responsibility toward the Puerto Rican government, still less to the Puerto Rican people and workers: obviously this does not favor the labor movement but obstructs it. Doubly true in the case of indigenous unions, but in lesser degree also true of North American unions.

Puerto Rican union organizations have made little progress in the last fifteen years. North American unions operating here have made little more, although they enjoy large economic resources, specialized legal aid, trained personnel, etc. The key to their failure is not hard to find. Colonial unionism simply doesn't pay.

Some thirty international unions (so-called because they have members in Canada) have done organizing work in Puerto Rico during the past decade, some for much longer. Apart from their paid officials—full-time organizers—they have a regional director named by the top AFL-CIO leadership. There is also the Labor Federation of Puerto Rico, supposedly functioning in the same way as state federations in the United States. San Juan also has a "Central Labor Council," consisting of delegates of North American international unions' locals.

In addition to these there are union federations such as the old Free Federation of Labor, the Island Workers' Union, the Union of Industrial Workers, etc. They function or purport to function as centralizing federations, but this does not mean that all independent unions are affiliated to one of them. In fact the most important unions unconnected with North American internationals have their own life and function independently. Among these are the Electrical Industry Workers, the Heavy Equipment Workers, etc. To complicate the picture further, the North American internationals do not confine themselves to acting within their respective jurisdictions. Each one of them— Teamsters, Boilermakers, Hotel & Restaurant Workers, etc.— competes in organizing workers of any and all industries.

Undermining established unions and raiding locals of one or another federation are common practice. This is aggravated by such other negative factors as the deluge of employer propaganda, the antilabor activities of certain lawyers' offices at the service of big concerns, the high percentage of unemployment, and the continuous threat of "removing the plant," the Yanqui corporations' standard form of blackmail. But among all these factors one stands out: the lack of a recognized labor leadership that would command the respect, if not admiration, of all classes—that could speak responsibly in the name of the working class. This Puerto Rico had in the past with Santiago Iglesias and the sizable group of Socialist leaders, and again in the first CGT period at the end of the thirties and beginning of the forties. Which brings me to my conclusion: until that new collective leadership emerges and takes on growing stature, the labor movement cannot hope to develop in step with today's and tomorrow's changes in Puerto Rico.

A revised version of a report read by the author at the National Leadership Seminar of the Pro-Independence Movement, Cidra, January 12-13, 1968; later published in the magazine *La Escalera* (January-February 1968).

Eduardo Seda Bonilla (1925–)

Anthropologist, sociologist, essayist. University studies in Puerto Rico and the United States; was professor at University of Puerto Rico, New York University, and Hunter College. Has contributed to specialized journals and participated in international anthropological and sociological congresses. His studies have often led him to Spanish America; for some years he lived in Mexico and Argentina.

Selected Bibliography

Seda Bonilla, Eduardo. *Lor derechos civiles en la cultura puertorriqueña*. San Juan: UPR, 1963.
————. *Interacción social y personalidad en una comunidad de Puerto Rico*. San Juan: Ponce de León, 1964.
————. *Requiem por una cultura*. Río Piedras: Editorial Edil, 1970.

The Crab Syndrome: Alienation and Pseudo-Conflict

One of the traveler's first impressions on arriving in Puerto Rico is the disorganization of the institutional life of society in every sphere. This disorganization gives the impression of what a friend calls "the crab syndrome"—that is, an exaggerated dispersion of behavior patterns which in other societies tend to stay within an ordered and coherent structure. To start with, the baggage doesn't turn up at the airport, the telephone to call the hotel doesn't work, the hotel can find no trace of the reservations, and we have to call a friend to straighten everything out. The highways from the airport are congested with traffic badly directed by inept police, and it would be no great surprise if the car broke down on the street and no mechanic could be found to fix it till Monday, this being Friday. During the time the car has to remain stationary on the street, one runs the risk that it will be pilfered piece by piece down to the last screw in the motor. The number of stolen cars is such that another friend has lost two in less than six months.

We might write off this first impression of disorganization as coincidental misfortune, but any such optimism will begin to weaken when we confront the chronic entropy characterizing other spheres of social life.

The traffic on the avenues is reminiscent of speed contests on the tracks of Indianapolis. As the *New York Times* remarked concerning Argentina, "Every motorist imagines himself to be a new Fangio, and many don't retire with as much luck." Cars and more cars moving so haphazardly that they look like crabs; shiny trucks resplendent with lights and such inscriptions as "My love!," "I am a bird without a nest," "Forget me not," "Captain Centellas," "Red Devils," "Sock it to me" pass in front and on all sides of us in a giddy whirlwind. Up ahead, two drivers have stopped in the middle of the freeway: they haven't seen each other for years and are deep in intimate conversation to the infernal accompaniment of a thousand horns demanding the right of free passage. Further on a driver has obstructed half the road for the purpose of changing a tire. Another pandemonium, with bellowed allusions to the intruder's innocent mother specifying certain parts of her anatomy.

Finally we get there. Our friend has two children, and but for their angelic little faces we would think we had arrived in purgatory. They are addressed as basilisks, demons, Barabbases, excrescences, Lucifers, and similar endearments, and they behave as if they were such. Now they have set up a howl because what our friend brought for Pepe isn't as good as what he brought for Yoyo; as Yoyo plays with his toy, Pepe tries to force an exchange, and since Yoyo rejects the deal, Pepe proceeds to beat him up.

The children's mother will under no circumstanes listen to the reasons for the outbreak of violence and punishes both equally, securing herself with the adage that "all children are alike." I would have liked to remind her of Gunnar Myrdal's riposte to the North American bromide that all men are alike: "But some are more alike than others." The importance of a year or two's age difference, in childhood and in adult life, cannot be compared. I would have liked to remind her that the sense of justice, the perspective of balance and reciprocity in human relations, respect for oneself and for the rights of others, confidence and security in observance of rules of the game, the feeling of fraternity and social responsibility—perhaps even that patriotism which we so badly need—depend on the security of the family environment.

Exiled to a corner of the living room, the children now contain their emotions with difficulty and carry on the cold war, execrating one another in an undertone with offensive, provocative gestures and words. They are unable to find behavior patterns that satisfy each one's need to express himself, not at the other's expense, not in spite of the other, but in complementary harmony. They are children and they "don't know," "they are ignorant," as the parents say. All the more reason to take the trouble to educate them properly—or isn't education a corrective for ignorance? "Well, that's how it is," our friends tell us, "they have rocks in their heads," "nothing penetrates." To determine just what it is that doesn't "penetrate" and why, one would need time to observe the family "crab syndrome." One word would sum it up, "inconsistency." Proposals of reward or punishment that are spoken with no remote intention of carrying them out; negligence as an excuse for avoiding the "bother" of looking after the children as human beings; arbitrary authoritarianism that forcibly imposes obedience without regard for the principles of respect for human dignity and justice.

On the cultural level the inconsistency shows itself in *umju, buche y pluma no más,* the *pelea monga,* and *"jaibería"** (true, the *jaiba* is a kind of crab), in paternalism and political opportunism and sadomasochistic authoritarianism.

Every Man for Himself

Wherever persons enter into disorganized contact, a state of high-tension nervous excitement culminates in outbursts of verbal and physical violence. Some exasperated people are waiting in front of a ticket booth and finally the most impatient ones break the line. Realizing that some have "sneaked ahead," the others stampede like so many crabs and the resulting hubbub is known as the "get the hell out" situation in which "every one for himself" is the watchword.

In the Country

We go out for a walk; now we are leaving the metropolitan area behind. We take a narrow, steep, curved road, the product of tortuous labyrinths in the minds of its constructors. The sky is deep blue, the air fresh and transparent, and the breeze carries

---

* This is a colloquial expression for the docile colonized.

the smell of wild flowers, the songs of birds and of tillers of the soil. Here man seems at peace with himself as he sweats and struggles to grub out sustenance for his family. But the man who labors in the country is becoming an anachronism. The ground he has so devoutly worked has never been his, and the youth of today has lost the love of the soil. The campesinos say there is no future in farm work and it is true. The octopus has turned around, the latifundist is no longer the absentee corporation man whom the newspaper *El Batey* once called "don Colmillú" and cartooned as a potbellied monster with gold watch chain and diamonds on his fingers. Today's "don Colmillú" wears a "Palm Beach suit" and a white collar; he is the speculator in land, the one who literally sells the motherland for cash to the highest bidder, whether he be Cuban, American, or from the planet Mars.

The Return Migrant

The young folk emigrate to the United States and the movie companies tell us they have no luck there, they don't make good in the big city because they don't learn to speak English. If one of these exiles returns he is often loath to take off his wool overcoat, regardless of the suffocating discomfort of heat and sweat. People remark that he "came back white" and "already chews up English." Soon he will start talking about "the bucks," "you know how it is," "men," "I got it from the boss." It's a great sensation to know he can "get by" in the English he has learned to masticate, and this is a sure qualification for a job in an American industrial plant, a hotel, or one of the service enterprises for tourists. "You know how it is" and "you gotta get in right with the boss" may secure him a job where only "whites" were previously employed. "There's no worse cradle than one of the same wood," his subordinates will end up saying.

The Labyrinth

"Christmas has come and the young people have taken jacket and tie from the trunk to go to the 'Ferryboat' terrace and put money in the jukebox and dance to its deafening music. Darling Miranda pressed a button on the jukebox to stop a record and the commotion heralding a melee ensued. Darling struggled with the people who were trying to interfere with her. You couldn't tell who she was mad at or whether it was really aggression she wanted to express. After a while, some bottles having been smashed and a few random blows exchanged, the 'brawl mania' cooled off."

In this community interpersonal relations are riddled with fear of the "labyrinth that blows up from under one's feet like a whirlwind without a hint of when or why."*

Alienation

The pseudocombative propensity of alienation has been very dramatically described in the most significant contemporary works of literature and science.

In Ortega's "mass" man as in "the alienated" of Robert K. Merton; in Erich Fromm's people who are "free from" but not "free to"; in Robert Lindner's "rebels without a cause," César Andreu Iglesias's "defeated and self-destroying," Octavio Paz's "pachucos," Camus' "strangers," Pirandello's "characters in search of an author," Paul Tillich's "fear of being" people, in the "men" and other such, we find the distorted caricature of what a creative and productive human being can become when he has gone astray for lack of generous and consistent institutional molds.†

---

* Eduardo Seda Bonilla, *Interacción social y personalidad en una comunidad de Puerto Rico* (San Juan: Ediciones Ponce de León, 1964).

† The author alludes to José Ortega y Gasset, *Revolt of the Masses;* Erich Fromm, *Escape from Freedom;* Robert Lindner, *Rebel without a Cause;* César Andreu Iglesias, *Los Derrotados;* Octavio Paz, *Labyrinth of Solitude;* Albert Camus, *The Stranger;* Luigi Pirandello, *Six Characters in Search of an Author;* Paul Tillich, *The Courage to Be.*

What these works tell us is that the rootlessness, frustration, and existential anguish that result from alienation produce reactions that are in the best of cases unpredictable, and of a violent nature in the worst.

The point I want to make here is that conflict is not a dissociative element on the level of human associative processes, except when those who sustain them are unaware what questions they involve.

According to Freudian theory it is a demonstrable fact that unconscious conflicts lead people to the most serious personality dissociation, but become manageable once they are transferred to the level of the conscious mind. There are many examples illustrating this, some of which stand out for their dramatic quality: cases of hysteria where the patient recovers his speech or sight, or recovers from total or partial paralysis, on becoming aware of jealous, hostile, or incestuous impulses which, being contrary to his moral sense, he could not admit to his conscious mind. In other words, dissociation is produced not by conflict as such, but by not recognizing what questions are in conflict.

One aspect of alienation in the Marxist sense results from lack of class consciousness: ignorance of members of a social class as to the natural conflict between its interests and those of other social classes. This position implies a theory of history and of historical consciousness. Presumably the classes dominating the media of communication and persuasion have small sympathy for people who try to discuss "controversial" questions in public.* "Public relations" is the order of the day and the sycophants are widely quoted. The sycophant's function as manipulator of public opinion is precisely that of keeping the multitudes ignorant of the atomizing and alienating controls of an arbitrary social system. Propaganda techniques enable the "public-relations man" to adorn with rhetorical tinsel the most iniquitous aspects of the social system, so that avarice becomes initiative, hatred and race and class prejudice become "good taste" and distinction, the

---

* Works like Gordon Lewis's *Puerto Rico: Freedom and Power in the Caribbean* are repeatedly turned down by publishers while inane or trite stuff like that published by Earl Parker Hanson under many titles is the object of painstaking attention from publishers of books and articles. (Author's note.)

rapacity of nations becomes protection of law and order, and imperialist actions in the name of anti-"kommunism" (as Juan José Arévalo wrote in *The Fable of the Shark and the Sardines*) become the "protection" of democracy.

In a recently published work Vance Packard describes with a wealth of detail how Madison Avenue "image-builders" manipulate North American consumers to ease the problem of capitalism's insufficient consumption. Through unabashed propaganda stratagems they hypnotize the consuming public with the most incredible fantasies of power, prestige, and grandeur. Erich Fromm in his *Escape from Freedom* has explained the destructive forces that moved the German people in the Nazi period. The frustration of the comfortable classes before the working class's growing power, and displacement of the aggressive energy of that conflict on to a scapegoat, set the stage for mass extermination of six million innocent lives. Like all cases of racial prejudice, anti-Semitic ideology in this case had the function of draining off aggressive impulses by turning them against a defenseless object serving as scapegoat, instead of against the arbitrary social system which really causes the aggression. The displaced energies of genuine conflicts empty themselves into prefabricated forms of pseudoconflict.

In nineteenth-century Puerto Rico a Spanish governor launched a program known as the "three Bs": that government's motto was "people who are entertained don't conspire," and the three Bs were *Baile, Botellas, y Baraja* (dance, drink, card games). During that administration cockfights and card parties provided the Puerto Rican multitudes with breathless enjoyment. The Spanish colonial regime manipulated the stormy winds of the Lares revolution, and Puerto Rico became a prize of war when the North American regime supplanted the Spanish by right of conquest.

Contemporary capitalist society suffers from acute alienating tendencies as a result of propagandistic manipulation by agencies expressly designed for the purpose. The basic function of the sycophant is to sharpen the individual's alienation by producing blind spots, myths, and scapegoats as a screen for the arbitrary forces to which he ought to respond with genuine aggression, since they are the true causes of his alienation. The screen not merely blocks his vision of the true causes but channels his hostility against an object unconnected with them, thus intensifying the alienation through pseudoconflict. At the same time the alienation produces a disequilibrium of genuine life experience, so that by way of escape the individual seeks self-awareness in blind pseudoconflictive expression. If it is aggression he wants to express, there is no true aggression in it, only crude and sadistic confusion. In other words, the conflict situation is experienced as a condition without meaning and tending toward greater alienation, instead of integration of the personality with itself and with others.

Marx's metaphor concerning a society bearing within it the seeds of another society can be applied to individuals who live with anachronistic existential perspectives and have intuitions of a new order. The birth of a new society, seen through this same metaphor, would represent the birth of that consciousness of the social order which is necessary to break the existential alienation imposed by the anachronistic order.

There is a metaphor that certain authors have applied to Puerto Rico: "Puerto Rico is the corpse of a society that was never born." Perhaps there is some truth in this; if there is, it would imply that a society can be left behind in its historical development, sterile to conceive the structural bodies necessary for the advance of history, its members in a state of chronic alienation.

Chapter III of *Caribbean Integration*, ed. Thomas Matthews (Río Piedras: Editorial Universitaria, 1967); reprinted in *Requiem por una cultura* (Río Piedras: Editorial Edil, 1970).

IV
Culture and Politics

Antonio S. Pedreira (1899–1939)

Born in San Juan. Essayist and literary critic. Studied in Puerto Rico, the United States, and Spain. Founder and coeditor of the journal *Indice* (1929–1931). Director of Hispanic Studies at the University of Puerto Rico, 1927–1933, giving courses on Spanish and Puerto Rican themes. He contributed first-class analyses of Puerto Rican literature and culture.

He was undoubtedly the major influence on the so-called "thirties generation" and one of the distinguished figures of Puerto Rican culture. His *Insularismo* has been among the most influential books written in the Island.

Selected Bibliography

Pedreira, Antonio S. *Obras completas.* 7 vols. Río Piedras: Editorial Edil, 1969.

——. *Hostos, ciudadano de América.* 1932; San Juan: ICP, 1964.

——. *De los nombres de Puerto Rico.* 1927.

——. *Aristas.* 1930.

——. *Bibliografía puertorriqueña.* Madrid, 1932.

——. *La actualidad del jíbaro.* Rio Piedras, 1935.

——. *El año terrible del 87.* San Juan, 1937.

——. *Un hombre del pueblo: José Celso Barbosa.* 1937.

——. *El periodismo en Puerto Rico.* Habana, 1941.

——. *Aclaraciones y crítica.* 1942.

Arce de Vázquez, Margot. "Antonio S. Pedreira, hispanista." In *Impresiones.* San Juan: Editorial Yaurel, 1950.

Flores, Juan. *The Insular Vision: Pedreira's Interpretation of Puerto Rican Culture.* Centro de Estudios Puertorriqueños, CUNY, 1978.

Maldonado Denis, Manuel. "Visión y revisión de *Insularismo.*" *Asomante* 19 (1963).

Meléndez, Concha. "Pedreira: autorretrato en su autocrítica." In *Figuración de Puerto Rico y otros estudios.* San Juan: ICP, 1958.

Quiñones, Samuel R. "Filiación de Antonio S. Pedreira." In *Temas y letras.* San Juan, 1955.

Insularism

The admiring tone which our complacency has created for measuring Puerto Rican reality will be absent from these pages. They are not the product of scientific analysis but have arisen, without spurious pretensions and responding to a personal disquiet, from a series of events and attitudes which I have submitted to the most genuine and disinterested reflection.

I do not claim that observations that are true for myself are so for others. If they contain internal contradictions and visible repetitions, these spring from the very vitality of the problem we are tackling. I am searching intuitively for the hidden significance of the events that have marked our course as a people. I am aware of the possible errors of judgment that inevitably lead to wrong conclusions. But since I am not aiming to write history or science, nor to do the job of statistical experts, I have let my good faith triumph over my personal misgivings. These pages, then, aspire not to resolve any problem but rather to pose one. They represent one of various positions that can be taken on a theme.

The question we seek to answer is: taking us Puerto Ricans as a whole, and in the long run, how and what are we? We want to put together the diverse elements in the heart of our culture and come upon the decisive points of our collective psychology. But we must bear in mind that if the many facets of an individual personality make the individual hard to define, it is much harder to define a people. And the difficulty mounts when, as in this case, one seeks to define an aggregate of human beings who have not yet been able to find a proper delineation of their collective life.

We have been tethered to an optimistic and sterile interpretation of history, from which arises the arrogance of thinking ourselves the *non plus ultra* of Antillean peoples. Enthusiastically addicted to rhetorical patriotism, we have persisted in deftly

251

concealing the pejorative sense to which honest reflection must lead us. To come upon the essence of our spontaneous manifestations of consciousness, we need to do some scavenging in the outskirts of officially written history and bring to light basic attitudes which by their very innocence eluded the canonical historian. From such suburban excursions, and from such moments ingenuously passed by in the professional amassing of paper, must we draw conclusions about ourselves.

It is time to have done with the slavish idolatry that tends to define our personality on the basis of alleged perfections which in fact were never more than aspirations. It is fashionable to affirm our virtues as if we had really fulfilled and lived up to them. What we ought and want to be is a far cry from what we have been and are. If one seeks to define an indefinable people that yearns in its delusions of grandeur to hide its errors and defects from itself and others, one must by way of compensation put some stress on its weaknesses to reach a reasonably impartial judgment. Firmly and undauntedly, then, and leaving due room for mistakes, we put behind us the bracing tropical music which only exalts positive values without noticing that they still belong in the category of yearnings.

Applause only produces healthy conformity, business-as-usual, and braggadocio. Pessimism and doubt are vital forces that move us to examine our conscience. Discussion clarifies thinking and tends to instigate corrective proposals. "There are pessimisms," said Rodó, "that in fact represent *paradoxical optimism*. Far from implying renunciation and condemnation of existence, they propagate by their distaste for what exists the need to renovate it." Whatever bitterness is in this essay is saturated with hopes of renewal.

We have always tended to measure the volume of our qualities by the fickle yardstick of politics. The point of view has oscillated according to the shifting of the base. Our politics has developed tragically in longings for more utility and participation. The useful, the necessary, the profitable have been norms of all the parties. And since we breathe politics and live politics—since in school, theater, journalism, club, office, and everywhere else the imperative and invariable theme is politics—we have developed an electoral attitude to measure things. This attitude varies with circumstances. Only yesterday it was a patriotic duty to be political; today it is a profession. Compare the politics of the nineteenth with that of the twentieth century and you will see the jump that has been made from principle to office, from sacrifice to success, from effort to attainment. Before, the dominant spirit was that of a general plan; now it is personal interest, concealed privilege at every step. Without minimizing the importance of our politics we must reject eleventh-hour ebbs and flows as a fulcrum for impartial judgment of the problem before us. The surge of the ocean is transitory although it comes from the bottom.

Nor can our qualities be measured by the sudden jump from one dominion to another, in which the progress in the two periods is compared. "Frivolous people," wrote Ortega y Gasset, "think human progress consists in a quantitative increase of things and ideas. No, no, true progress is the growing intensity with which we perceive half a dozen cardinal mysteries that are the convulsive and unceasing heartbeat of history." Let us see whether those mysteries exist for us and what they mean. Or at least let us try to bring the essence of our character to the surface. Speaking of Puerto Rico in his *La agonía antillana*, Araquistáin writes: "Obsessed as everyone is by political concerns, few can relax enough to take an interest in the essence of life and of things."* Our wish is to penetrate into that essence.

In this desire to make an analytical construct of our character, we have had to restrain constantly recurring evasions and concentrate on revelations that can form a pattern. The complexity of the matter requires us to reject exceptions which, because there are so many of them, would drown in doubts the need for the synthesis. We know, and indeed would so wish it, that many of these evasions will hover in the reader's mind to provoke disagreement. But if we were ruled by scruples, we would not have written these pages.

Having indicated the direction our interpretation will take, we should also clarify what we understand by culture. Simple references generally take shelter in the convenient and inadequate

---

* Luis de Araquistáin, *La agonía antillana* (19??). The author is a Spanish Socialist.

definition that makes culture a private matter of knowledge or morality. We believe with Ludwig Pfandl that "culture does not mean *Sum* or *Synthesis* of all spiritual or civilized components, but rather the external world, the environment so handsomely described by Carlos Justi as the ether of things."* The repertory of conditions that give tone to events and channels to the life of peoples; that peculiar reaction to things—ways of understanding and creating—that sorts humanity into national groups: this is what we will mean by culture here. Vital intensity is more than progress.

To define this cosmic rhythm of the problem without serious errors, and locate in it the syntax of the Puerto Rican genius, we must not lose sight of these zones of quantitative quality into which culture is commonly divided: universal, national, and individual. Oswald Spengler in his controversial *Decline of the West* divides the first into two great phases, the ancient culture of Apollonian soul and the Western of Faustian soul: serenity and anxiety. Within these broad terms Spain is no more than an attitude in the scale of Western culture, and we an American expression of the culture in Spain. And it is this national aspect that interests us. Even reducing the complexity of the matter to such simple terms it is not easy to pin down our particular idiosyncrasy, because in these days we cannot exclude the Anglo-Saxon expression which the United States is slowly filtering into our Hispanic essence.

I see three supreme moments in our people's development: first, passive formation and accumulation, beginning with the discovery and conquest and ending in the last years of the eighteenth and first of the nineteenth centuries; second, awakening and initiation, dovetailed into the first and ending with the Spanish-American War; third, the present period of indecision and transition. In the first we were no more than a faithful prolongation of Hispanic culture; in the second we began to discover an idiosyncrasy of our own within that culture; in the third we have wanted to continue developing this, but with the modification of a new expression of Western culture (the Saxon)

---

* Pfandl was a well-known German Hispanist, specializing in the Golden Age.

superimposed on its growth. For the moment I am not interested in discussing the result of that injection but in pointing out the discontinuity of our own evolution, which has never fully matured.

We have had birth and growth but no rebirth. We emerge from one transplantation and head into another without ever completing the outline of our own idiosyncrasy; not that we have altogether lost it, but that it is transitory in the present historical moment. And what we call our idiosyncracy—without claiming that it is on a par with the Spanish or Anglo-Saxon expression of Western culture, merely recognizing the temporary subjection of the former—is the sole cause for concern in what we here call insularism. The whole system of conditions in which it floats historically is what we will understand here as Puerto Rican culture.

If we isolate in this way the concept of our international dependency, we at once confront the fact that what Spain brought us is infinitely superior to what we have created: we have not made a language, nor an art of our own, nor a national philosophy. Like so many other peoples we have not only failed to make the most of the indigenous element, but have lacked the bountiful interpretation of life, the leap into the abstract which is the proof of a people's solidity and maturity. Culturally we were and continue to be a Spanish colony. And yet within the harmony of our race we have the beginnings of our own rhythm which, if it has not come fully into the foreground, has succeeded—as with other peoples—in differentiating itself a little from the general order that Spain created in America.

This preliminary effort should be taken as a sheaf of provisional reflections on the way to elaborating some data which I find indispensable for defining the Puerto Rican people. Any dismemberment will result in damage to our people as a whole. No one should expect remedies that I cannot offer. I am not an alienist. My purpose is rather to point out the diverse elements that can make sense of our personality. In response to the question that insistently interrupts my sleep, I have written this personal essay: it is sewn together in the desire to do away with theoretical renovations. Instead of mending the rags of the motherland with the thread of lamentation or patches of indifference, I rise to suggest that we adorn her beautifully with our duties.

This book, then, attempts to pick out the vital rhythm that defines us. After reading it all through to write this preface, I note that many ideas stick up like stumps without proper development. They are like seeds newly sown, waiting for the reader to make them sprout.

I resort to the essay because, as the word itself suggests, it is a malleable form in which much is begun and nothing is finished.

From *Insularismo,* 1934

Margot Arce de Vázquez (1904-)

Essayist and critic. Went to Spain in 1928 and studied with Tomás
Navarro Tomás and Américo Castro. Her doctoral thesis written there
on Garcilaso de la Vega is an important contribution to Golden Age
studies. On return to Puerto Rico she entered the university's Department of Hispanic Studies, where she remained until retirement in 1970.
As a professor she shaped several Puerto Rican generations; at the same
time she has been very active politically on behalf of Puerto Rican
independence.

A number of her essays deal with Puerto Rican literature, especially
Palés Matos, Luis Llorens Torres, Carmen Alicia Cadilla, José de Diego.
Apart from literary criticism she has been much concerned about Puerto
Rico's linguistic problem.

Selected Bibliography

Arce Blanco, Margot. *Garcilaso de la Vega. Contribución al estudio de la lírica española del siglo XVI*. 1930; San Juan: UPR, 1961.

————. *Impresiones*. San Juan: Editorial Yaurel, 1950.

————. *Gabriela Mistral. Persona y poesía*. San Juan, 1958.

————. *La obra literaria de José de Diego*. San Juan: ICP, 1968.

————. In collaboration with Laura Gallego y Luis de Arrigoitia. *Lecturas puertorriqueñas*. Sharon, Conn.: Troutman Press, 1966.

————. "Los adjetivos de la *Danza negra* de Palés Matos." *Ateneo Puertorriqueño* 3 (1939).

Esau

And Isaac loved Esau, because he did eat of his venison: but Rebekah loved Jacob. And Jacob sod pottage: and Esau came from the field, and he was faint: And Esau said to Jacob, Feed me, I pray thee, with that same red pottage; for I am faint: therefore was his name called Edom. And Jacob said, Sell me this day thy birthright. And Esau said, Behold, I am at the point to die: and what profit shall this birthright do to me? And Jacob said, Swear to me this day; and he sware unto him: and he sold his birthright unto Jacob. Then Jacob gave Esau bread and pottage of his lentils; and he did eat and drink, and rose up, and went his way. Thus Esau despised his birthright.

Gen. 25: 28-34

March 2, 1967, marked the fiftieth year since the Jones Law became Puerto Rico's organic charter. Its minimal political reforms* were conceded in exchange for forcible imposition of U.S. citizenship on the country's inhabitants, against their frequently and publicly expressed will. The law's despotic and disgraceful provisions turned the small group of high-principled citizens who rejected the imposition—because their birthright was not for sale—into pariahs in their own land. It did not banish them from the country but took away their fundamental civil rights while not exempting them from compulsory service in the U.S. Army. That would have been too much to ask!†

Puerto Rico's Honorable Governor has dedicated the whole of this month of March to commemorating the fiftieth anniversary of the imposition of U.S. citizenship on Puerto Ricans. The legislative chambers for their part approved a Joint Resolution, and

* See José de Diego, "El Nuevo Bill Jones," *Nuevas campañas*, 1916, pp. 243-276. (Author's note.)

† Ibid., pp. 263-265. (Author's note.)

the Honorable President of the United States sent the Puerto Rican people cordial—and how ironic!—felicitations on their enjoyment of fifty years of compulsory foreign citizenship.

The initiative for the celebration came from the "Exchange Clubs" (I wouldn't know their name in Spanish nor their real purpose). They opened the ball with a so-called "Caravan of Truth," a designation testifying perhaps to a rich sense of humor.

These events are a repeat of the same dangerous mystification of historical truth which has operated, for example, with respect to another date, July 25, 1898, although in the case of March 2, 1917, it has gone much further and involved much more serious distortions. July 25 was chosen to celebrate the approval of the Free Associated State Constitution which was supposed to solve the colonial problem in Puerto Rico; and probably July 23, 1967, has been chosen for a plebiscite, supposedly to decide our people's definitive constitutional status. The nearness of this date to July 25 would seem to indicate an intention to make the latter also the celebration day for the result of the plebiscite, which has to be victory for the Free Associated State formula. But of course! For the conditions under which the plebiscite will be held offer no sort of guarantees that democracy will reign immaculate over the voting. We need hardly look beyond the fact that one of the constitutional formulas before the electorate is backed by an Island government which disposes of all the machinery of power and will be both litigant and judge.

Choice of the July 25 date seems to be deliberate rather than accidental. Could it conceal the intention to expunge the memory of a historic fact, the invasion of Puerto Rico by North American troops on July 25, 1898? Those troops arrived in full panoply of war; they had bombarded San Juan on the morning of May 12 of that year, without warning to its defenseless and unwitting inhabitants who had made no offensive move against the aggressors. Far from that, many deluded Puerto Ricans nursed an honest belief in the democratic and liberating principles of their gratuitous and unexpected enemies.

Despite the libertarian promises of General Miles, commander of the invading army, a military government was set up which abolished all the freedoms granted by Spain in the Charter of

Autonomy; and the occupation warriors submitted innocent Puerto Ricans to excesses and outrages to their physical and personal dignity. Members of my family were horrified eye-witnesses of these misdeeds in Caguas and in Aguas Buenas.

But these slick prestidigitators have turned July 25 into a "glorious day" for celebration by the Puerto Rican people. (In our people's Hispano-Christian tradition, July 25 is also the day of the Apostle Santiago, patron saint of Spain who on a white horse led the Spaniards to victory against the Moorish invaders at the battle of Clavijo. Now it has been transformed into a day to celebrate the arrival of other invaders.)

Historical Truth

History cannot be falsified with impunity; regardless of politicians' opportunistic or lucrative perversions, its truth will always shine through. The men who governed Puerto Rico between 1902 and 1917 (fight against the Foraker Law and the Executive Council) loved their country and saw clearly the primary importance for our people's sovereignty of having their own citizenship. On two separate occasions* the Chamber of Delegates, which was the people's real representative, voted a unanimous protest to the U.S. Congress against the imposing of U.S. citizenship on Puerto Ricans. Luis Muñoz Rivera, then resident commissioner in Washington, likewise registered his protest with firmness and patriotism. On the record for anyone to read are his historic speech in the Congress affirming Puerto Ricans' right to their natural citizenship, and his letter to de Diego predicting failure for his efforts. The position of both Muñoz Rivera and de Diego corresponded with that of the overwhelming majority in the country. But the will of the governed was of no concern to the United States' democratic Congress, and it imposed its conditions: either U.S. citizenship would be accepted with the reforms, or there would be no reforms. Muñoz Rivera erred seriously in

* February 6, 1913; July 14, 1913. (Author's note.)

concluding he had no alternative as a politician but to give in. But this does not justify those who now applaud his error by picturing him as the champion of U.S. citizenship, a title devoid of truth which tarnishes his illustrious memory. De Diego called the Congress's action a "brutal ukase."

The Puerto Rican people did not know how to say a virile "No!" through the mouths of their leaders, and settled for compromise. Instead of cleaving to the principle of our inalienable rights, they sacrificed them in exchange for some reforms which actually meant little in liberalizing the colonial situation. One need only mention the absolute veto over legislative decisions which the Jones Law conferred on the North American governor; the legislature's almost total deprivation of power over the budget; the absolute control over public education conferred on the North American education commissioner; and the enthronement of the Auditor as an imperial grand vizier.* . . . According to de Diego, instead of "law to provide Puerto Rico with a civil government and for other purposes," it should have been called "law to rivet a despotic government on Puerto Rico and for no other purpose."†

What motives had the U.S. Congress for so unscrupulously betraying the principle in its own constitution? Let us cite the historian Ada Suárez Díaz. In 1917, "the United States has already completed its domination over the Caribbean basin. From 1898 it possessed Puerto Rico and from 1901, through the Platt Amendment, Cuba. It has acquired the Panama Canal, has occupation troops in Santo Domingo and Haiti, and . . . will close the semicircle with purchase of the Danish Virgin Islands."††

So the aims of future North American policy in the zone come into focus. For those aims a firm hold on Puerto Rico was expedient. U.S. citizenship would provide a formidable obstacle to our country's right to its full freedom and sovereignty; Puerto Ricans would have to fight tooth and nail to remove it; perhaps like the southern states they would have to resort to violence.

There was another way in which imposing their citizenship

---

* José de Diego, op. cit., pp. 243-265. (Author's note.)
† Ibid., p. 243. (Author's note.)
†† "El Instituto José de Diego," *Asomante*, 12, 4 (1966), pp. 54-55. (Author's note.)

suited North American interests in that period: it enabled them to conscript Puerto Ricans and send them to die on the battlefields of World War I.

Citizenship and Sovereignty

Citizenship in a state is based on the people as a nation: it becomes a kind of juridical expression of its national being and its political substance. It should logically respond to deep realities of the collective spirit. The U.S. Supreme Court recognized it as such when it affirmed in the Dred Scott case: ". . . the people and citizens are synonymous terms since both define the political body in accordance with our republican institutions, and comprise the sovereignty that sustains power and directs the government through their representatives."*

And in the Tobin vs. Walkin Shaw case the Circuit Court declared, referring to the Guadalupe-Hidalgo treaty, "if they [the inhabitants] had not continued being Mexican citizens, nor had become citizens of the United States, an entire people would be deprived of its civil rights. They would have had no status as citizens, would owe no allegiance, and would have remained in the anomalous position of a people without a country."†

"The Court," comments de Diego, "makes allegiance—that is, sovereignty—a derivative of citizenship, and even ends by paralleling the concept of citizenship with that of country."††

In the United States the procedure by which a foreigner acquires North American citizenship is called "naturalization." The term is very significant: it implies that those who "naturalize" themselves as U.S. citizens "denaturalize" themselves as citizens of their own country, hence no longer owe it the duty of allegiance. In fact they deny their own country, turn their backs on

---

* José de Diego, "Valor jurídico y político de la ciudadanía puertorriqueña," *Nuevas campañas*, p. 210. (Author's note.)

† Ibid., pp. 211-212. (Author's note.)

†† Ibid., p. 212. (Author's note.)

it. It is in this "denaturalized" situation that the imposition of U.S. citizenship leaves us Puerto Ricans since March 2, 1917.

Such a serious decision as changing nationality would seem most honorably made by one profoundly desiring the adopted citizenship, believing the adoptive country to be better and more worthy of love than the natural country, identifying totally with the new country, forgetting his own and feeling no ties of loyalty to it. For in the case of armed conflict between the two states, his new citizenly duty would oblige him to fight against the land of his birth and kill his natural and true compatriots. And whoever adopts foreign citizenship and renounces his own solely to turn his ambiguous position to material advantage deserves to be plainly labeled "opportunist." Decent people deny neither their country nor their natural citizenship. If they do, they also deny themselves. If the natural country's situation is not to their liking, their compelling duty is to remain loyal and fight to improve it. History is full of infamies committed for practical motives and political realism.

Citizenship is the sole foundation of popular sovereignty; the latter is the power emanating from the former. "The acquisition of foreign citizenship should be based on a stipulation by the contracting parties and by individual consent that the voluntary nature of the citizenship determines the legitimacy of the sovereignty by the concurrence and reciprocity of both concepts in public law."*

Since this principle was ignored when the United States imposed its citizenship on us, and voices will always be raised to denounce the imposition, its legitimization is clearly one aim of the coming plebiscite. And those who believe in the possibility of a sovereign Free Associated State are victims of a hallucination: as long as Puerto Ricans are U.S. citizens—and after the plebiscite, voters for statehood or Free Associated State status will be such by their own consent—total and exclusive sovereignty will reside in the U.S. federal government. Even statehood cannot give us full sovereignty because it likewise leaves the federal government with jurisdiction in decisions that are decisive and most binding.

* Ibid., p. 210. (Author's note.)

At the same time the Caribbean political situation leaves no doubt as to present North American intentions concerning Puerto Rico. With a Cuba governed by Castro; an unstable Dominican Republic on the verge of revolution, fresh from a new U.S. military intervention-occupation, and with a Washington stooge as President; and with a Venezuela in continuous agitation, it is naive to think the United States would recognize full sovereignty for Puerto Rico. Events of very recent occurrence confirm this. To cite only three:

—The new U.S. attempts to prevent the Puerto Rican case from coming before the United Nations Decolonization Commission.

—The refusal to transfer to the Puerto Rican government the Castle of El Morro, a historical relic without military value which by some magic or other has been metamorphosed into a U.S. "national historic monument."

—The North American Senate's $10,000,000 appropriation to extend its military based on our soil, especially the huge Roosevelt Roads base.

The "Free Associated State" label was dreamed up with the aim (already misfired) of shutting up both independentists and statists—the former in their aspirations for full sovereignty, the latter for federally limited sovereignty.

Only under independence could Puerto Rico really enjoy sovereignty and display the natural citizenship corresponding with its national being, with its history. (I start from the assumption that no true Puerto Rican exists who denies that Puerto Rico *is a nation with its own way of being and with a history.*) And all of us know that the sole "status" we can demand with full reason and right, and even take for ourselves should it be refused to us, is independence. A decision by the people, and the calling of a constituent convention of the Puerto Rican republic, would suffice: the right to independence and sovereignty is a natural right, sanctioned by the best and purest norms of international law and most authentic principles of democracy. Under statehood or as Free Associated State we can never shake off the decisions and will of the U.S. people.

Certain Puerto Rican politicians—those most closely tied to

Washington and to the potent North American financial enterprises now dominating our country's economy—have resorted to the falsehood that the sovereignty concept is now obsolete and irrelevant. They hope with that to confuse their compatriots about the true and real value of sovereignty, to deceive them into renouncing their legitimate and most relevant aspiration to attain it. It is true that, for the common good of humanity, modern sovereign states enter into international organs and treaties under which they freely yield some of their political powers. But is that the case with Puerto Rico? In no way! One can only renounce something that one possesses; what is the possessor of nothing going to renounce? At the same time one may ask: has the United States renounced its full sovereignty? Is it prepared to do so? All that is happening today suggests the contrary. And how many countries have claimed their independence by revolutionary or peaceful means from the end of World War II till now? What was the UN Decolonization Commission created for?

Odd that those politicians should have chosen the word "obsolete," a Latin barbarism which according to Corominas* has fallen into total disuse in the Spanish-speaking world. Such gibberish, without real meaning for simple people, may perhaps inspire in them that vague respect which they feel for the unknown (one recalls the coercive power of the Sacristan's Latinisms over the angry rustics in *Divinas palabras*).† But the more cultivated ear immediately perceives the contemptuously intended putdown of champions of sovereignty as out-of-date ignoramuses. It is laughable to see these politicians restoring the barbarism "obsolete" to Puerto Rican speech and literature to discredit the allegedly archaic concept of sovereignty. Good taste has always rejected the use of worn-out, pseudoerudite barbarisms as intolerable affectation. Unnecessary to mention that those who think sovereignty for Puerto Rico "obsolete" find sovereignty very up-to-date and admirable when the United States exercises it over us, or tries to exercise it over any people on the planet.

* Joan Corominas, Catalan linguist and author of an important etymological dictionary.
† A play by Ramón del Valle Inclán (1920).

"Denaturalization"—Dehumanization, Corruption

These distortions of historical truth, this negation of positive human values, this almost supine realism and pragmatism, have produced a corrosive subversion of our people's moral life, along with a series of myths and catchwords designed to anesthetize their conscience and lower their healthy vitality. (In exoneration of the Puerto Rican people we must recall that they have been subjected for sixty-nine years to perpetual indoctrination, a propaganda scientifically contrived to weaken and destroy their national conscience—a genuine "brainwash" with devastating results.) Substantially contributing to the creation of these myths and catchwords has been the semantics of the government party and of a daily press at the service of North American interests, the declared enemy of our country's independence.

Neither the Popular nor the Republican Statehood party nor the newspaper *El Mundo* is unaware of the tremendous power of the word, both to spread truth and to spread lies; and they know especially well the mental confusion producible by half-truths. Thus we cannot be surprised by the almost total disappearance from Puerto Rican speech of such words as *motherland, patriot, patriotism,* whose elimination is designed to blot from our collective memory not only the concepts but the feelings and emotions they rouse. When we independentists use them—the only ones who do—we are generally put down as dreamers, romantics, old fogies, reactionaries, and, worse, as subversives and communists. I have always wondered why they propagandize so favorably about communists when they fear and despise them so! Another method is the discrediting of words like *nation, national, nationalism* when applied to Puerto Rico. The positive value of those concepts is carefully avoided and their exaggerated use is stressed, as if there were no other kind of nationalism than the imperialist and the Hitlerian. Curiously, no one criticizes North American nationalism, one of the most virulent of our epoch. But most curious is that *nation, national* appear in certain kinds of newspapers and on the lips of certain kinds of politicians, not referring to Puerto Rico but to the United States—and then it becomes most praiseworthy to be a "nationalist"! For our real country the humble adjective "local" is reserved. "Our local flag," said an otherwise admirable woman friend to me, referring to the flag of Puerto Rico. The *national* flag is that of the United States!

To strangle Puerto Ricans' natural love of country, a feeble kind of universalism is preached to us. I say feeble because real and fruitful universalism can only be conceived as unity of all sovereign nations to work for universal good; and in such a unity Puerto Rico, still not a sovereign nation, could only participate as an appendage of the United States—if that country's government would grace us with an invitation.

The natural, human, spontaneous thing is to love above all what is your own and closest to you. That is the only take-off point for a broader love, which would always be somewhat abstract unless animated by deep historical vision, great abnegation, and genuine charity. And "charity begins at home.". . . Things are asked of poor, weak Puerto Rico that were never asked of other peoples: to renounce its national sovereignty, give its blood for a foreign country, consider that country as its motherland, be loyal to two flags. . . ! (But don't we know what happens to he who serves two masters?) In the case of "obsolete" sovereignty we have seen that the semantic game works through the use of contemptuous language.

In the official language and that of some newspapers the independentists are described as "separatists" or "subversives." It is pertinent to ask, is Puerto Rico really bound to the United States by ties of race, language, culture, idiosyncrasy, customs, history, geography? Or by political ties of juridical equality and mutual interest? Have we Puerto Ricans transformed ourselves into authentic North Americans? Obviously not! So what are we separating ourselves from? The United States "possesses" us, as it has said many times. "Possession" does not necessarily imply "union," but on the contrary a juridically and ethically illegitimate relationship as far as the rights of people are concerned.

"Subversive" is the term for those who subvert order; but to have validity, order has to be founded on truth, equity, freedom, and justice. Is it suggested that the political and economic order existing in Puerto Rico responds to those requisites? In external

policy, and to a great extent in internal, we are completely subordinated to the all-embracing will of the U.S. Congress; our economy is ruled by the laws of that congress, which legislates in its
own country's interests as it has to do, and by the will of the great
North American financial groups controlling almost 80 percent
of our wealth. A few days ago the *San Juan Star* reported the
concession to North Americans of the right to exploit our mineral
wealth over nearly one-third of our territory. And it was denied to
Puerto Rican bidders!

We the so-called "subversives" want freedom, sovereignty, possession of what is rightfully ours, equity, justice: in other words,
real democracy. The true subversives are those who support, applaud, and connive in the existing economic and political *disorder*
in Puerto Rico.

The clever and effective official propaganda has also created
some myths and catchwords tending (as we are told) to "change
the image" of the United States in Puerto Rican and Spanish
American eyes. (Note that this "image-changing" is done with
obvious political and propaganda motives, not for love of truth
nor to correct injustices.) With this in mind Popular Party leaders
have visited Spanish American countries, and foreign officials
have been invited here on top of the flood of assorted conventions
that come every year. For all this the Puerto Rican taxpayer
pays—and pays plenty.

Let's look at some of these myths and platitudes:

Status is not "at issue." (It turns out to be very much so.)

Nothing bad can come to us from Washington. (What price the
minimum-wage law? Compulsory military service? The coastal
navigations? Etc.)

Independence would be the end of Puerto Rican economic progress.
(Or the end of our economy's domination by foreign concerns?
Progress has gone ahead in Jamaica, in Israel, and in various
recently liberated African countries.)

Originality of the Free Associated State formula. (According to Rubén
Berríos in his *San Juan Star* column, the same formula was proposed by the North American colonists of 1776. People had also
thought of it here.)

U.S. citizenship is the world's best, offering the most guarantees to citizens. (What about the British? The French? The Chilean? The Mexican? . . . Are they not equally good, giving citizens equal protection?)

Puerto Rico the "showcase of democracy." (What about the report of the Governor's Commission on Civil Rights? And compulsory military service without representation? And the triple political police—Internal Security, FBI, CIA? And the political prisoners treated like common criminals? And the federal government's power over Puerto Rico? And etc., etc., etc.?)

Puerto Rico's great progress as a result of the association. (But is there any real association, equal to equal, or does one of the associates have almost total powers over the other? And haven't even African countries progressed over the same period? Look down from any Santurce skyscraper on the belt of slums, the ring of pain and poverty that surrounds the opulent hotels and banks and ostentatious mansions of the rich. And the poverty of the rural communities? And the crisis of our agriculture?)

Two citizenships, two anthems, two flags, two loyalties. (But are they of equal worth? Do they carry the same obligations and prerogatives? Is Puerto Rican citizenship available to North Americans? Do they want it? What protection does this nominal, paper Puerto Rican citizenship afford to us, the minority who want it effective and real, against political-police persecution and the calumnies of certain newspapers? Can it rescue us from going to Vietnam, to that most dubious and gruesome of wars which has absolutely nothing to do with us?

The benefits of industrialization. (Very true and palpable, but they are pillars of sand. And what have they cost us? By official statistics more than 75 percent of our wealth is in the hands of North American absentee corporations, which for ten years will pay no taxes to the people of Puerto Rico and which are drawn here by lower wage scales than they would pay in the United States. And when our minerals begin to be exploited, the percentage of capital in foreign hands will be even larger, plus the very serious threat to the fertility of our soil, the purity of our water, and the health of the population, failing urgent preventive measures. As for our already languishing agriculture, it will thus be finally and definitively destroyed.)

Economic freedom must take precedence over political freedom. (To my knowledge, history provides no proof of this, but to the contrary. Without political freedom no economic freedom is possible. It was just because they needed economic freedom that the thirteen American colonies had to rebel against England and free themselves politically.)

The Free Associated State formula is as estimable as independence. (It is the essence of a thing that makes it worthy of esteem. It is not made so by the definitions of interested officials and politicians.)

A genuine analysis of the reality, without rationalizations, would destroy such myths and catchwords. But under their influence the Puerto Rican people have suffered a dangerous subversion of values, so that most of them are now psychologically disposed to accept "a cat for a hare," to deny themselves as a nation, to dehumanize themselves. Here are some examples of what I mean:

When a distinguished group of Puerto Rican intellectuals warned the country of the danger of North American atomic installations in the Ceiba and Aguadilla military bases, very few supporting voices were raised in response to the natural instinct of conservation and in defense of their own lives. Instead a campaign of defamation and mockery was launched—in which certain university professors notably joined—culminating in the contemptuous catchword, "document of extermination." Why did they jeer at this warning to the Puerto Rican people? Simply that they thought it a "betrayal" of the United States, whose right to defend its own security at the expense of Puerto Rico's destruction they upheld at any price. Some months later *Fortune,* a magazine notoriously above suspicion, confirmed the document fore and aft by pinpointing Puerto Rico as one of the world's surest and most dangerous targets in the event of atomic attack!

When a North American policeman died under Nationalist fire in the attack on Blair House, Puerto Rican schoolchildren—presumably by initiative of the authorities—contributed a substantial sum (for them) as a gift to the unfortunate widow in compensation. If those children did the same for the unfortunate widows and orphans of Puerto Rican policemen killed in the Nationalist revolt of 1950, I have no knowledge of it. Of course there were not even condolences for the unfortunate orphans and widows of Nationalists who fell in that struggle. One of the most disquieting signs of our times, says the Catholic philosopher Gabriel Marcel, is the ease with which the worst and vilest crimes are forgiven while *there is no forgiveness* for political crimes.* Last December, in preference to pardoning the political prisoner Blanca Canales, the traditional gubernatorial prerogative of Christmas clemency was suspended.

A Puerto Rican father whose son was killed in the Vietnam War publicly proclaimed that he was proud of it and would give his remaining sons to the same fate. Don't tell me this is an isolated case: it is a fairly general attitude in the country, as shown by the repeated attacks on the "Committee for Sixto Alvelo." Yet it is fair to say that there has recently been an awakening of the Puerto Rican national conscience in some sectors of public opinion, which fills us with hope.

The eminent Italo-German theologian Romano Guardini has said that a people sacrificing its freedom in exchange for security and material possessions inevitably ends in corruption.† That is the terrible danger that threatens our people, and of which these examples are alarming symptoms. Symptoms that point to the service of false gods, to the concealment or distortion of truth, to contempt for or insensitivity to deep and vital human values; to a kind of general holocaust-wish in furtherance of the political and economic interests of a country that is not our rightful mother-land and has kept us under a colonial regime from 1898 until today. Such aberrations are leading many Puerto Ricans to rebel against truth, against the spirit and the freedom that are the essence of humanity. From there to totalitarianism is only a step.

> Then Jacob gave Esau bread and pottage of lentils; and he did eat and drink, and rose up, and went his way. Thus Esau despised his birthright. . . .

March 25, 1967

---

*Gabriel Marcel, *Les Hommes contre l'humaine* (Paris: La Colombe, 1951.) (Author's note.)
†Guardini is well known for a book on Christ, *Der Herr.*

Nilita Vientós Gastón (1908–)

Born in Sebastián, Puerto Rico. Lawyer, teacher, and writer. First woman director of the Ateneo Puertorriqueño, a position she held longer (fifteen years) than anyone in that institution's history. Founder and editor since its inception (1945) of the journal *Asomante*, a genuine cultural bridge between Puerto Rico and the rest of the Spanish-speaking world, now extended in the journal *Sin Nombre*.

Has worked for more than twenty-five years as a lawyer in the suits initiated by the people of Puerto Rico to recover lands from latifundist corporations. In 1965 she won the Puerto Rican Supreme Court judgment to the effect that "the language of our people is Spanish, a reality that no law can change."

She was for many years producer of the TV program *Puntos de vista*. Has been a tireless champion of the Spanish language as mainstay of Puerto Rican destiny. Her reviews and articles have been collected under the title *Indice Cultural* and she has written a book on Henry James.

Selected Bibliography

Vientós Gastón, Nilita. *Introducción a Henry James.* 1956.
————. *Impresiones de viaje.* 1957.
————. *Indice Cultural*, Vol's I, II, III, and IV. 1962–1971. These volumes include a large number of brief essays, published in various periodicals.
————. *Consideraciones a un ensayo sobre Puerto Rico.* San Juan: Ateneo Puertorriqueño, 1967.

The Supreme Court of Puerto Rico
and the Language Problem

No aspect of Puerto Rico's history tells us more about the drama of its political situation than the language problem, the struggle against so-called bilingualism—the notion that Puerto Ricans should also consider as theirs a foreign language, English. Only in a nation without sovereignty does the right to place its own language above any other come up for discussion. Since 1898 when Puerto Rico became a U.S. possession, everything possible has been done to make English the official school language. The history of public education since then is the history of the school administrators' different and contradictory standards concerning the language in which instruction shall be given. A continuous and impassioned polemic rages over a question that can only arise in a colony.

The object of all education is to form a national conscience: knowledge and appreciation of one's own reality, perception of what is peculiar and distinct in it. Contrary to what is preached or accepted as dogma here for obvious reasons, national is not the negation of universal: it is the only road to arrive there. Our history and literature are not given their due importance in the classroom. Puerto Rico's past is almost *terra incognita* for the Puerto Rican student. Education is always part of a political program. As the Argentine educator Luis Reissig writes, "it is the highest of man's political functions: an education without politics is inconceivable." Politics gives the teaching profession its basic orientation, since all schooling responds to an educative philosophy. In Puerto Rico education reflects the dangerous ambiguity of our people in the face of the three solutions to define our destiny: independence, the so-called Free Associated State, and statehood. As long as no one knows why Puerto Ricans are educated, and the teacher doesn't know whether he addresses the

275

student from the vantage point of his own country and of a land that is his but belongs to another, there will be no education in Puerto Rico. We will suffer through systems, theories, arbitrary standards, but we won't have a genuine national philosophy of education with a universal thrust. The educational philosophy of a colony is hostile to the authentic education of the people colonized. Pedagogy in Puerto Rico is at the service of Americanization. Education cannot divorce itself from politics.

Among the most interesting and least known aspects of this fight to preserve our language are the proceedings that have taken place in our highest court of justice, the Supreme Court of Puerto Rico. It has handed down four judgments on the problem. Even superficial study of these proceedings brings out once again how stubbornly and persistently our people has fought to save itself by saving its language. The fact that a people resorts to the courts to preserve its language is in itself an accusation against our colonial regime, a regime that by its very essence is the negation of justice. Such a study also brings out that the Supreme Court, by its unfortunate decisions in 1948 and 1956, has contributed to the prevailing confusion about language; not until 1965 did it concede the exceptional importance of the problem.

The first collision between the Supreme Court and the language problem was in 1905.* The question at issue was the text that should prevail in the interpretation of a law—whether the Spanish or the English. The court ruled: "There can be no doubt that the English text, the one signed by the governor, is the law that must apply." This shows that seven years after the U.S. occupation of our country, the juridical system already displayed the confusion that would continue to characterize it, the inescapable ambiguity that the attempt to harmonize civil with common law would produce. Two distinct juridical traditions confronted each other, a situation which has prevented the Supreme Court from elaborating a juridical system responding to our reality. The implantation of another system's juridical proceedings and terms, and constant reliance on decisions of U.S. courts, affected the language of the legal profession just as medical education in

---

* Cruz vs. Domínguez, 8 DPR 580. (Author's note.)

English created a physician who often didn't know the Spanish word in the medical lexicon.

Not until 1948—forty-three years later—did the court consider the problem again. The case concerned the validity of a bill approved in the ordinary session of 1946, instructing the education authority that "as from the 1946–1947 school year teaching will be exclusively in the Spanish language" and making the study of English obligatory. The bill was approved to end the anarchy in the educational system resulting from the different and contradictory standards and changes established to impose English. At the end of the 1911–1912 school year the substitution of English for Spanish had almost been achieved. In 1913 parents and teachers rose in protest. Public opinion forced the Education Department to order teaching in Spanish in the first grade. In 1914 and 1915 members of the Chamber of Delegates, especially José de Diego, came out against teaching in English. Between 1915 and 1931 Epifiano Fernández Vanga published a series of articles on bilingualism, later collected in *El idioma de Puerto Rico y el idioma escolar de Puerto Rico,* calling the educational system "criminal and wretched. . . . No country treats its language as a subject in its schools. All treat it and consider it as *the* subject." Some titles of publications in that period are revealing: "The Horror of the Puerto Rican Public School," "The Curse of Bilingualism," "Neither American nor Puerto Rican: Our Schooling Is Barbarous."

In 1933 the Teachers Association, which had stood up for teaching in Spanish since its first assembly in 1912, held a referendum in which the overwhelming majority voted for teaching in Spanish. A committee was appointed to request the education authorities for the necessary reforms. In 1933 Education Commissioner José Padín introduced a reform of exceptional importance. Padín, who in 1916 had made a study of teaching in English, was the first commissioner to recognize the obvious: that English is a foreign language for the Puerto Rican child. He ordered that Spanish should be the sole vehicle of instruction in elementary schools and that English should be taught as a subject in the seventh and eighth grades. When José M. Gallardo succeeded Padín in 1937, President Roosevelt said it was his government's policy to make the Puerto Rican people bilingual. The new commissioner abandoned the ruling of his predecessor and introduced a series of changes. Adrian L. Hall, supervisor of the Educational Department's English section, has pointed out that between 1898 and 1965 no less than seven different systems of teaching English have been put into effect.* In 1942 the Superior Council of Education, the organization that directs the university, recommended that university teaching be in Spanish and assigned its secretary, Pedro A. Cebollero, to make the study of Puerto Rico's linguistic policy which we cite here.

The chairman of the council, Chávez, said in a discussion of the language problem on February 19, 1943:

... no one's permission has to be asked to teach English in a part of the United States such as is Puerto Rico. . . . Any language other than English should be secondary in any American territory. . . . The United States would not be the nation it is today if it taught in Spanish in New Mexico and California, in French in Louisiana, in Italian or Jewish in New York.

I suggested in an article about the council members' statements that the Puerto Rican legislature should pass a law making the language problem a question of public order (reason of state), and instruct the education commissioner that all subjects be taught in Spanish. I also discussed the authority of our legislature to pass such a law.†

The language bill was vetoed by the interim governor, Manuel A. Pérez. On March 21, 1946, the legislature passed it again. The governor vetoed it for the second time and sent it on April 30, 1946, to the director of island territories and possessions in the Department of the Interior, for submission to the U.S. president under the terms of the Organic Charter then in force. The bill reached the Territories Division on May 6 and was sent to the president on August 7. On August 13, 1946, Pedro Parrilla Montáñez, as a father with parental authority over his five children, brought suit in the San Juan District Court against the

* San Juan Review, June 1965. (Author's note.)

† "La legislatura y el problema de la lengua," El Mundo, March 21, 1943 (i.e., three years before the legislature approved the bill). (Author's note.)

education commissioner, Herbert H. Martin, to compel application of the legislature's decision. He submitted that since the bill had not been vetoed by the U.S. president within the ninety days prescribed by the Organic Charter, it had become law. The legal question at issue narrowed down to determining when the ninety days, which Article 34 of the charter stipulated for a veto, began: whether from the bill's arrival at the president's office, or from its reception by his agent, the Territories Division director. The plaintiff asked that the case be heard by a collegiate court of five judges, and this was conceded because of the question's importance. While the suit was in the works, on October 25, 1946, the U.S. president disapproved the bill and sent it back to the new governor. The court found on February 25, 1947, that the ninety days began from the submission of the bill to the Department of Interior:

> The time spent by the department in studying the bill and making recommendations was part of the period fixed for presidential action. If it had been otherwise, the intention of the Congress to fix a definite time limit for the governor's veto, at the expiration of which all bills approved by the Puerto Rican legislature would become law, could in fact be annulled by indefinite procrastination in the Department of Interior.

The bill was ruled to have been law since August 4, 1946. On February 28, 1947, the new education commissioner, Mariano Villaronga, appealed to the Supreme Court—then consisting of five judges, four Puerto Ricans and a North American—which revoked the district court ruling on January 28, 1948.* According to the decision handed down by Judge Angel de Jesús, in which Presiding Judge Martín Travieso concurred, the law contained nothing on the issue to justify the inference that the Territories Division was an agent of the president, and the delay in the Department of Interior could not deprive the president of his veto right. Judge Snyder concurred for another reason: the law "does not require the governor to submit the bill to the president within a specific period." Associate Judge Roberto H. Todd

* Parrilla vs. Martin, 68 DPR 90. (Author's note.)

clearly saw the absurdity of the court's rejection of the district court's ruling. The other judge, Borinquen Marrero, ruled himself out because he had been one of the collegiate court judges considering the case in the district court. Thus the decision expressed the opinion of three judges, two Puerto Ricans and a North American. The plaintiff appealed to the Boston Circuit court on February 24, 1948, but gave up on March 17 for lack of funds to meet the expenses involved—which included among other things English translations of all the essential submissions and documents. But the suit did not end in that court. There was a further appeal to the U.S. Supreme Court.

No argument is necessary to understand the colonial situation revealed by the case. Here was a people compelled to go to court to legalize the use of its own language, Spanish, in the education of its children, defeated by legal technicalities and by the will and pleasure of the president of the linguistically and culturally different nation that dominated it. The case throws dazzling light on the contradictions and ambiguities of Puerto Rican collective life. The legislature asks for education in the Puerto Rican's maternal language; the governor opposes it for political reasons—for there are no pedagogical reasons; the U.S. Department of Interior, out of forgetfulness or negligence hard to explain, delays sending the bill to the president and brings on the lawsuit; the education commissioner, some of whose predecessors have introduced reforms along the same lines as the law in dispute, feels obliged to sustain the attorney general's position that the law is invalid; the U.S. president throws it out after the question has been raised in the island courts.

The confusion in which we live prevented the Puerto Rican Supreme Court from seeing the importance of the case, not only on the question of teaching in Spanish but on the incidental question which it raised: the powers of the island legislature. As Raúl Serrano Geyle points out in his analysis of this lamentable decision, the court, relying on rigid technicalities, laid down

> . . . a new limit on the functions of the legislative power. No importance was conceded to the real framework within which relations between the president and the Territories Division of the Department of Interior, and between that division and the governor of

Puerto Rico, are evolved. . . . A magnificent opportunity to make
the Puerto Rican regime more tolerable was thrown away.*

In other words, the court with its decision leaned over in favor
of the United States and against the Puerto Rican people.

On the basis of the case, the use of Spanish for teaching in
schools was administratively ordered by the educational commissioner for the 1949–1950 school year. But despite the affirmation
of this principle, which was also that of the Higher Education
Council for the university, it was still called in question in elementary and secondary teaching and was not respected in two
university faculties, medicine and odontology. In 1962 a fierce
debate arose after a new education commissioner promised to
"keep it unalterably in force" and said it was "not only good for
public but also for private schools." The problem of private
schools' right to teach in either of two languages, Spanish or
English, emerged more glaringly than ever. Many of these
schools, in the main religious, insisted they were not obliged to
teach in Spanish—a situation resulting in two teaching systems
with different tendencies and philosophies: one imposed by the
government, the other on their own initiative by private schools.
Only in a colony can a group of citizens, for the benefit of the
country dominating it, reject an educational rule which is not
merely rooted in unquestionable pedagogical principles but is the
only one assuring survival of that colony as a nation, as a subject of
history.

In 1956, eight years after the Parrilla case, the Supreme Court
again confronted the language problem.† The lawsuit arose from
a property registrar's rejection of a document in English presented by a North American corporation. He said he was under
no obligation to deal with English documents; his office required
no knowledge of that language; his staff contained no translators,
and there was no protection for third-party rights—a basic element in mortgage legislation—if a document were drawn up in a
language unknown to most people who consulted the property

* *Revista Jurídica*, University of Puerto Rico 17, no. 3 (January-February 1948).
(Author's note.)
† R.C. Communications vs. Registrador, 79 DPR 77. (Author's note.)

register. The court ruled that although Spanish was "our vernacular language," both "English and Spanish became official languages in Puerto Rico" with the 1902 law on languages to be used in the island government's departments, courts, and offices. As for the inevitable limitations on publicity imposed by use of a foreign language, these "are dissipated by the legal requirement to employ competent translators and interpreters where necessary."

This ruling, as lamentable as the one in the teaching-language lawsuit, helped deepen the confusion about the situation of Spanish in Puerto Rico. The court fell into the serious error of placing the language of the United States on the same level with Spanish, the language of Puerto Rico. The error was not offset by calling Spanish "our vernacular language," a timid admission betraying insecurity before an obvious fact: neither individually nor collectively can one put in the same category the maternal language and a foreign language—in Puerto Rico's case, Spanish and English—no matter what a law may say. This the court finally came to see in 1965. But there was no concern about the eclipse of cultural values resulting from deformation or loss of the vernacular.

As significant as the court's majority opinion were the concurring one of Judge Lino Saldaña and the dissenting one of Judge Emilio S. Belavel. The first because it showed the true reasons for the ruling, the background that explains it; the second because it expresses the criterion of those who understand the complex nature of the problem. Saldaña found that

> . . . bilingualism is an economic necessity. Any legal order impeding the free and effective use of the English language in business can only retard our economic development and smother our people's vital needs without benefiting our culture in any way. The juridical question posed by this case must not be confused with the cultural problem which consists in adding one language to another without both being destroyed.

Belavel found:

> As a matter of reality, Puerto Rico is not a bilingual community. It has not been so in the past and, following the recent rectification of

certain educational standards to the effect that the Puerto Rican's basic education must be in the vernacular language, it is less likely to be so in the future. . . . Languages belong more to a strict jurisprudence of values than to a jurisprudence of interests. . . . Languages are so closely linked with the values of moral sovereignty at the foundations of subject right, that any imposition of an official language different from the individual's natural language can become an endless source of resentment, an outcome which would not be healthy for the true goals of a political association between peoples.

The court consisted at that time of nine judges, eight Puerto Ricans and one North American.

Eight years later, in 1964, came the fourth lawsuit when a North American corporation was accused of not submitting the annual report required by law, and the firm's lawyer asked that the report be accepted in English since he was "not sufficiently familiar with the Spanish language." The public prosecutor opposed it. The judge, López Pritchard, admitted that granting the petition meant virtual paralysis of judicial proceedings since court employees knew too little English and needed everything translated; yet the law invoked by the defense—dating from 1902, and interpreted by the Supreme Court in 1956—was "so clear and conclusive" that he had no alternative. The public prosecutor, Carlos Noriega, clearly saw the consequences of the ruling and refused to accept it. "This," he said, "means the gradual undermining of our country's culture; it is a crime against the human being's basic principle of expressing himself in his own language . . . ; we are the majority; we don't see why a minority has to impose a language that is foreign to us." The words used by the judge to justify his position are exceptionally interesting. By insisting that he was not "judging an ideological question," he in fact recognized the existence of a situation in which that "ideological question" came up day after day: the struggle between Puerto Rican ideology and assimilationist ideology. A North American lawyer's right to use his language in a Puerto Rican court is just one aspect of this struggle, in which Puerto Rico's survival as a people is at stake.

The prosecutor's argument obliged the attorney general, the

Justice Department official responsible for bringing state cases before the Supreme Court, to decide whether an appeal should be lodged. Observe the odd situation in which these two officials—the attorney general and the secretary of justice—were placed when they had to support the public prosecutor's position and move against the judge's ruling. It amounted to the state calling in question the 1956 decision declaring the existence of two official languages. It showed that our dangerous ambiguity in face of vital problems was a reality in the very heart of the administration of justice. For in the last analysis, the appeal was the same as asking: what must be the language of justice in Puerto Rico?

Since I worked at that time as assistant attorney general, and the language problem always concerned me, I asked the attorney general to have me represent him in the case. Within this article's limits I will list just two of the main arguments I used in favor of Spanish as the court language: (1) that the text of the 1902 law did not have the authority with regard to the English language that the court decision in 1956 attributed to it; (2) that if the Supreme Court upheld Judge López Pritchard's ruling it would go against Puerto Rican reality. In support of the first I submitted that when the law spoke of the use "without distinction" of Spanish and English in all public offices except municipalities and municipal and police courts, it established an important and marked difference between the two languages. It decreed the use of English and Spanish only in what we might call higher-type offices employing and frequented by the more educated and prosperous classes. It confirmed Spanish as the language for offices closer to the people. It was not conceivable that the legislature would declare official a language which did not prevail in all ramifications of government throughout the country. Even in the period when the law was passed, at the outset of North American domination when many thought they could change language as easily as dress, the legislators realized it was not possible to impose total use of English on the Puerto Rican people.

In support of the second argument I submitted that the individual and collective tendency was to speak the Spanish language and concern ourselves about its conservation. Among examples of this tendency I cited the use of Spanish for teaching in public schools and in the university (with the exception of the medical and odontology faculties); the creation of the Institute of Puerto Rican Literature and the Institute of Puerto Rican Culture; the fact that laws were now drawn up in Spanish and that, despite the law of 1902, English had never been used as the official language in any island court.

On June 30, 1965, the Supreme Court, consisting of nine Puerto Ricans, unanimously pronounced Judge Pritchard's ruling to be without effect.* To avoid an open declaration that their ruling implied derogation of the law invoked by the accused corporation, and revocation of the 1956 ruling, the judges found

> that the determining factor with respect to the language to be used in judicial proceedings in courts of the Free Associated State does not arise from the law of 1902 . . . : it arises from the fact that the medium of expression of our people is Spanish, and that is a reality that cannot be changed by any law. The law of 1902 can only have guidelines authority. . . . Spanish being the language of Puerto Ricans, judicial proceedings in our courts must be pursued in Spanish.

The ruling is extraordinary for the meager juridical scaffolding on which it rests. So logical and natural did their criterion appear to the judges, so inevitable within the reality they were living in—so clearly did they see the importance and consequences of their ruling—that Byzantine language was not needed to justify it. They understood that confirmation of the lower-court position meant disappearance of the Puerto Rican lawyer and his replacement by the North American lawyer, and destruction of the Puerto Rican judicial arm of the government. They declared the existence of a reality so live and inescapable "that it cannot be changed by any law."

The ruling marked one more victory for our language: juridical sanction for what was already a fact in the judicial branch. Taken together with the administrative rule of Spanish instruction in public schools and university (despite the assimilationists' continuous onslaught), the legislative and judicial use of Spanish

* Pueblo vs. Tribunal Superior, 92 DPR 596. (Author's note.)

(with some exceptions) shows that against all efforts to implant bilingualism, the Puerto Rican won't surrender his language as easily as he surrendered his land. For the most confused among us, if he is authentically Puerto Rican, knows that his country's salvation as a people hangs on the conservation of Spanish.

It would be interesting to analyze—as space prevents my doing here—this Supreme Court decision along with that of 1948, in which misused legal technicalities prevented teaching in Spanish by law; and with that of 1956 which, placing the economic factor ahead of the cultural, sought to put English in the same category as our language and supported bilingualism.

I would say that one basic reason for this drastic turnabout was the nature of the question posed—the language of judicial proceedings. Here was the language problem touching the court on the raw, making it see clearly for the first time that the Spanish language had to be defended on all fronts; so vital was the question that the judges had to discard law to do justice. The ruling shows the judicial process in its best aspect: that behind the judge delivering verdicts stands a person knowing and feeling himself part of the society in which he lives, whose values he has to sustain.

It is impossible to exaggerate the importance of this ruling which, by what it says and how, takes in much more ground than the specific question posed. One has to believe that it closed the door on further contention about bilingualism. Yet our history since 1898 shows that bilingualism, like some mythological monster, sprouts a new head as soon as the last one is cut off. The debate on language will only end when our political destiny is decided.

Published in *Casa de las Américas* 70 (January-February 1972); reprinted in *La Opinión* (Buenos Aires), May 14, 1972

Manuel Maldonado Denis (1933–)

Professor of sociology and political science. Has contributed to many Puerto Rican and international journals on various aspects of national literature and culture. Was editor of *Revista de Ciencias Sociales* of the University of Puerto Rico. Has traveled in Europe and Spanish America.

Selected Bibliography

Maldonado Denis, Manuel. *Puerto Rico: An Historic-Social Interpretation.* New York: Random House, 1972.

————. *Puerto Rico: mito y realidad.* Barcelona: Editorial Península, 1969.

————. "Puerto Rico ante su futuro político." *Cuadernos* (Paris) 52 (September 1961).

————. "Puerto Rico: problemas y perspectivas del momento político actual." *Cuadernos Americanos* (July-August 1962).

————. "Nueva York, la ciudad más grande de Puerto Rico." *La Gaceta* (México) (February 1962).

————. "Visión y revisión de *Insularismo.*" *Asomante* 19 (1963).

————. "La temática social en la literatura puertorriqueña." *La Torre,* 11 (1963).

————. "Apuntes preliminares sobre la *intelligentsia* puertorriqueña y del Caribe hispánico." *Revista de Ciencias Sociales* (1964).

————. "Las ciencias sociales en Puerto Rico durante los próximos veinte años." *Asomante* 20 (1964).

————. "¿Declina el movimiento independentista puertorriqueño?" *Revista de Ciencias Sociales* 9 (1965).

————. "Ideologies and Attitudes among the Spanish-Speaking Intelligentsia in the Caribbean." *Social Research* 33 (1966).

————. "A Review of *La Vida* by Oscar Lewis." *Current Anthropology* 8 (1967).

————. "Situación de los intelectuales en América Latina." *Cuadernos Americanos,* (July-August 1968).

————. "The Puerto Ricans: Protest or Submission." *The Annals of the American Academy of Political and Social Science* 328 (1969).

————. *Puerto Rico y Estados Unidos: emigración y colonialismo.* México: Siglo XXI, 1976.

————. *Hacia una interpretación marxista de la historia de Puerto Rico y otros ensayos.* San Juan: Editorial Antillana, 1977.

————. *Puerto Rico y Estados Unidos: emigración y colonialismo.* México: Siglo XXI, 1976.

The Intellectual's Role
in Puerto Rico Today

To talk about the intellectual's role in here-and-now Puerto Rico is to have to take sides on the problems of our country. Why is the intellectual's position here so problematic that we are forced to discuss what his "role" should be? Could it be merely that the place of the intellectual in the world we inhabit is far from clear? What is the root of this particular question? I suggest that it lies in the conscious or unconscious abdication of intellectual responsibility by those who are now helping to mystify the problems our people face, as contributors of their undoubted talents to the Puerto Rican art of "sugar-coating the pill."

Julien Benda in a famous book spoke of the "treason of the intellectuals," meaning the intellectual bankruptcy of that part of the European "intelligentsia" who, fascinated by the prevailing irrationalism, had turned their backs on the Western rationalist tradition.* In our different context we could use the title of Benda's book to pass equally severe judgment on the Puerto Rican intellectuals who have placed personal convenience, political power, or the even more degrading pursuit of merchandising words, ahead of the critical and radical function proper (in this writer's opinion) to the intellectual.

As one who does not beat about bushes, let me say that my proposition rests on a previous political commitment and hence on an existential commitment. I do not see the intellectual's mission as removed from politics, nor do I think the university should be a "house of study" where politics is only conducted in a whisper—sometimes a murmur—with the "tonic" imprint that those interested in preserving Puerto Rico's present power structures seek to place on higher education. Everyone knows that verbal liberalism for outside consumption, as practiced by those

* *La Trahison des clercs* (19??).

289

actually holding public power in our country, has not been a mere ideology of convenience or ideological fetish but has served to mystify our colonial situation for Puerto Ricans and for the world. And why should we be surprised? Do we not find that classic exponent of liberalism, John Stuart Mill, defending in his famous *On Liberty* the tutelage (read, imperialism) of some countries over others? Then it should not startle us that his later disciples, from John Dewey and Ortega y Gasset (despite their differences), to Rexford Tugwell and Jaime Benítez, have found in the arsenal of liberal arguments not only a defense of the capitalist system but—particularly Benítez—a native justification of the metropolitan regency. Thus we cannot see the intellectual as an isolated being cut off from any connection with the human, with the all-too-human of which Nietzsche speaks, since isolation itself is already a posture—in this case, one of evasion—before the social world he has been called to inhabit. His posture, like it or not, is the result of his confrontation with the society he lives in—by way of either accepting, justifying, criticizing, or reforming it.

The reality of today's Puerto Rico leaves no room for evasion or fetishism. For let no one be deceived: Puerto Rico is not and is far from being that utopian "ultima Thule" that the well-paid press agents and mass communications at the service of imperialism would have us think. In the face of our colonial reality—in itself an insult and a threat to our integrity and identity as a people— only one posture is possible for the Puerto Rican intellectual: the critical, the radical, the iconoclastic. And this means subverting by critical analysis the personal and collective alienation directly resulting from the colonialism in our country. Or if you prefer, the Puerto Rican intellectual's job in this moment of history can be none other than the anti-imperialist one of unmasking colonialism in all its facets, showing it in its true light as it is: an economic and political system based on economic exploitation, political control of the weakest by the strongest, and cultural assimilation of the colony to the metropolis. In the face of this stark and melancholy fact the only possible position is that of struggle. The rest is nothing but mystification, fetishism, evasion, treason to the intelligence.

I think that no other country of what Martí called "Our

America" poses the problem of collective and personal alientation so agonizingly as Puerto Rico. For the intellectual unwilling to lend himself to the colonial game, alienation takes on a singularly painful form: his voice is drowned by the government-controlled communications media, by the "big press" represented by the SIP,* by the collective hysteria shamelessly stirred by Cuban exiles in Puerto Rico. At times he is weighed down by feelings of impotence. Puerto Rico is where imperialism has its firmest grip, so firm that it can allow itself the occasional luxury of an "academic" show of protest. This often drives the intellectual, in his struggle for self-expression, to stridence or shock treatment to try to awaken lethargic consciences. The struggle has to be waged on all fronts, taking advantage of every breach offered by the system itself, with continuous hammering and an implacable critique of the causes and effects of the iniquitous system that gnaws at our spirit.

Thus in my view the Puerto Rican intellectual must take as departure point for any analysis of our society the most radical and most profound fact about here-and-now Puerto Rico: its character of colony of the United States. As an additional point of departure he must take the alienating, dehumanizing effects of any colonial "status." Seen in this double light, the intellectual's commitment must be clear: a commitment to authentic, radical humanism and not to the servile and partial humanism of the "liberals," who would rationalize the presence here of an imperial boss-nation. I am not off course referring to the conservatives, the "ultras." *They* don't wrap themselves in the mantle of hypocrisy but always show themselves as what they are: those who say no to the twentieth century, the Goldwater-warmonger types dreaming of a revival of fascism. But in Puerto Rico this lot have no figures of comparable intellectual stature to the liberals. From the standpoint of the ideological, not the economic or political, struggle, lions in sheep's clothing are much more pernicious than tigers who don't conceal their stripes.

The unmasking of lions and tigers forces us into the role of the "subversive." All radical humanism such as we espouse must start

* Sociedad Internacional de Periodistas.

from a previous assumption: that one cannot accept men's professions of what motivates them without first analyzing the concrete interests behind the professions. In other words, all ideas
can be traced to a determinate interest; "abstract" principles as
such do not exist; one cannot conceive of ideology as something
separate, removed from the socioeconomic framework. What lies
concealed behind the bombastic pronouncement of the politician
or the ferocious editorial of the "big press"? Here is the mission of
the intellectual, most especially of the Puerto Rican intellectual.
For Puerto Rico is the land of concealments *par excellence*. Here
colonialism has taught us always to call things by other names,
never by their own. That is why I always remember Camus when,
referring to the war in Algeria, he said the intellectual's mission at
that time was "to clarify definitions to disintoxicate spirits, even
against the current."

This clarifying operation is appropriate here in Puerto Rico
provided that one does not claim what Camus would never have
claimed concerning Algeria: that the problem is a semantic one of
mere definitions. The intellectual cannot lend himself to that
game of semantic legerdemain in which the analytical operation
ends by creating a dusk in which all cats are gray. (Herbert
Marcuse in his book *One-Dimensional Man* has unmasked the
political implications of a philosophy like that of linguistic analysis, whose verbal gymnastics are so helpful in justifying all existing power structures. And although we have no representatives
here of this school with deeply English roots, we do have a group
of liberal intellectuals who lend themselves to the word-juggling
game.) Once the heavy machinery at their command goes into its
crushing imitation of a juggernaut, the original meaning of words
and the realities they represent disappear before a political *diktat*
as to the truth of our society and our world. The political attempt
by colonial ideologists to implant George Orwell's *1984* "doublespeak" as everyday language would be funny if it were not so
tragic. All this babel reminds one of Luis Palés Matos's lines:

> Jaula de loros tropicales,
> politiquendo entre los árboles
>
> Cage of tropical parrots
> Politicking in the trees

Like the happy intuition of someone who knew what he was talking about.

This colonial politicking—in which hollow and pompous rhetoric unites with perennial celebration of the "Alliance for Progress" and "showcase of democracy"—covers itself with a mantle of the most absurdly unfeasible ideals from our viewpoint as a North American colony. Sleight-of-hand with vital questions becomes the order of the day, while all the catchwords made fashionable by the imperialist system and its controlled "big press" are repeated *ad nauseam*. The control of propaganda and education media is such here in Puerto Rico that not even comic strips are exempt from the indoctrinating function in favor of the free-enterprise system (read, "free world"). Of course this is a continent-wide phenomenon, but our vulnerability—given our impotence—is much greater than that of our brother peoples. If there is a historic example of that "brainwashing" of which capitalist ideologists like to accuse socialism, it is Puerto Rico. One need but talk to the man in the street, subject to the most varied influences and attempts to control his thinking, to realize that the success of a system such as we endure does not necessarily depend on the use of violence (except when the system is threatened); it has sufficient economic and political means to indoctrinate whole generations in the rationalization of their own slavery.

The fact is that no purely verbal analysis of Puerto Rican society is possible unless one is willing to juggle with the real question that should concern every good Puerto Rican: the economic, military, political, and cultural absorption of Puerto Rico by the power that holds imperial sway over us. This is such a palpable, patent, and radical fact that only by total obfuscation of the critical faculties can one avoid its implications for our existence as a people. For this, neither more nor less, is where it's at. The rest is concealment and mystification of reality to serve the unspeakable ends of the country that has the power in the so-called "free association."

It may well be objected that what I have said is nothing but "politics." I concede it in advance. But I then ask: what aspect of collective life can be considered as detached from politics? Does not the intellectual have an inescapable responsibility to take political positions on the reality of our country and our world? I believe he does and that he has no alternative to "commitment." But that commitment should be understood as radical concern about man's fate and the full development of man's faculties. It implies a decision about colonialism and neocolonialism, which still strive to perpetuate the exploitation of man by man and the dominion of powerful peoples over weaker ones. It further implies that nowadays one cannot adopt a cynical-sage posture toward the world of one's time without abdicating a responsibility that goes beyond the spiritual peace of the monk: the responsibility of determined struggle to make the present world—irrational even within its bewildering rationality—more humane, more peaceful, less subject to sudden explosions that imperil the very existence of civilization.

While the colonial situation makes this responsibility especially heavy in Puerto Rico, it should be extended into solidarity with all peoples and people who are in the fight for freedom against those who would deny it. The Puerto Rican intellectual's international posture must link hands with that of countries and minorities exploited by the great colonial powers, just as long as they suffer the same evils that afflict our land. He must fully identify with the national liberation of all peoples in face of their greatest enemy, imperialism.

It is fashionable in certain Puerto Rican intellectual circles to be constantly "celebrating Puerto Rico." Participating in these celebrations are of course the communications media and the economic and political interests they represent. We have here a Puerto Rican version of what C. Wright Mills called "the American Celebration." An integral part of it is the effort to rewrite Puerto Rican history in such a way that it appears to begin in 1898 or in 1940—or perhaps those two dates are to be seen as stages that become reconciled in 1964 in a marvelous synthesis. Its daredevil acrobatics at times resembling a circus, the celebration features talk of a Puerto Rican "crossroads" where all would be *couleur de rose* were it not for a few romantic writers and liberal "traitors"; of the miraculous intervention by an envoy of Providence who descended upon us in 1940; or of the political party that monopolizes patriotism and has moved into ever higher gear the delivery of our patrimony to the economic interests of the metropolis. All these versions of "history" have one general drift, clearly political: that the average Puerto Rican should identify with the opulent societies, but above all with the world's most opulent, the United States of North America. And for this the propaganda machinery is on hand; later it will stir the aforesaid ideologists' pronouncements into a potion which will end by having us insist like the Orwellian characters that 2 + 2 = 4. With the reservation of course that the ideologists' sophisms may reach the point of assuming we believe (if this suits the imperium) that for all practical purposes 2 + 2, when considered in the light of the colony's spiritual fathers, really = 5.

Yes, there are people who want to hasten the arrival of 1984 in our country. The masters of Orwellian "doublespeak" hope to make use of the powerful machinery at their command to apply the "big lie" in the ever-fertile context of the colony. Thus, for example, the road all American peoples should follow is not the Cuban revolutionary road but that of "free association." As for the Afro-Asian peoples, they are "backward" and, as the Congo illustrates, "cannibals." We Puerto Ricans cannot, these political parrots insist, detach ourselves from the "civilizing" mission of the Anglo-Saxon countries! As creators of false awareness, as the most servile defenders of fetishisms, intellectuals at the service of colonialism do the ideological job of maintaining our country's collective alienation. "He who is incapable of ordering himself can only obey" is a well-known Nietzschean aphorism. In their obsequiousness these conscious or unconscious footmen of U.S. colonial and neocolonial policy have lost what is needed to order oneself, the fortitude to say to the oppressor: NO. So their business is obeying, servilely, as they do—although from time to time an attack of nationalist hiccups comes along to provide temporary balm for their consciences.

In this day and age the Puerto Rican intellectual cannot accept the thesis that his basic identification must be with industrially advanced countries just because, in a world closed off by our rulers' political *diktat,* a few gentlemen say so. Here too these word-merchants need to be ideologically and politically unmasked so that out of the remaining detritus may arise the shining truth kept hidden by native and metropolitan colonialists. We must tell our people that their place is with the Afro-Asian and Latin American countries which have suffered and are suffering colonialism and neocolonialism: countries that "know from inside the entrails of the monster,"* to borrow Martí's famous and here most pertinent phrase.

The job to be done is truly formidable. It implies no more nor less than confronting a whole economic, military, and political system which has infinite resources and crushing power to propagandize and coerce. But today's world offers us no alternative to ideological and political struggle against these dehumanizing, often blind forces which could put an end to civilization by consummating the holocaust. As Marcuse says, this one-dimensional and alienating society offers the intellectual no other road than "subversion" through thought. And that, as I see it, is the intellectual's mission in Puerto Rico today.

Originally published in *Asomante* 21, no. 2 (1965)

---

* The phrase is from Martí's last letter, to Manuel Mercado, May 18, 1895; see José Martí, *Our America: Writings on Latin America and the Struggle for Cuban Independence* (New York: Monthly Review Press, 1977), pp. 439-443.

Alfredo Matilla (1937–)

Born in Valencia (Spain); came as a Republican exile at age seven to Puerto Rico where he later did his university studies; obtained a doctorate at New York University. Has written critical works on Spanish, Spanish American, and Puerto Rican literature. Familiar with contemporary narrative, especially the work of Mario Vargas Llosa. Has published some stories and poems in Spanish American and European journals. He prepared an anthology of current Puerto Rican poetry, *The Puerto Rican Poets* (Bantam, 1972), together with Iván Silén. Has taught at Goucher College, Brooklyn College, and the State University of New York at Buffalo.

Selected Bibliography

Matilla, Alfredo. "Las comedias bárbaras y la guerra carlista." *Atenea* (Puerto Rico) 3 (1967).
————. "Las comedias bárbaras como una obra expresionista." *La Palabra y el Hombre* (México) 44 (1967).
————. "Las Comedias bárbaras como una sola obra dramática." In *Valle Inclán: An Appraisal of His Life and Works.* New York: Las Américas Publishing Co., 1968.
————. "La toma de conciencia en Miguel Delibes." *La Torre* 65 (1969).
————. "Los jefes y las coordenadas vargasllosianas." *El Urogallo* (Madrid) 4 (1970).
————. *The Puerto Rican Poets.* New York, 1972.
————. "El asesinato de Augusto César Sandino (1934)." *Claridad,* February 2-8, 1979.

"The Broken-English Dream":
Puerto Rican Poetry in New York

allá no hay adoquines
allá no hay castillos

there they don't have paving stones
there they don't have castles

Etnairis Rivera

Puerto Rican poets in New York can be divided into two main groups: those who write in English—born or at least raised in the United States—and those who write in Spanish, "birds of passage" in the city or people who opted for temporary exile. In either case, a discussion of Puerto Rican poetry in New York presupposes a specific political stance on the Puerto Rican experience; for the fact that nearly a third of our population is now out of Puerto Rico, and that those million-odd people use their language in the midst of a foreign culture and work situation, is the result of a special relationship between the United States of North America and our island toward which we cannot be indifferent.

The metropolitan panacea loses its magic for the Puerto Rican emigrant when he confronts classical exploitation, along with racial and cultural discrimination, in North America's sociopolitical structure. Like other colonial groups, the Puerto Ricans mainly centered in New York learn to manage the language of the country to which they must pay their tribute of labor—in this case, English. At the same time the myths and mores and culture of the Puerto Rican, transmitted perhaps through the subculture of slum or ghetto, live on as bonds with the past that liberate them in dreams from the horror of spending the strength of their hands in a place where they are completely foreign.

The New York Puerto Rican is a person displaced from his own soil and penned up in northern city barrios. He is a U.S. citizen by unilateral U.S. decree (Jones Act of 1917), but a second-class one (like the Indian, black, Chinese, and Chicano), with all the responsibilities toward the system that drinks his blood and with few of its privileges. From this confusion of worlds is born our poet of New York, traumatized by the language of the oppressor, conscious of being radically different from his surroundings. He is moved by compulsion to shape a vision of reality that records his implicit and explicit *rejection* of that other universe which is nevertheless his most immediate point of reference. For his poetry Puerto Rico signifies a unison of roots and future, the cultural heritage and the goal of liberated culture. Between these magnetic poles is the clamorous present of New York's streets and barrios and drugs and poverty:

> Spics going to the cooker
> never realizing they've
> been cooked
> Mind shook, money took
> And nothing to show for it
> but raw scars, railroad tracks
> on swollen arms
> And abscesses of the mind.*
>				Felipe Luciano

The metropolitan language shaped against the metropolis. Lapses into Spanish are frequent, as if to rest the writer's foot on his Puerto Rican floor:

> the corners full with wide-eye zombies
> of the strange parts trying to buy a night for
> themselves / mary lou & plate of mofongo / sunday
> morning / sunshine / sitting back eyes closed /
>				(Víctor Hernández Cruz)

or in search of the indigenous: *"Jíbaro,* my black beauty" (Luciano). Sometimes the mere mention of certain words keys us in to a community where Spanish is the password:

> The first Spics on the block
> Proud to belong to a community

---

* Poems in English in original.

Of gringos who want them lynch
Proud to be a long distance away
From the sacred phrase: *Qué pasa*
Pedro Pietri

The English used by the New York Puerto Rican is more significant than the interpolated phrases and words in his first language, for it is an English learned from the adaptations of other oppressed groups who came before. Thus we find cross-bred strains such as this with black slum English:

We are the real Americans
We *was* here before Columbus
We *was* here before general electric
We *was* here before the ed sullivan show
Pedro Pietri (our emphasis)

The mental agility imparted by city life, and above all the peren-nial armor-plating against the needle-jabs of the ghetto (heroin, poverty), keep them convoluted into the same linguistic intensity. Language pulled out of the asphalt, out of experience in per-petual motion:

The grocery stores were outnumbered by
Funeral parlors with neon signs that said
Customers wanted No experience necessary
A liquor store here and a liquor store
Everywhere you looked filled the polluted
Air with on the job training prostitutes
Pimps and winos and thieves and abortions. . . .
Pedro Pietri

Language with a new drive in Puerto Rican poetry, since for the first time the industrial proletarian masters the machinery of letters. The Puerto Rican poetry of New York has no academic antecedents in the Island. Its poetic roots are in music (both Puerto Rican and black), in "jive" (which stabs reality from a viewpoint repudiating the U.S. "white" world on almost all levels), in the streets, the subway, the barrios where average North Americans fear to tread. It recognizes no influence from the immortal poets, nor even from modern ones. It is a poetry hand-forged out of the anguish of enforced exile. If the immediate point of contact is the black ghetto, the core or matrix is the unarguable fact of expulsion from two worlds: the Island and the United States. The fusion of its inherent Puerto Rican, proletarian, and minority-group elements compels it to embrace everything and at the same time not to take root in any known and specific perspective—in short, to create one of the most original poetic universes in contemporary literature.

The New York poets look at the condition of their people with intemperate fury. As frequent in their work as in that of the Island poets are insults, attacks on the symbols of power, calls to armed struggle, to revolution against the oppressor:

> And when the revolution comes
> very, very soon—You shoot, and I'll shoot
> You shoot and I'll shoot, you shoot and I'll shoot—
> And unless you shoot straight,
> I'm gonna get you
> before you get yourself!
>
> Felipe Luciano

Felipe Luciano conceives his poetry as bullets speeding toward the revolutionary target. Of the three New York poets I am mentioning here, he is thematically most limited (up to now) by political slogans, because he *has* to write at times about guns and injustices. And this could take us to a cardinal problem: the marriage of art with historical reality, and the ethical justification of art. For if it is true that in capitalist societies the intellectual and the creator should be the equivalent of an ideological shock-troop vanguard, it still remains to be determined up to what point and above all how we must understand this postulate and who will be the arbiter of its limits. I don't propose to analyze this now. My sole interest is to note that in Luciano's case, I think, the party line more than once obscures the poetic line; or better said, Luciano is sometimes unable to fit his revolutionary urgency into an artistic structure that would enrich it on another level, in this case the poetic.

The verse of Victor Hernández Cruz is diametrically opposed: calibrated, calculated, literary. There is knowledge of North American lyric poetry (white and black) and of some literature that exists beyond the ghetto, like upside-down nostalgia. There is the mind of the poet. Hernández Cruz is the contact between New York's Puerto Rican poets and the foreground world. (I am not of course suggesting he is a bona fide ambassador like Piri Thomas: I refer to a vision of New York reality moistened by an earlier literary tradition.) One of his work's outstanding characteristics is the introspective line—a mobile eye that has closed in sleep after a banquet of objects. His words have direct velocity: their journey is controlled. In him the literary line eclipses social commitment. Due to the kind of introspection to which objectivity drives him, seeing things with a photographic poet's eye, his message falls short of striking a balance between poetry and the historical moment in which he lives.

Pedro Pietri's verse, on the other hand, is a subversive act. There is no political banner as with Luciano, nor self-searching as with Hernández Cruz (and remember that all of them start from rejection of the North American world). The diffuseness I find in Hernández Cruz is more a problem of essence, which I don't see as arising from this dual expulsion: there is only "poetry," and this would take us back to what we said before. Pietri maintains a strong cohesion in the community where the impossible is bound up with the incredible. He speaks the language of the subway, of the advertising that jumps at you from all sides, of the TV, of cockroaches that kill themselves leaving a seven-page typed suicide note which is the poem. He speaks the way his people in New York do. Students dig it, revolutionaries, the kids of "El Barrio" or the South Bronx, ordinary folk. His poems are subversive because for the dark world-view of the alienated they substitute a militant poetic reality, and because they prod the Puerto Rican into awareness of himself and his surroundings. It is a poetry that consumes itself with great speed, devouring itself like a suicidal firefly. Its language consists of a chain of magic metaphors, of onomatopoeic sounds and unwonted rhythms; an assault on the idea, a violation of English and Spanish with clichés turned inside out, a convulsive direction like that of the streets he visits. And through all his verses there is deep recognition of the fraudulence of things. Pedro Pietri's poetry is the first liberated proletarian creation of Puerto Rican literature. He has been able to couple the intimate with the collective, the accessible with the mysterious, the commonplace with the intricate.

The poetry written in New York in both languages shares a common basis with that of the Island: the enemy is the structure of North American power—neocolonialism and imperialism, whether exported to Puerto Rico or consumed internally. Today and perhaps since the Yanqui invasion of '98 our verse is overwhelmingly a sperm of struggle for liberation of the Puerto Rican essence. The clearest difference between the New York and the Island compositions may be that the class base from which they take off is proletarian in the former, middle in the latter. This gives rise to great theoretical problems because some current Island poets want to create proletarian literature guided by a revolutionary coordinate: that art, and above all the art of the word, should come out of the people and their historic needs and return to them—not necessarily to enlighten them (paternalism, basically elitist) but to help radicalize them within the power structure of a neocolonial situation.

This group—I refer especially to the *Guajana* and *Palestra* poets*—*seeks* simplicity of ideas, rhythms, themes; *has to seek* a vocabulary cleansed of the politico-poetiç rhetoric which has characterized our literature in this century till now; and *proposes* to reach the worker, the people. They require the marriage of theory and practice. And they achieve it, although at times the poetic slogan is above the reality-flight conjunction. This is because literature in Puerto Rico has always been, and still is, the heritage of the bourgeois classes. Of course I speak not of anonymous verse but of what appears in books and journals. The creative person on the Island has a double battle: against external political oppression (both by foreigners and by their Creole agents) and against the internal bonds that would hold him in a predominantly petty-bourgeois tradition of literary militancy.

The Puerto Rican poet in New York, on the contrary, writes from *within* the dispossessed classes and speaks particularly to them. Thus his language sprouts from the very convulsion of the street; it has already reached the readers or hearers *before* being put into verse. In this sense the poetry of Felipe Luciano and of Pedro Pietri, more than the others', takes on its deepest dimen-

* Groups of young poets and their journals. See introduction, pp. 11-42.

sion when read aloud before the popular groups that have made it possible. It is a poetry of the people that never leaves the people: it begins there and it returns there. Thematically the poets writing in English do not try to embrace political abstractions. The urgency imposed by the barrio has frontiers in the rivers that cut Manhattan. The immediate enemies are those that destroy man here and now: the daily violence, vertically imposed; the drug pusher, the police, the storekeepers selling garbage on installment, the professional politico, etc. One of the few times when this "antipoetry" addresses itself to an ideal is Luciano's poem to the *jíbaro*, in which he exalts the Puerto Rican essence through its peasantry. But this is the need for roots, the return to beginnings—to the island countryside—of the Puerto Rican emigrant to the United States.

Those who write in Spanish have as it were one foot in the poetry of the Island and the other in the estrangement of their New York-raised circle. (I don't mention here those writers who compose verse detached from their historical moment, nor those who put poems together by quantitative accumulation of lines.) The Puerto Rican poet living in New York "exile" feels the pressure of language in a different way from the one staying in the Island. He launches an attack on reality which is also an irruption into Spanish from the starting point of real Puerto Rican speech. On the whole (excepting the *Victor Campolo* of Luis A. Rosario Quiles and some poems by Billy Cajigas) poetry within Puerto Rico seeks a more or less constant equilibrium between academic or dictionary Spanish and the language of the Caribbean street. It avoids mixing in English words and anglicisms although these are common usage among most of the country's social strata. There is a reason for this. Ever since the North American occupation, Puerto Rico has had to protect (better, defend) its culture— its language—in every imaginable way against the assaults of transculturization spurred by neocolonialism. In this sense the struggle has been exemplary. But it is also true that today, some generations after the defenders of New York the other metropolis's language and customs took the road to Hispanicization, Spanish in Puerto Rico has undergone a series of changes whose consequences can't be foreseen. Perhaps they are not yet irrever-

sible but they constitute at this moment a truth of our people that
must be mastered and analyzed from all possible points of view.
Due to the proximity of English, both directly and through the
Spanish of a million-odd Spanish-speaking New Yorkers, the
"exiled" poet, while retaining deep in memory the speech forms
of his island past, picks up from daily life the speech that is all
about him without fear of thinking himself either more or less
colonized. The word of the invader is turned against him. In this
the poets in Puerto Rico and those in New York make clear
contact. Both use the language as if they were consuming it; both
confer various levels of meaning on words; both want to violate
the idiom, in the one case moving toward the Puerto Rican and in
the other away from the English:

> y descubro que el insomnio
> se está burlando desde el radio
> como si yo fuera el señor banquero
> ja-ja ja
> y no me gustan los ojos sin esprines.

> and I find that insomnia
> is being made fun of on the radio
> as if I was Mister Banker (ha-ha-ha)
> and I don't like springless eyes.*
>   Iván Silén

> . . . trying to forget
> english as I remind myself
> I never did speak english . . .†
>   Victor Hernández Cruz

The New York verse in Spanish, like the latest in Puerto Rico
and that written in English, abounds in obscenities, insults,
tabooed words, the language of gutter and ghetto. The change in
vital intellectual perspective, the contact with different political
ideas, thrust into this overseas work an idea of poetic material
which must necessarily reflect these new trails. Julia de Burgos
made this clear in her New York verses before she died.

---

* Spanish in original.
† English in original.

Another tie binding them to the *Guajana* and *Palestra* poets is their social background: all from the more or less successful middle class, all university-educated. But perhaps because they are a bridge between extremes and have access to other experiences, the "exiles"—bourgeois by birth and education—see political commitment as also a militancy of language and poetic structure, to advance the reconciliation of the Puerto Rico and New York poles. This in no way means that a poet like Silén thinks English will some day become the language spoken by Puerto Ricans, far less that that would be desirable. But it does show the awareness of these poets that the changes in Puerto Rican culture since 1898 point in a direction ever more remote from the "pure" Hispanic. It is precisely in this "impurity" that our roots are to be found—from the moment when the first Taíno fell, from the moment when the first African was shoved on to our shore and when Sotomayor and Guanina united their banners.* If three million Puerto Ricans say *suiche* for the light switch, our literature doesn't necessarily have to say *interruptor;* if we say *parquear* for car parking, we don't have to write *aparcar.* What is bad is not the use of anglicisms, or of neologisms taken from Uncle Sam's hat, but the notion that we must put these words into our poetry because there is no other way to grapple in literary form with our reality. North American cultural penetration is such that it reaches into the popular imagination, and it is there that the living language of the street is born.

Here let us note that while working-class Puerto Ricans use words taken from English—but always Puerto Rican-ize them, changing them into our Spanish—the middle and upper classes, more subject to colonialism of the mind, transplant English words and whole phrases into Spanish with the greatest of ease. This linguistic castration has an impact on our culture, but it is the product of our bourgeoisie's imitative affectations. The popular strata in our island intuitively resist such cultural penetration. One must say that the battle for Puerto Ricanhood against assimilation by the United States is cause for amazement, for after

---

* Refers to the legend of the Indian woman who falls in love with the conquistador and betrays her people.

seventy-three years of exploitation and military, economic, and political intervention, Puerto Rico still expresses itself in its own Spanish and still clings to its traditions and customs. The big changes up to now have been economic: from an agrarian colonial system to a capitalist one of consumption (Puerto Rico, some 39.5 miles broad and 106 long, is the *fifth largest international market* of the United States of North America) from which a great number of workers have to emigrate to the metropolis, hungering for better economic conditions.

The "exiled" poets point to their linguistic-social reality not from the perspective of smiling fealty, but as testimony of what we hope will one day be considered a parenthesis of less than a century when we learned many useful things and how to reject many others. What will survive of this flirtation with suicide we don't know, but the poets of New York attest to the fact that it is there, it exists; and they do so with a more violent language than the poets on the Island, where resistance to English by progressive groups takes on crusade dimensions—with reason, as I have explained—though it sometimes means distorting the cultural reality of the Puerto Rican.

Among the poets writing in New York, the only one keeping a more or less "hispanic" vision of the language is Iris M. Zavala (1936–). The others, Jaime Luis Rodríguez (1936–), Iván Silén (1944–), Angel Luis Méndez (1944–), and Etnairis Rivera (1949–), are rooted in the Puerto Ricanhood of our day-to-day Spanish. Zavala's themes go with the structure of her language: internationalization of protest, revolution on all possible fronts and in all possible epochs:

> Nunca conoceré tu rostro
> mis palabras no apagarán
> el ruido de los aviones y las bombas
> no veré el mundo que defiendes
> > guerrillero de Vietnam
> > de Cuba
> > de Bolivia
> Miguel Cruz, Eric Zamora, Li Tuan Quynh . . .
>
> I will never know your face
> My words won't silence

the noise of the planes and the bombs
I won't see the world you defend
 guerrillero of Vietnam
 of Cuba
 of Bolivia
Miguel Cruz, Eric Zamora, Li Tuan Quynh . . .*

Of these poets, Zavala is the one who most puts the reader in mind of certain schools of Western verse. Linguistically and thematically she avoids nationalist introspection and, with that, the backward leap into nostalgia. Hers is a poetry that always looks ahead or is set in the universal historical preterite.

Angel Luis Méndez's verse speaks of New York, of the present, the daily round. He builds words into constructions with roots in a naked feeling of the Puerto Rican's radical solitude in a city that is doubly accursed—by the violence of its composition, and because it is the metropolis that destroys us. Of them all, Méndez is the most introspective, the least "narrative":

> tratar de poner la mano sobre todos los sueños quedos y sin nombre regresar por las noches al vacío que producen las tardes de sol cuando penetran a los rincones donde se quedó en cuclillas una espera, un recado, una llamada, un vaso de ron, una nota en la puerta sin timbre, la bicicleta . . .

> try to put one's hand on all the quiet and nameless dreams return at night to the emptiness that the afternoons of sun produce when they penetrate the corners where a hope remains squatting, a message, a call, a glass of rum, a note at the door without a stamp, the bicycle . . .

In contrast, Etnairis Rivera and Iván Silén write a basically narrative verse in which things are told, tales of poetical plunges into external reality (New York), or into the past (childhood days in Puerto Rico), or into myth (Silén's recent ventures into classical mythology). Narrative is perhaps more evident in Etnairis Rivera, as can be seen in his long poem "Letter to Manuel." These poets

---

* For a more thorough understanding of these poets, A. Matilla and Iván Silén, *The Puerto Rican Poets* (New York: Bantam Books, 1972) and Roberto Márquez, *Latin American Revolutionary Poetry: A Bilingual Anthology* (New York: Monthly Review Press, 1974).

sing the recovery of the world of the past, of the language of a whole epoch, and the search for the language of today connected by constantly shuttling planes, in unison with the ineluctable presence of the Puerto Rican in New York and his struggle for liberation.

Silén starts out from a revolution-committed vision shot with anarchistic individualism. His verse is a mixture, with varying doses of the very intimate and the very public. His images, like Pietri's, rediscover the prodigal magic of things; but Pietri, detaching the magic from the things, winds up in surrealism, while Silén looks at reality through spectacles fogged by Trotsky and Breton. This brings us back to the difference of social and cultural context between the two groups. Silén's language echoes the talk in the street. He explores the creative possibilities of the rhythm and syntax used both by ordinary people and by sophisticated Latin American poets. (The same goes for Jaime Luis Rodríguez. His work, in which he is very hard with himself, brings out the anguish of Puerto Ricans beneath the colonial incubus.)

Puerto Rican poetry in New York oscillates between the extremes of Spanish and English, as does the fate of Puerto Rico itself in this hour. The synthesis will be national liberation, the day when Puerto Ricans will no longer be split between the imposition of colonialism and the agony of the metropolitan slum—the day when we awake from this dream in broken English.

Revista Instituto Estudios Puertorriqueños (Brooklyn College) 1 (1971)

Eneida Vázquez

Eneida Vázquez is a professor at the School of General Studies, University of Puerto Rico, and president of the Consejo Puertorriqueño de la Paz.

Union Organization of Women in the Puerto Rican Labor Force

In Puerto Rico women began joining the forces of production on a massive scale in the first decades of the twentieth century. This was not due to a momentary discovery by big capitalist entrepreneurs of how unfair they had been to women by restricting them to the narrow confines of domestic life, as they had been in previous centuries when our society was predominantly agrarian. The new needs of the capitalist system brought women into employment in the needle and tobacco industries at starvation wages. The greater integration of women into the country's productive forces was an essential characteristic of the accelerating industrial process in Puerto Rico. It was a development typical of capitalist and industrializing societies, with the result that today the female half of humanity produces a third part of material goods.

However, it rested upon the great contradiction of maintaining discrimination against and inequality of women. While they were brought into the productive forces, society did not create the necessary mechanisms and adjustments such as adequate child-care centers, laundries, cafeterias, etc., as required by the new situation of women leaving their homes to work. The result has been double exploitation of the woman: as a worker, in the sense that she shares with male work mates the exploitative situation to which all labor is subjected, and as a woman, since she is paid less for the same work; there is prejudice against hiring married females; and she is penalized for something that is essential to her nature—motherhood—so that she faces the incredible situation of a 50 percent wage cut just when she needs more to meet higher family expenses. An interminable list. But along with this exploitation as a worker goes the exploitation in the home, which she suffers by virtue of being female. Thus we have the woman's double burden: a worker in the shop and a worker at home.

Although no constitutional right to work exists in Puerto Rico (remember what the U.S. Congress did with the famous Clause XX of Article 11 of the draft constitution "reported" by the Puerto Rican Constitutional Convention, which included the economic rights of citizens), we hold that every human being should have it without sexual or any other distinction. As concerns women, this has to be clarified, for there are many myths about why women work. It is commonly said that a woman works because she wants to and not because she needs to. If we start from the premise that every human being should have the right to work, and furthermore that it is each citizen's responsibility to contribute to social production according to capacity, the point of view changes. All women capable of working should do so, as should men. In a society like ours, which does not instill in its citizens the value and dignity of work, the overwhelming majority of women work not because they want to or because they see it as a citizen's duty, but out of economic necessity: the continual rise in the cost of living and low pay make the woman's wage essential to maintain the home. The woman has the function of providing for the home as her man has. But her contribution to the home finances is little appreciated and tends to be minimized. There is an attempt to sell the notion of a frivolous, superficial female who works only to buy herself a lot of cosmetics and pretty clothes, and to disregard the economic situation that compels her to work whether she wants to or not.

In general, it should be noted, women's incorporation in the labor force has not displaced men. An important fact, for one of the most effective antiworker weapons is divisionism, the fomenting of resentments between sectors of the labor movement, in this case between men and women. In large part the jobs taken by women, apart from generally being less well paid, are jobs that one might describe as an extension of the role our society assigns to women: nursing, teaching, secretarial work, various service tasks, and light industry like the needle trades.

There is another very revealing fact to illustrate social patterns in Puerto Rico and how these impede women's integration into the productive forces and limit their development. It concerns the civil status of Puerto Rican women workers. Statistics from 1971 show that the highest work participation by women is by the group aged 20-24, and from there it begins to decrease. A possible explanation of this is that family-life pressures and the increase of children force women to retire from the labor market, at least for a few years.

The fact stands out that the participation rate of single women—unmarried or divorced—is considerably higher than that of married women. The highest participation in 1971—47.6 percent—was that of divorced women, followed by married women with absent husbands (26.8 percent) and with present husbands (22.7 percent). The lowest participation was by widows (9.6 percent). We find these figures impressive, and many factors need consideration in analyzing them. The divorced group in the labor force was almost twice as large as the next highest group. We might conclude that the divorced woman is free to decide if she will work or not, or that she has no option since her economic situation as an independent person forces her to work.

Many arguments about this problem, which we cannot go into here, could be advanced. But the much higher percentage of divorcees in the country's labor force is what springs to attention. One way or another it means that family life as it is structured in Puerto Rico—the man-woman relationship and the subordination of woman to man—is a weighty factor in the woman's possibilities of work.

The figure for the next highest group, married women with absent husbands, strengthens the argument. It seems that with respect to integration in the labor force, having or not having a husband makes a big difference. This reinforces the fact that on the labor-union level, a great proportion of the women members who actively commit themselves to specific tasks are also divorced. Among other factors, what clearly makes the big difference is whether a woman has a man who restricts her initiative and ties her down to home responsibilities.

We would underline the point made above, that the problem we are dealing with rests upon a terrible contradiction. On the other hand, the Puerto Rican labor movement confronts the enormous difficulty and necessity of organizing our workers into unions. Among those workers is the female sector, scattered through various industries, businesses, agencies, and work centers. It is in this context that discriminatory practices against women, our prejudices and incorrect attitudes toward the female sector, operate negatively against our unions' efforts to organize women. One result is that the mentality and attitudes fostered in female workers, which most male workers see as so positive and seek to perpetuate, become a sometimes insurmountable obstacle to more effective organization of the working class. Said in another way, this mentality turns women into one of the boss's prime weapons to hold back the workers' struggle for their social and economic rights. In this context women could become the great antilabor reserve of the boss and of the capitalist system in general.

It is important that the leadership of Puerto Rico's organized labor movement become aware of this problem and take correct attitudes and positions in their practice, overcoming old antifeminist prejudices. We know that this is far from an easy task. We also know—it is an obvious fact—that until now that leadership has been and is almost exclusively male, with a few honorable exceptions. For example, we know of very few women who are presidents of unions. The preeminent maleness of the labor leadership imprints its male stamp on the trend of the working class, contrary to the best in   ests of the female sector.

This is a sad reality, although in many of our unions most or a good part of the membership is female, sometimes with an extraordinary fighting spirit, as in the case of telephone workers. Yet the directing bodies, the state or national steering committees, call them what you will, are overwhelmingly composed of males. Of course we must add that this is not an exclusively labormovement phenomenon but typical of all Puerto Rican society. The basic premise behind it, let us not forget, is that in our country as in many others we women have been conditioned to feel inferior, dependent, secondary, docile, and complementary to men, never as equal and capable human beings. Thus we have been taught to see ourselves and thus men have seen us.

When we speak of union organization, we refer to the unions' efforts to achieve representation of the employees by a group qualified to bargain collectively, mainly regarding terms and conditions of work. But before that representation is obtained, the problem of organizing the workers must be tackled.

Apart from the boss's brutal pressure, the chief obstacle to this process is the workers' lack of class consciousness. Many are not aware that the jobs they hold and the pay they receive are due to their own exertions and not to the boss's generosity. Within this line of thought many never grasp the fact of the abysmal conflict between their interests as workers and the boss's interests, and don't understand how the boss lines his pockets by the sweat of the workers while always opposing pay raises and improvements in wages and working conditions. For that reason, as long as he can deal with each worker individually without the strength that a union gives, he will try by all means to do so.

This lack of class consciousness in many working-class sectors is very similar to what happens with the women, who, despite their double oppression as workers and as women, are for the most part unaware of it—so that many women are first to defend their own oppressive situation.

Combined with the fact that there is no consciousness of the value of labor, since workers believe they owe their well-being to the boss, lack of class consciousness makes it very difficult to sell the union to the workers. Yet no matter how softly the message is expressed, in reality the seed of class consciousness and conflict of interests is being sown.

When it comes to women the situation is much worse. The woman is conditioned to be passive and submissive: she is trained from birth to submit to the man in authority, starting with the father, the brother, the sweetheart, the husband, and in our case the boss. The picture becomes far more complicated when the problem of female submission to the authority-figure is added to lack of class consciousness and of consciousness of the value of labor. For example, signing the union card would be an act of rebellion against the authority-figure. How could a submissive creature do such a thing?

Linked to the problem of submission to the authority-figure is that of credibility. Whom should the working woman believe: the boss, who is her authority-figure and to whom she thinks she owes her job and well-being, or the labor organizer who attacks him and his authority?

Supposing, however, that she has been moved by the organizer's message; the problem arises that women don't take decisions by themselves without consulting the authority-figure at home, the husband. If the husband is prounion, sometimes there is no problem; but we must say "sometimes" because many men don't see what is good, natural, and right for them as being good for their wives. If the husband is antiunion, the union probably has no chance whatever of convincing the wife.

Apart from the initial obstacles to women signing up, when the boss begins fighting with all he has against the union and the workers sympathetic to it, women are much easier than men for him to dissuade. This does not mean that men are not also scared off by the boss's pressure, nor that many women don't stand their ground before his attacks. Our point is that due to her particular mental traits and the role our society assigns to her, the woman is much more likely to give in.

Another factor to consider is that there are areas in the Island where the male unemployment rate soars because the kind of industry established there requires what is called female labor; so that you have the woman working while the man is idle. This situation, doubling the woman's load by making her the sole provider on top of her responsibility for home chores and minding the children, has great implications for the whole problem, apart from the devastating psychological effects on the man of feeling he contributes nothing to the home.

In these cases the woman's wage is the only source of income so that, if she loses her job, there is nothing to sustain the family. Remember that in our society the woman is raised to understand that the family is her special function and her role as mother and wife takes precedence over everything: that being her life's basic mission, her main responsibility is the security of the family, and it becomes much heavier when this security depends on her own economic contribution. In such cases even women who are for the union don't support it for fear of being fired and endangering the family's economic security.

With this general outline of the problem, we may ask ourselves: what can the labor movement do about it? Our point of departure is that with some exceptions the leadership of the movement, as we have pointed out, is overwhelmingly male. Let us start by suggesting that the *compañeros* and *compañeras* generate their own discussion of the problem, facing up to both the personal and the collective contradictions involved. This discussion should address itself to the question: to what extent is the development of the labor movement, and of the whole process of transforming our society's political and socioeconomic bases, affected by discrimination against women and the usage of boxing them into certain roles and tasks? We believe we have given ample illustrations of this point.

Secondly, following this line of thought, it is imperative to develop a well conceived and planned campaign to incorporate women in the various leadership levels of the labor movement. It is not enough to accept certain points among the overwhelming realities before us. It is not enough to accept a theory: the policy of bringing women into the movement must be demonstrated in practice. We submit that as part of the Puerto Rican labor movement's strategic goals for the next years, this matter should be given its proper importance—especially when, as we have seen, women can potentially become the great antilabor reserve of the bosses and of the whole capitalist structure in Puerto Rico.

Here we must face up to the objection raised by many *compañeros*, that it would be incorrect to nominate officers for the mere fact of being women. This often-raised objection needs serious examination, for if we follow the thought behind it, save in exceptional cases, we can only conclude that the male exclusiveness we have had till now must be maintained, because women have less union experience and know-how than men. But how could it be otherwise if women have always been denied the chance to develop under equal conditions, if women have been condemned to underdevelopment in countless areas because these belong in men's exclusive domain?

The point we want to make is that, to deal with the problem, the option before the unions is to define a policy of integrating women on all levels. Not in a "token" way—look, we have a

woman and we don't discriminate—but with the seriousness the
problem deserves. It's a matter of starting to think about women
as real possibilities for different tasks and administrative posts. Of
breaking the habit of automatically considering men for certain
functions. Of providing favorable conditions and styles to promote female participation. And, given equal conditions, of pushing a woman forward for a post even though a male candidate
shows himself in some ways more qualified—remembering that
the competition she must face is an unfair competition with
centuries behind it, and that women can never catch up unless we
struggle on a high level of consciousness and with some forced
marches. We recall many nominations of men who have turned
out to be complete flops. So why not give women a chance? Or is it
that we women are more demanding, and criteria which are
applied to us are not applied to men?

The third point, an extension of the first, is that many men as
individuals show prejudicial attitudes toward women, even
toward women in their own union. Sometimes it also happens
that women have negative attitudes toward members of their own
sex who are militant and show aptitude for leadership. For this
reason it should not surprise us that when a union elects its
leaders, the women generally don't consider candidates of their
own sex, or choose to vote for males rather than for females who
have demonstrated their commitment and capacity to lead. It
would be interesting to ask many of the *compañeros* and *compañeras*
who exemplify with their commitment the defense of the working
class's true interests, whether they appraise women with the same
eyes and criteria as they do men; whether they don't often reject a
woman *a priori* as a union member or, once she is a member, as a
candidate for militant tasks; whether they don't fall into the
contradiction of preventing their own *compañeras* from undertaking such tasks in their own unions, parties, or organizations of
interest to women. This may be the most painful point since it
implies facing up to attitudes and prejudices which have been
internalized for centuries, and which are one of the sustaining
pillars of the exploitative system we live in. Hence we must lay
siege to it from every flank, starting with ourselves as individuals

and bearing in mind what the poet said, that it is in the intimacy of the home that one knows the true man.

Fourthly, we would propose a policy of naming women as organizers. We face the contradiction that even in sectors with a predominantly female labor force, the organizers are male. However, female organizers should not be installed to deal exclusively with female sectors, but also and without discrimination in male sectors. Among other things this could lead to the formation of a capacitated and committed female leadership within the Puerto Rican labor movement. The unions should at the same time develop a policy of engaging female lawyers with know-how in the labor field. With respect to women, this area is truly a desert.

Panorama, April 29-May 5, 1977; excerpts from a paper presented to a 1976 trade-union leaders' seminar on behalf of the Federation of Puerto Rican Women.

Pedro Juan Rua (1943–)

Studied at the New School where he specialized in Sociology of Politics. Professor of Social and Political Sciences at U.P.R. Has published articles in the island and the U.S.

Selected Bibliography

Rua, Pedro Juan. *Bolívar ante Mary y otros ensayos.* Río Piedras: Ediciones Huracán, 1978.

————. "León Trotsky y Puerto Rico." *Revista Pensamiento Crítico* (1978).

————. "Ideología y pseudo-radicalismo en la pedagogía y la practica de la ciencia política." *Revista ciencias sociales* (1979).

Sociological Notes on Contemporary Puerto Rico

1. What made it possible for Yanqui monopoly capitalism to transform the old relations of production in agriculture into what they are now? Any attempt to explain it would have to start by considering: (a) the world capitalist crisis ("depression" of the thirties) which, as it developed, destroyed with particular intensity the solidity of the sugar cartels; (b) the political consequences of that crisis, which objectively disorganized great petty-bourgeois and middle-class sectors and radicalized them toward nationalist positions (of fascist tendency in imperialist countries, national-liberationist in colonial countries); and (c) the clear post-"world"-war preponderance of Yanqui imperialism relative to other imperialist countries, generating the inevitable need for an immediate, aggressive expansion of the Yanqui industrial base and broadening of its captive markets.

2. The forties were the only decade in Puerto Rican history presenting the plain alternative: reform or revolution. A profound change was demanded in the social relations of production and the utilization of productive forces, given the incurable crisis of agrarian capitalism, the intensified class struggle in the countryside, and the rise of anti-imperialist nationalism. We say the "only" decade because the national movement of the nineteenth century's third quarter—the Lares movement led by Betances—did, it is true, have a revolutionary option to the extent that it could perhaps have put a sector of the Creole bourgeoisie clearly in power; but it had no real reformist option. The abolition of slavery, just and necessary as it was, did not imply deep changes in production relations since it involved what was at that time a relatively small sector of the productive forces. Thus the real alternative was stagnation or revolution.

3. The social groups led respectively by Albizu Campos and

325

Muñoz Marín were middle sectors in social decline or precarious equilibrium, in process of proletarianization or of lumpen-proletarianization (especially Muñoz Marín's) but with a significant difference. The elements brought together by Albizu were strictly speaking middle and petty bourgeoisie engaged in entrepreneurial and commercial activity and facing annihilation as a fraction of a class. Muñoz articulated the previously frustrated ambitions of intermediary elements in the liberal professions and the small technical and administrative elites to climb in the social scale. Hence, to some extent, the respective intensities of their radicalization, and hence the claim (as Juan Antonio Corretjer has always insisted) that the direction of nationalism was seriously anticapitalist; their dismemberment as a class, and the objective difficulty of their reconstitution as such, brought the Nationalist movement close to the people in a much more real sense. In this context it is interesting to contrast the social position of the Nationalist leadership in the thirties and forties with that of the largely working-class organizers and executors of the heroic military actions in the early fifties. But let us remember that while there were indeed objective elements making access to socialist study difficult for the Nationalists, that situation was aggravated by the Puerto Rican Communists' sectarian attitude toward nationalism on some occasions.

4. The change finally generated by the conjunction of national and global forces was made viable by the specific agent of the change, the Popular Democratic Party (PPD). We all know the roots of that transformation: forced "industrialization" through massive ingestion of imperialist capital in the context of global emigration of the "surplus" population toward the United States. But there is one aspect of that process which has been insufficiently stressed: the agrarian reform, which the PPD instituted in its first years of colonial administration through the 500-Acres Law and the Land Authority, and the creation of various important public enterprises (cement, glass, containers, etc.), accumulated certain social savings whose real function was to help finance the penetration of imperialist capital. The first infrastructure projects, subsidies, and loans that the PPD administration vouchsafed to the imperialists came largely out of Puerto

Rican socialized labor. This enables us to define precisely the tragicomic achievements of Muñoz Mentiras,* and to perceive once again that the weapons of public conversion of capital is only revolutionary and truly progressive when it is in the hands of workers' power, of the proletarian dictatorship.

5. It is true, as has so often been said, that the "Free Associated State" (ELA) is on the one hand a co-optative concession by imperialism to the rise of revolutionary struggle in Puerto Rico, particularly the 1950 rebellion. But at the same time—and with emphasis—ELA must be seen in the framework of its special character as a superstructure strikingly coincident with the real structure of profound changes in production relations and in utilization of the productive forces during the last quarter-century. Hence we understand the extent to which the removal of the PPD administration represents a destabilization of imperialist power itself. And this gives us some idea of the ephemerality of the PNP government† and of the small interest, in terms of foreseeable strategy, that imperialism has in effectively annexing Puerto Rico.

6. The socioeconomic performance of the "Popular Party Era" unquestionably covered a lot of ground, in terms of speed and of the class and structural changes it generated in our country. This attests to the essential nature of our epoch: it has favored Puerto Rico's transformation from a purely colonial structure of domination to a neocolonial stage of imperialist domination, maintaining the framework of classically colonial forms. That is: Muñoz Marín and popularism—again, tragicomically—brought about in Puerto Rico, without the form of independence and with none of the earned prestige of the neocolonialist leaders in Africa and Asia, some of the same changes that those leaderships implemented in the independence framework. And that is of crucial importance, since from it arises the fact that in today's Puerto Rico, colonialism (military occupation, direct juridical control, deculturation, etc.), and neocolonialism (capture of the imperial-

---

* Muñoz Mentiras literally means "Muñoz Lies," a phrase used by Pablo Neruda to describe the leader of the PPD.

† The Partido Nuevo Progresista, the party favoring "statehood," actually in government after obtaining a plurality in the 1976 elections.

ist governing apparatus by intermediary native elites which the apparatus generates, etc.) overlap in one solid aggregate, in one and the same dominating structure. To shake one is to shake the other, and vice versa: today in Puerto Rico anticolonial tasks (national unity, antimilitarism, cultural consolidation, etc.) and antineocolonial tasks (breaking the hold of industrial monopoly, worker resistance, preparation for revolutionary seizure of the state apparatus, etc.) are both equally revolutionary and of equal priority. Anticolonialism and struggle for socialism are today objectively two distinct currents within one and the same process, and this suggests the source of the essential difficulty of rooting the neocolonialist versions of independentism (mainly PUP) among the masses: historically speaking, neocolonialism is a stage that begins to grow obsolete in Puerto Rico. The political programs of Antonio González*—though unfortunately he doesn't see it—were carried out by Muñoz a quarter-century ago. Further to be noted is the growing immediacy that the transition from independentism to socialism is acquiring on the ideological level, and here we find the explanation.

7. Puerto Rico in the seventies is a society showing all the indices and contradictions of a bourgeois neocolonial formation of great development, in the sense that almost all possible "advanced" forms of monopolist expansion and domination have been manifested here (petrochemical complexes, expansion of insurance corporations, massive penetration of publicity and propaganda enterprises and of automated complexes on all levels). As has been broadly recognized, this implies that the struggle against imperialism in Puerto Rico has assumed great universal significance and will do so increasingly; and the Puerto Rican revolutionary experience will have very special educational relevance for the progressive forces not only of many dominated countries but of the imperialist countries themselves. The new class formation generates the most fertile soil for this process: (a) dominated proletarian and salaried urban classes already exceeding 50 percent of the working population (see U.S. Population

* Antonio (Toño) González, leader of the PUP, which attempted, until its demise, to develop a fully pro-United States "sovereigntist" movement.

Census, U.S. Bureau of the Census, *General Social & Economic Characteristics of Puerto Rico* and the various writings of *compañero* Angel Agosto); (b) a growing professional sector in process of proletarianization (see *U.S. Population Census y Nueva Lucha,* 1970); (c) a numerically large entrepreneurial and commercial petty bourgeoisie, increasingly anti-Yanqui and beginning to move closer to the revolutionary movement. The explosive potential of this situation stands out if we note that, speaking precisely, no labor aristocracy has taken shape in Puerto Rico, partly due to the skimpy unionization of workers in the Popularist period. Trade-union colonialism indeed exists in Puerto Rico, but it suggests more a juridico-political than a sociological phenomenon. Keith Terpe, Agustín Benítez, Efraín Velázquez, and their hangers-on are a wretched handful of stooges representing no cohesive formation whatsoever.*

8. It is urgent to define more precisely the role of the ex-Cuban exile community and where it fits into the social structure of today's Puerto Rico. This is no mere ethnic or foreign pressure group. Nor is it a community whose members, existing on various economic levels, occupy various positions in the class structure (*gusanos†* of the bourgeoisie, petty bourgeoisie, proletariat, etc.). Such a haphazard classification might imply expectations that these groups would move in the same direction as these classes, with some sectors joining the struggles for our country's rights. The ex-Cubans, over and above any internal differences, form a community *sui generis* which acts and will act in a body as an intermediary of capitalist domination. It is furthermore unlikely that the next generation of *gusanos* can become significantly acclimated or Puerto Ricanized. As a colleague recently pointed out, this is not an emigrant community but an exiled one: it comes not like others to build a new world and a new life for itself, but to establish a beachhead from which to try to reconstruct and restore a world that is lost. For that purpose it has set up in a very

---

*A small group of trade union spokesmen, mainly from the Seafarers' International Union, who attempted unsuccessfully to organize a broad anti-nationalist union movement.

†Literally,"worms" revolutionary Cuba's term for its counterrevolutionaries. (Translator.)

short time a well-articulated complex of institutions of all kinds, merging almost all of its members into a social amalgam like a special subculture. Tentatively, for what it is worth, we suggest that the social category of people-class, with whom Marx sought to explain the Jewish community's position in the capitalist development of Europe, might throw some light on the situation. The Jews' competitive, saving, inventive, technical, and planning skills—the substantial patrimony from the peculiar experience of the Disapora, their historic exile—enabled them, although they were primarily a cultural formation, to occupy a particular class position. In the same way the exiled ex-Cubans, likewise a primarily cultural formation but endowed to a considerable extent with these skills, collectively support imperialist relations of production and execute, transmit, or become a filter for exploitation; they play in this sense a class role in their relation with the productive forces. They are certainly not a "people-class" on the mode-of-production level, nor a primary determinant of the dynamic of conflict and change in our society, but perhaps they are indeed one on the level of our concrete social formation. If these considerations correspond at all to reality, it means that our country's revolutionary forces cannot wait until the Day of Judgment to elaborate a systematic policy against this group. In our country few Puerto Ricans have not had oppressive, discriminatory, or humiliating experiences with this group, and the consequent resentments run deep. To the same extent that the imperialist masters are not a direct presence for many Puerto Ricans, the latter experience oppression as coming primarily from the *gusanos*. The policy to be devised by the revolutionary forces must then be aimed at mobilizing this experience to help explain the overall situation of imperialist domination, in which the *gusanos* play a key role as economic, ideological, and (let us not forget) armed spearhead. In years to come the intermediary crust of ex-Cubans—especially in the framework of any eventual openings between revolutionary Cuba and the Yanqui state—will become more belligerent and will attempt to strike against the struggles for our country's rights (we have had a foretaste of this in the attack against the Conference on Puerto Rico and the

Caribbean in New York).* So we should be on our toes; and although there is some danger of a small war, let us consider the possibility that it could invigorate us and hasten the resolution of the "big war." Also we must bear in mind the undeniable connection between the ex-Cuban exiles and the massive proliferation of the drug traffic in our homeland—a much more serious cultural and economic contamination than we like to realize, and which we also have to confront. To make our position quite clear, let us stress that our policy toward the ex-Cubans must be based on the revolutionary principle that, regardless of his national origin, any foreigner who genuinely participates in the struggles for our rights is and will be a Puerto Rican co-national.

9. Seen from the perspective of the tremendous class-structure transformation during the Popularist era, the lack of mass support for the independentist ideology in the fifties and sixties becomes more comprehensible. On the one hand the radicalized rural proletariat of that time (which undertook such memorable actions) and the nationalistic campesino sectors,. in the course of their forced transition from country to city, underwent a new process of disintegration and dismemberment as classes to reappear in a different structural situation. It was not then to be expected that, given the precariousness and difficulty of the sudden change, they would maintain their previous levels of consciousness and radicalization. The historic conjuncture of neocolonialist industrialization in Puerto Rico inevitably produced a cultural rupture among the masses on every level which, during a certain interim, kept them from perceiving and critically reflecting on their concrete conditions of existence. The new occupational and generational set-up had to be more or less completed before the people's national and social conscience could really take on new life; this began to solidify in the early sixties. At the same time the middle strata, petty bourgeois, "professionals" and so on, along with the student elements who now increasingly support the national-liberation and socialist movement, were for concomitant reasons still in process of gestation.

* An important symposium on Puerto Rico, organized by U.S. progressives, where several books were placed by an admittedly "gusano" group.

10. With the end of the PPD administration in 1968, a considerable sector of independentism, especially of the PIP, began posing "polarization" as the key to eliminating centrist positions in our country. We regarded this appraisal as overhasty at the time, for the precise reason that the PNP could only maintain its predominance by effectively occupying the "free state–ist" position. This is so because—and we socialists must get it through our heads once and for all—Yanqui imperialism is not strategically interested in the foreseeable future in integrating Puerto Rico as a "state of the nation." Such an objective would be much less congenial than the present situation to the Yanqui imperialist monopolies' desire for superextraction of surplus value, since "statehood" would impose local and federal tax contributions, the extension of federal minimum-wage legislation, some federal control over the use of capital, "ecological" control, etc. There is not and has not been in recent Puerto Rican history any annexationist party with decisive Yanqui support; indeed, national socioeconomic and political groups of any kind insisting on "state-ist"demands are quickly called to order by imperialism, if their positions show any likelihood of prevailing in the country. Among the first to become aware of this was Luis A. Ferré.* If the Ponce pseudohumanist immediately dropped his platform "promise" of a plebiscite, it was when it was pointed out to him that this was a blind alley; for had the annexationist proposal prevailed "democratically," the PNP would have fallen into serious discredit before the inevitable Yanqui negative. Particularly for imperialism this situation was dangerous, since it would have unmasked before the country the character of its neocolonial domination and deep contempt for "democratic" wishes, and could have stirred an intense nationalist reaction by the people. Of course—we won't deny it—our present tie with the United States, within a federal machinery retaining a certain degree of autonomy from the economic base, always leaves open the possibility of annexation. True, also, that in terms of support, imperialism always plays two or more party cards through one or another of its many political financing agencies.

* An important industrialist, leader of the Statehood Party, and governor of Puerto Rico 1968–1972.

Nevertheless, today and for the visible future, imperialism prefers to quarantine the casinos rather than play any but the face-up card, that is, the Jack of Clubs of Trujillo Alto.*

Thus the essential objection to annexationist ideology is that it is really an illusion, a phantasmagoria, an imaginary probability. And this is precisely what gives it its profound ideological character in the Marxist sense: a veil, a screen, a crude mask for the exploitative relations in which we all live. In sum, it is an irrational mentality which permits certain middle and upper-middle strata to soothe and alleviate their painful class insecurity and to rationalize their authoritarian character-structure and their inferiority complex. It is in these sectors that annexationism retains important support; among native groups of the high corporate bourgeoisie, who are in tune and in perfect time with imperialism, such support is comparatively rare. So oppressive is imperialism—and thus we must put it to the people for their enlightenment—that *it is not* interested in any kind of assimilation of our people: not to federal political institutions (remember the stillborn idea of the presidential vote), not to the dominant Anglo-Saxon culture. Cultural assimilation is certainly a category applicable in some senses to the intermediary native elites and bourgeoisie, who find that "good American" thinking and values are useful to them. At the same time, dialectically, it is from some of these sectors that some disaffection arises (a live example, Eladio Rodríguez Otero, et al.)† with the watchword of strict antiassimilationism which has positive mobilizing value for those sectors. But it is not a category applicable to the people. The people are not subjected to assimilation but to deculturation, to the plundering of their national and historical consciousness and its substitution not by the dominant Yanqui classes' values, attitudes, and norms of conduct (calculating competitiveness, aggressive egoism, mastery of the Anglo-Saxon language, awareness of civil rights, esthetic pseudohumanism, appreciation of the value of aristocratic intimacies and of unproductive idleness, utilitarianism, trivialization of convictions, erotism, religiosity, etc.), but by

* Luis Muñoz Marín.
† A well-known "hispanista" intellectual, former president of El Ateneo, an important traditional cultural institution. He died recently.

an amorphous and dislocated structure of values and morals which absorbs like an indiscriminate sponge the accumulated irrationalities of that system; which swallows or vomits, as the case may be, the concoctions dictated by ideological propaganda and publicity mechanisms. That is to say, a vacuum on the cultural level, period. That is what is intended, not "acculturation" or "transculturation." From this perhaps springs our peculiar sensation of lack of identity.

To recapitulate: recapture of the colonial administration by the PPD is, from whatever perspective, in greatest consonance with the stability of imperialist objectives and seems, from the look of things, to point toward disintegration of the annexationist current and thus to a probable ultrareactionary tendency in some PDP sectors. This could show itself in a link-up of these sectors with the violent assaults against the national movement, in harness with the ex-Cuban community. Yet even if the fleeting rise of the PNP were not a mere political breeze, that brief episode will have been important, as has repeatedly been said, in helping to weaken attitudes of paternalistic, fuehrer-accepting dependency among the people (examples of which we have recently seen very close to us) and impressing the people with a sense of their own power. This is one of the secondary variables explaining why the people are getting nearer to a critical attitude, to the posing of political questions, and to an opening to possible change.

Marcia Rivera Quintero

Marcia Rivera Quintero is a sociologist and president of the Center for the Study of Puerto Rican Reality. Her work focuses on slum formation in Puerto Rico and the incorporation of women into the labor force. She has published many articles in Puerto Rican newspapers and magazines.

Puerto Rican Women in the Economic and Social Processes of the Twentieth Century

With the introduction of capitalism as the dominant mode of production in Puerto Rico, the process of incorporating women into economic, political, and social life began too, in proportions unparalleled in the previous centuries of our history. Nevertheless, this process did not produce a situation in which women were considered the equals of men in rights and duties. In fact, new forms of domination arose which we should examine and counter.

It is not easy to reconstruct the historical processes through which the incorporation of women into social and economic life was produced. Our history, even recently, is a history in which women are absent, when a woman appears it is in exceptional situations, where a woman or a group of women stand out for some special reason. And while this is true in relation to the processes that have occurred in the twentieth century, it is much more tortuous to try to seek out our women in the history of the nineteenth century or earlier. As a consequence, the reconstruction of these historical processes is a slow, tedious, but fascinating task. Those women among us who have decided to undertake it have had to begin with an analysis of the most basic data regarding our economy, and have had to examine incomplete and rather general statistical sources prior to presenting some hypotheses concerning these processes.

In this preliminary study, we should like to begin by sharing some findings of research that is still in progress; therefore, it will frequently be the case that we will not present clear, precise, and definitive explanations of many of the processes we have begun analyzing. Furthermore, we would like to share some of the forms, methods focuses, or ways of approaching the study of the woman question that might be helpful to future research which,

337

we hope, will be undertaken by new generations of historians and social scientists.

Before entering into a discussion of the economic and social processes of the twentieth century, we should like briefly to summarize the situation of Puerto Rican women in the nineteenth century. During practically the whole nineteenth century (as in earlier periods), there was no feminist movement in Puerto Rico and very little participation by women in economic life, that is, in the production of goods or services for the market. Since the conquest and colonization by the Spanish, women had been carrying out an essentially reproductive function, and they represented the center of the family unit. As long as the precapitalist mode of production predominated in Puerto Rico, the productive activity of women was directed only toward the production of goods with use value, but without exchange value, that is to say, toward the type of production that is not directed to the market. This production of use values but not exchange values occurred basically in two forms. On the one hand, the activity of women in the home obviously constituted, and still constitutes, work, but not work of the kind that culminates in the production of a good for the market. Each time a woman prepares a meal, mends clothing, cleans the house, or bathes a child, she is indeed working, but her relationship to production is different from that of the artisan who makes a product for sale or of the worker who sells his or her labor power in exchange for wages.

On the other hand, during the nineteenth century women did participate somewhat in tasks involved in agricultural subsistence. The dominant mode of production during practically the whole century was the hacienda or plantation. Since at that time land was the economic element in greatest abundance, it was common for the owners of the land to allow the peasants free use of some of it in exchange for their work on the hacienda. The *agregado* peasants, as they came to be known, cultivated their borrowed lands and produced some agricultural goods for their own sustenance. This production was not aimed at the market, but rather at family consumption. There are repeated indications in the literature that Puerto Rican women participated in some aspects of this agricultural production, especially during harvest time, and in the care of animals for domestic consumption. The type of female labor that agricultural production implied was not monetarily defined: it was use value and not exchange value production. Before the nineteenth century, when almost all Puerto Rican peasants were independent producers for personal consumption, the tasks carried out by women seem to have been similar to those they carried out during almost all of the nineteenth century.

There is no evidence that Puerto Rican women participated significantly in remunerated agricultural work during the nineteenth century. By 1899, the Census of Occupations shows that there were only some 1,868 women employed in agriculture, which represented less than 1 percent of all agricultural workers.

Nevertheless, we have yet to examine the historical impact on women of the regulations of the work-card and pass-book. Even though we cannot here enter into detail about the very important considerations of the situation of the labor market during the nineteenth century, it would be worthwhile briefly to summarize the situation during that period.

During most of the nineteenth century, the owning classes in Puerto Rico constantly complained about labor shortages for farm work. There were also repeated expressions of discontent with regard to "idleness and negative attitudes" on the part of the day-laborers. Throughout the century, the Spanish Crown used various measures—many of them repressive—to combat vagrancy and the shortage of workers. Among the most important of these were the work-card and the pass-book. In 1838, the Spanish governor, Miguel López de Baños, ordered, in the Edict of the Police and Good Government, that "every citizen must own sufficient property to provide himself with the means of subsistence; otherwise he must place himself in the service of another person who will provide him with the resources with which to attend to his necessities." This edict, besides establishing the obligation to work, stipulated sanctions to be applied against those who violated it. These regulations were to be implemented by requiring everyone to carry a card that stated for whom he worked.

With similar aims in mind, but with a broader scope than López

de Baños' edict, Governor Juan de la Pezuela promulgated, in
1849, the pass-book law, to substitute for the work-card law. It is
very important to study the process of the incorporation of
women into economic life in order to learn the impact of these
regulations on Puerto Rican women. In both cases, the regulations contain clauses which indicate that they were also applicable
to women. The Police and Good Government Edict of 1838 (the
work-card regulation) says in this regard: "Peasant women who
live in their huts and who are not known to have an honorable
occupation for subsistence, are also legally required to sign up for
work on a hacienda."

Because of the way the regulation is written, it is not clear, and
we have not yet found evidence in documents of the period, if
being a "housewife" constituted "an honorable occupation for
subsistence" or not. But given the family relations of that period
and the creole and Spanish traditions and customs, we can de-
duce that the wives of day-laborers who could support them were
not obliged to work outside of the home.

The regulation of day-laborers which the pass-book law imposed in 1849 says at the beginning of Article One: "All persons
who, because of lack of capital or industry, must work in the
service of another, either in field work, in the mechanical arts, in
cartage, or in domestic service with an agreed-upon wage, shall be
considered day-laborers." Already in this regulation there is a
specific stipulation regarding domestic work in the residences of
the plantation owners. Although we do not have a basis for
measuring the effect these regulations might have had on the
incorporation of women into remunerated work, it is obvious that
by the end of the century there were a large number of women
employed as domestic workers. The 1899 census data show that
among servants, washerwomen, cooks, and others with similar
tasks engaged in salaried domestic work, there were 37,404 women, which represented 78.4 percent of all employed women.
Table 1 presents a summary of female employment by sector for
1899. Note that the proportion of women workers in agriculture
is only 3.9 percent, which tends to indicate that the regulation
regarding day-laborers did not seem to have resulted in the
incorporation of a substantial number of women into agricultural

work as a way of resolving the problem of labor scarcity. Why did more women not enter agriculture, given that sector's great need for labor power? The ruling classes preferred, instead, to establish the obligation of women workers to work in paid domestic service—in occupations which would serve to buttress the social domination of one class over another, and in which women were subject to constant economic and social exploitation.

The second sector of female employment of some importance in 1899 was seamstresses. Sewing—the making of dresses and other clothing—was clearly a craft-type of activity, but since it took place fundamentally in the home it was not affected by developments that began to occur at the end of the century in the artisan sector. Beginning in the 1940s, the thousands of women involved in sewing were thrust into the process of proletarianization which occured with the establishment of clothing factories, themselves a product of the new development strategy for Puerto Rico; until then, sewing remained an activity that took place inside the home.

Table 1

Female Employment by Principal Sectors, 1899

Total women employed	47,701	100%
Paid domestic work (servants, washerwomen, cooks, etc.)	37,404	78.4
Manufacturing (sewing,* making straw hats, other)	6,389	13.4
Agriculture	1,868	3.9
Commerce and transportation	1,729	3.6
Professionals (teachers, nurses)	311	.06
Women without remunerated work	433,281	

* The category of seamstresses which is classified under the heading of manufacturing employed 5,785 women, an equivalent of 90.6 percent of the manufacturing section.
Source: War Department, Report of the Census of Puerto Rico, 1899, Tables XXIV and XXVI.

As we see, the remunerated jobs for women at the end of the nineteenth century were in large part an extension of the type of work women do in the home. It is important to point out that the few professional women employed in 1899 were concentrated in teaching and nursing. In teaching, women represented 30 percent of the total, and in nursing 50 percent. In both occupations the participation of women increased substantially beginning in 1899, and these sectors came to be areas of virtually exclusively female participation. The incorporation of women into teaching can be traced to the last twenty-five years of the century, and already by 1873 reports of the period indicate the presence of women teachers throughout the island.

It was not until after 1898 that the incorporation of Puerto Rican women into the production of market goods and services began in a significant way. The greater participation of women in economic life in an independent manner led to their integration into the social and political struggles of the time. During the first three decades of the twentieth century, the economic structure of Puerto Rico changed fundamentally, from a mode of production based on precapitalist relations (the system of haciendas and tenant farming) to a capitalist economy dominated by the system of sugar cane plantations. With the transfer of political power from a mercantilist colonialism to an imperialist colonialism in 1898, and the development of a capitalist mode of production, we see the displacement of the traditional agricultural economy by other growing sectors.

The capitalist economy, from its beginnings, recognized the advantages of the incorporation of women into the work force. Like other societies in which a capitalist mode of production developed, the immediate incorporation of women into wage work was evident in Puerto Rico. The development of capitalism in Puerto Rico and elsewhere increasingly opened up work opportunities for women. But that opening up of opportunities did not come from the beneficence of the system or from a recognition of the capacities and the undervaluation of women, but rather from the craftiness of the capitalists who simply saw that women were easily exploitable because of their "virtues" of "docility," "submissiveness," "sense of responsibility," and the fact that they made fewer concrete demands.

In order to achieve the expansion of imperialist capitalism in Puerto Rico, the development of a new social structure to take the place of the social life of the nineteenth-century hacienda was needed. To this end, the implementation of an economic policy aimed at weakening or eliminating numerous haciendas and small farms (by means of, for example, tax laws, limitations on credit for commercial production, and financing of works which would benefit large-scale cultivation of sugar cane in the coastal regions) was important, as was the encouragement of public education aimed at preparing citizens who would be able to serve the needs of the new economic structure.

The Incorporation of Women into Wage Labor During the First Decades of the Twentieth Century

In this article we wish to examine the impact of capitalism on women during the first decades of this century. Public policy aimed at weakening or eliminating the numerous haciendas and small farms, in order to open the way for the establishment of absentee-owned sugar cane plantations, had important consequences for the whole organization of social life in Puerto Rico, and resulted in the massive incorporation of women into the ranks of workers. Women were recruited for the workshops, the factories, and for employment in private homes, in heretofor unequaled numbers. We wish, therefore, to examine the scope of this incorporation and the working conditions under which it occured.

While the cultivation of sugar cane on plantations was facilitated through economic measures detrimental to the hacienda structure, large numbers of tenant farmers and peasants migrated to those areas where new economic opportunities were opening up. The organization of production on the haciendas permitted the peasants to use the land for subsistence farming in exchange for their work on the hacienda. U.S. sugar corporations, with the help of the first governors' economic policies,[1]* were able rapidly to acquire a large amount of land for sugar cane production. The establishment of the plantation disrupted the hacienda's social organization and obliged tenant farmers and small peasants to choose one of two alternatives: to become wage earners—proletarians—on the plantations, or to move to the urban centers and participate in a process of proletarianization similar to what was occurring among the artisans, especially among the cigar-makers.[2]

Women also migrated to the urban centers in large numbers

*Reference notes will be found at the end of the article.

and they, too, having radically changed their way of life, joined in the search for work. Numerous women earned a precarious living for themselves and their families in paid domestic labor. Others, as we shall see, worked at various jobs in the manufacturing industries which were beginning to develop.

The change in the structure of the haciendas also resulted in a substantial increase in the country's commercial activity, since it was necessary to import the bulk of the food needed for consumption, as well as the machinery and the equipment for the developing plantations. The growth of the commercial sector, together with the expansion of the economy's manufacturing sector, which began in the first decades of the century, radically altered the country's job structure.

The impact of these changes on Puerto Rican women was considerable. First, a substantial increase in female employment occurred in the first decade of the century. Between 1899 and 1910, the total employment of women increased by 61.2 percent, while that of men increased by only 17.7 percent.[3] The development of new businesses and the influx of capital seeking investment and a cheap labor force made the greater participation of women in the country's work force an imminent reality. It is important to point out that similar tendencies were observed at the end of the nineteenth century in those countries that began their capitalist development with the Industrial Revolution. For example, in England during the period between 1871 and 1891, the total employment of men increased by 7.9 percent, while that of women increased by 21 percent; and in Germany during the seven-year period between 1875 and 1882, the increase in employment was 35 percent for women, while for men it was only 6.4 percent.[4] What happened in Puerto Rico in terms of the incorporation of women into the labor force in a general way parallels what occurred in other countries where capitalism was developing.

Let us now examine the sectors into which women were incorporated and the impact of economic policies on this tendency.

We find that, in absolute terms, paid domestic work continued to be the principal source of employment for women during the first three decades of the twentieth century, but its relative importance declined as other employment possibilities for women opened up. So we see that the sector of paid domestic labor represented 78.4 percent of female employment in 1899; this proportion diminished to 58.7 percent in 1910, 37.5 percent in 1920, and 27.7 percent in 1930. This percentage was stable between 1930 and 1940, but by then it no longer constituted the primary sector of female employment.[5]

The thousands of women working in domestic service were at the bottom of the ladder in terms of wages and working conditions. The exploitation to which they were subjected forced many domestic workers to consider finding a job as a factory worker, a tobacco-leaf stripper in a workshop, or an embroiderer at home, as the hope of liberation from their exploited condition. And to that situation we must add the terrible burden which weighed on thousands of women when they had to leave Puerto Rico. Official policy saw the emigration of domestic workers as a possible contribution to the solution of the economic problems the country confronted during the 1930s. Through the Labor Department, programs were set up to place women as live-in domestic workers in the United States: between 1930 and 1936, 1,537 Puerto Rican domestics were placed in New York City alone. And the demand for this type of work, principally in New York, Chicago, Newark, and Florida, was the basis for the setting up of private U.S. agencies devoted to recruiting domestic workers in Puerto Rico and taking them to the United States. Such is the case of Mr. Edgard S. Roll's Castle, Barton and Associates, and of others who will go down in the history of Puerto Rico as infamous traffickers in human pain and as exploiters of women.[6] Articles in the newspapers of that period tell of the despair of the domestics who had emigrated and found salaries lower than promised, jobs without contract, longer working hours than agreed upon, and slave-like treatment on the part of the employers. It should not surprise us, then, that the women aspired to other types of work.

The manufacturing sector offered some work possibilities for women beginning in 1898. In particular, there was a tremendous increase in the employment of women in cigar-making. We should recall that, in addition to the impact of the new colonialism on the sugar industry, the tobacco industry underwent substantial changes beginning in 1898. From being an importer of cigars, Puerto Rico became an exporter, and by 1910 cigars represented 13.5 percent of its exports.[7] The participation of women in this industry increased dramatically; they were principally employed as strippers, a job for which they were paid the lowest wages in the industry. In 1899, there were only 60 women employed in cigar-making, but by 1910 there were already 3,204, and by 1920 there were 8,573. This was the sector in which female employment grew the most rapidly during the first three decades of the twentieth century.

Through the incorporation of women into the tobacco industry, their participation in working-class struggles began to take on real importance. In many cases the women strippers became symbols of the militant struggle. Their work in this industry also encouraged their incorporation into political struggle. These workers had a decisive influence on the declarations and the struggles of the Socialist Party, which was founded in 1915 by the proletarianized artisans and the workers in the sugar cane plantations. The Socialist Party encouraged full participation of women in the party's internal structure and advocated woman and universal suffrage long before either was granted.

Another important sector in terms of female employment during the first three decades of the century was the home-sewing industry. This sector, which was made up of embroiderers and seamstresses, who for miserable wages made handkerchiefs, baby clothes, blouses, etc., represented the bulk of female employment in 1930. They then served as a base for the development of the manufacturing industries—textile, clothing, and others—which gained increasing importance in Puerto Rico in the 1940s and 1950s.

The working conditions in this industry were horrendous. In 1933 an extensive study was carried out under the auspices of the federal and local Labor Departments, published as *The Employment of Women,* in which the abuses and the onerous working conditions in the industries employing women were exposed. In those days, more than 50,000 women worked at sewing and embroidery at home, in return for wages of less than three cents an hour. Women who worked at home had to put up with payment in goods instead of money, and often the withholding of wages by unscrupulous and exploitative intermediaries. The exploitation to which the women who joined the work force in those first three decades were subjected is clearly shown in this study. Capitalism did not incorporate women into the labor force because it considered them equal to men, but rather because it could exploit them more easily.

Notes

1. José A. Herrero, in *Mitología del azúcar*, Cuadernos de CEREP, no. 5, mimeo, examines in great detail the economic policies of the first governors and the impact of these on the hacienda structure.
2. A. G. Quintero, "Socialista y tabaquero: la proletarización de los artesanos," *Sin Nombre* 8, no. 4 (March 1978).
3. Data taken from the censuses for 1899 and 1910.
4. A. Bebel, *Woman Under Socialism* (New York: Labor News Press, 1904; reprinted by Shocken Press, 1970), pp. 169 and 172.
5. Figures calculated from data from various censuses between 1899 and 1940.
6. We have reconstructed this process from reading newspapers, especially *El Mundo* up to the 1950s; it is part of a more extensive work entitled *Las condiciones del empleo doméstico asalariado*, in press.
7. A. G. Quintero, "El Partido Socialista y la lucha política triangular de las primeras décadas bajo la dominación norteamericana," *Revista de Ciencias Sociales* (Puerto Rico), March 1, 1975.

Educational Policy and
Female Labor, 1898–1930

In addition to an economic policy, the establishment and expansion of capitalism in Puerto Rico required the development of public education directed at preparing citizens who would be able to serve the needs of the new system. We wish to present here some notes that may serve as a guide for the study of that process.

The organization of the economy dominated by the system of sugar cane plantations which began around 1898 required the training of personnel with both manual and industrial skills, which in turn required an infrastructure of services in which professionals were very important. For example, engineers, accountants, lawyers, were needed. Thus, the educational policy that was to be implemented had, from the start, two fundamental objectives. First, the metropolitan power considered it indispensable to expand elementary education to the Puerto Rican masses so that they could learn to read, write, and understand the basic principles of the new institutions which would be developing and so that they could learn more easily some of the skills necessary for their eventual incorporation into the work force.

Second, it was also necessary to prepare professionals who would serve the new enterprises. As early as 1906, Commissioner Samuel McCune Lindsay, who was one of the most influential ideologues of educational policy for Puerto Rico, had declared that the educational problem on the island was a double one: that basic instruction had to be provided to the masses, and that it was also necessary to develop some future leaders—those who could go on to positions in government, trade, and the professions, through higher and university education.[1]*

These two aspects of educational policy had tremendous reper-

* Reference notes will be found at the end of the article.

cussions on Puerto Rican women. The public school system in Puerto Rico was expanded enormously in the first three decades after the change in "masters" from Spain to the United States. There are reports showing that in 1898, 85 percent of the population was illiterate and that by 1925 this percentage had been reduced to 45.5 percent.[2] In 1898, there were 29,182 pupils enrolled in the country's schools, with an average expenditure of $4.14 per pupil, while in 1925 enrolment was up to 230,120 students, at an average of $30.23 per capita.[3] Women were a part of this expansion from the first, with the massive entry of little girls into the elementary schools.

The purpose of primary school expansion was to fulfill the aims of that educational policy. One of these aims, which *was* accomplished, was to wipe out illiteracy rapidly. Another was to see to it that the Puerto Rican masses understood the basic principles of the new social order, and to that end the textbooks which were used from the first grade up were vital. The references in the readers for the first few grades regarding social, ethical, and moral values, the nature of justice, and so on, were aimed at developing well-behaved, understanding pupils, passive beings, and at inspiring in them devotion and love for the institutions which would become the mainstays of the social and economic order of the new regime.[4] And among these key institutions was the family. The vision of the family was not altered by the new educational policy; its minor modifications did not propose to subvert the prevailing patriarchal order, but on the contrary to serve as support for the acceptance of other more drastic and basic changes in Puerto Rican society. Within the family, the role of housewife continued as the principal function of the woman, although women were already beginning to appear in evidence in some other occupations, such as, for example, those of embroiderer or seamstress.

This vision of women permeated educational policy both at the elementary and higher levels. Elementary education had special provisions for girls. Half their time at school was to be spent in the study of reading, writing, health, civics, home economics, and *simple* arithmetic (for the needs which they might have as housewives), and the other half was to be devoted to learning the needle

crafts.[5] Of course, this was aimed at developing personnel with
the skills needed to join the growing needle trades, which paid
very low wages and in which gross exploitation of women's work
was the rule. This industry was of vital economic importance for
Puerto Rico, and it became the second largest sector in terms of
volume of exports between 1930 and 1940.

For men, schools on the elementary and secondary levels offered courses in agriculture and other vocational arts. In agriculture the emphasis was on apprenticeship for work in "the
country's important agricultural enterprises," that is, in those
which the new form of economic organization was developing:
the sugar cane plantations.[6] The purpose of the educational
policy had, then, the effect of facilitating the preparation of a
huge male and female work force to attend to the needs of the
new economic structure. In the case of women it had the double
effect of reaffirming their subordinate position in society
through their education for the world of the home, and of achieving their integration into the labor force as cheap labor in those
economic activities which were extensions of the type of work that
women do in the home.

Through the other purpose of educational policy—the training of professionals, high-level technicians, and government
functionaries—a significant number of women were also incorporated into social and economic life in the first decades of the
century. This process has not yet been studied in all its complexity
and depth, but the data which we have demonstrate the importance the expansion of the professional sector had for Puerto
Rican women, especially in terms of their incorporation into
teaching.

In order to extend public education to the whole population
and thus accomplish one of the purposes of public education, it
was necessary to recruit and train teachers who would be able to
carry out the tasks of teaching literacy and adaptation to the new
social institutions. Women, because of their "virtues" of "docility," "sense of responsibility," and "natural love for children,"
generated by the manorial world of the haciendas, came to constitute the motor force of school education under capitalism.

Since 1873 the presence of some female teachers in the few

existing schools in the country had been noticeable.[7] By 1899, census figures show that there were 246 women teachers, representing 30.4 percent of the total. This proportion increased rapidly in the first three decades of the twentieth century and the 4,254 women teachers in 1930 constituted 75 percent of all teachers.[8] Women teachers came to virtually monopolize primary education. In the first two grades of elementary school almost all the teachers were women (99 percent in first grade, 94 percent in second grade). Women represented more than 50 percent of teachers in all levels of teaching except that of supervisors and assistant supervisors, where they represented only 4.4 percent and 11.7 percent respectively.[9] Capitalism built on women's early participation in teaching, which existed since the nineteenth century, to incorporate women massively as teachers. However, as we can see from the data, decision-making and supervisory positions continued to be dominated by men.

Women teachers took up the banner of the suffrage movement in Puerto Rico. Their basic demand was equality of opportunity in the selecting of the island's governors and they based this on demands for equality of educational opportunity. In 1917 the first suffragist organization—the Puerto Rican Feminist League (Liga Femenina Puertorriqueña)—was formed, with the principal aim of encouraging woman suffrage and promoting the participation of women in education and other fields. However, suffragist groups never incorporated into their ranks other groups of women who had organized collectively in order to promote struggles for equality and social justice, that is, working-class feminists. Both were movements of female militancy, but they had different focuses, each reflecting different class values and positions.

The emphasis on the development of professionals also resulted in the incorporation of women into nursing, social work, and other occupations. Nursing steadily increased its proportion of women, until it became almost exclusively female. In 1899, nursing was equally divided—50 percent men and 50 percent women—and by 1930, women represented 94.4 percent of all those employed in that sector.[10] In the same way, although not as rapidly as in nursing, office work began to become concentrated in women's hands.

There is still a great deal of research to be done regarding the impact of educational policy on the incorporation of women into the labor force in the first decades of this century. In this article we have merely sketched some of the processes which resulted in the concentration of women into certain types of occupations and their nonparticipation in others. The bases for the segregation of the work force were laid down through these processes and we must continue investigating them in order to be able to understand the situation of Puerto Rican women today.

Notes

1. "The Public School System of Porto Rico," in *Register of Porto Rico* (San Juan: Luis E. Tuzo and Co., 1903), p. 78. See also the review by Isabel Picó de Hernández, "Americanización o proletarización, comentarios en torno al libro de la Dra. Aida Negrón de Montilla," *Revista La Escalera* 5, nos. 5-6 (1971).
2. Teacher's College, *A Survey of the Public Educational System of Porto Rico*, 1926, Ch. 1.
3. Calculated on the basis of data presented in ibid.
4. The Teachers College report (pp. 190-193) cited above discusses the basic elements in these new text books, in particular the books *Lectura Natural* by Isabel Keith Dermott and the "Children's Readers" by José González Ginorio.
5. Ibid., p. 215. The special curriculum for elementary school girls is described.
6. Ibid., p. 208.
7. Among other reviews of the period, Leonor Catala, "El desarrollo de la instrucción" in *Album histórico de Yauco*, ed. Francisco Lluch Negroni (Spain, 1960) reports on the development of the school system in Yauco, making reference to the incorporation of women into teaching.
8. Data from the censuses, section on occupational statistics, 1899 and 1930.
9. Teacher's College, *A Survey of the Public Educational System of Porto Rico.*
10. Censuses, 1899 and 1930.

Frank Bonilla (1925–)

Presently Director of CUNY's Centro de Estudios Puertorriqueños and professor of Sociology in the Doctoral Program (CUNY). Taught at MIT and Stanford. Has written many articles for scholarly journals here and abroad.

Selected Bibliography

Bonilla, Frank. *The Failure of Elites.* Vol. II in *The Politics of Change in Venezuela.* Cambridge, Mass.: MIT Press, 1970.

————— and Myron Glazer. *Student Politics in Chile.* New York: Basic Books, 1970.

————— and Frank Girling, eds. *Structure of Dependency.* Institute for Political Studies, Stanford University, 1973.

————— and History Task Force, Centro de Estudios Puertorriqueños. *Labor Migration Under Capitalism: The Puerto Rican Experience.* New York: Monthly Review Press, 1979.

—————. "The Young Puerto Rican in New York: The Search for a Culture." *The Morningsider* (November 1960).

—————. "Cultural Pluralism in the University: The Case of Puerto Rican Studies." *La Revista* (Institute of Puerto Rican Studies, Brooklyn College) (1972).

—————. "Industrialization and Migration: Some Effects on the Puerto Rican Working Class." *Latin American Perspectives* 3, no. 3 (1976).

—————. "Mamá Borinquen me llama: Puerto Rican Return Migration in the 70s." *Migration Today* (April 1979).

Beyond Survival: Por qué Seguiremos Siendo Puertorriqueños

One of the burdens of the wealthy is that they must from time to time take stock of their possessions. Thus when a people become the simple possession of another, one of the experiences the colonized must face is to periodically see themselves and all that is theirs coldly assessed by various agents of the overlord. In Puerto Rico this process began very soon after the arrival of the first U.S. occupying force. In March of 1889 Acting Secretary of War G. D. Meiklejohn called on department commanders in Cuba, Puerto Rico, and the Philippines to report "upon the existing state of the inhabitants and the national resources of the islands." A sizable outline of required information was provided which was to be transmitted "together with general observations as to opportunities for investment."[1]* Reporting from Arecibo to Brig. Gen. George W. Davis, the military governor of Puerto Rico, a certain Captain Macomb wrote in that year:

> But the people—and I discuss the poor, working class—are, upon the whole, a gentle, patient, uncomplaining lot, living in ignorance and penury, generally polite, and willing to work in a plodding, undemonstrative way. Their very gentleness has permitted the unjust scale of wages they receive to become the custom.[2]

The captain dutifully went on to note that "in the United States general education and the newspapers and labor unions forever prevent such abuse." In the nearby district of Aguadilla a fellow officer, Captain Dentler, found things much the same.

> The people seem willing to work, even at starvation wages, and they seem to be docile and grateful for anything done to them. They are emotional, apt to make idols of some one of their number, and to be led about by him only to pull him to pieces later on.[3]

* Reference notes will be found at the end of the article.

Across the island in Ponce, Lieutenant Blunt had apparently
come upon slightly more stubborn human material.

> The natives are lazy and dirty, but are very sharp and cunning, and
> the introduction of American ideas disturbs them little, they being
> indifferent to the advantage offered.[4]

However, Blunt's premonitions about the unresponsiveness of
the natives to the virtues of things American were not widely
shared. The more affirmative view stated forthrightly by the aforementioned Captain Dentler was that "when American ideas are
once inculcated into the people, they will never let go of them and
will benefit from them."[5]

What are we to make of the fact that seventy years of increasingly elaborate social-science research on Puerto Rico and its
mainland offshoots has added practically nothing to the imagery
of the Puerto Rican current among our U.S. overseers that could
not readily be inferred or extrapolated from the 1900 impressions of the Dentlers and the Blunts? Are Puerto Ricans as a
people as transparent, uniform, and unchanging that our essential qualities could have been captured so quickly, once and for all,
by the untrained eye of the first American occupation force?
Neither these appraisals nor much of the subsequent formal
research have a great deal to do with the questions to which
Puerto Ricans really require answers. These depictions are, on
the contrary, successive salvos in a mind-warping exchange that
has disfigured and scarred mentalities among both rulers and
ruled. This fragmentary and distorted self-knowledge constitutes
a crippling heritage from which, I believe, none of us so far has
achieved more than partial deliverance.

Puerto Rican Inferiority

The case for Puerto Rican inferiority has many strands and all
have been subsequently embellished since the turn of the century.
Many of these recurrent themes would seem on the surface to
have little to do with politics. Yet the way in which such issues are

posed, the rationales that are appealed to in explaining alleged shortcomings, and the paths pointed to as solutions have enormous political consequences. All individuous stereotyping, however hackneyed and timeworn, has political content and overtones.[6] We do not need to dwell very long here on the more obvious forms of social rejection implicit in such crude forms of labeling. Are Puerto Ricans by nature and choice noisy, foulmouthed, garish in dress, truculent, and oversexed? These may be taken as good reasons to avoid Puerto Ricans as neighbors and work mates and to remove one's own from schools frequented by Puerto Rican children. But such images have an adverse political effect chiefly when Puerto Ricans themselves begin to believe they have something to gain by fleeing from their own kind. The more corrosive features of the legend are thus those that destroy the bases of solidarity among a people, that undermine their political confidence, that systematically throw into question their capacity for self-government, and that arbitrarily close off to them desired features. The essential components of the carefully cultivated myth of Puerto Rican political inferiority have been handed down practically unchanged since their appearance in their most ingenuous form in the War Department report that has been cited.[7] The Puerto Rican, we have been told in countless ways since then, is by disposition docile and submissive. His political impulses and capabilities are primitive (as measured against a falsely idealized mainland standard). He is dependent on outside (U.S.) leadership and models to break the hold of poverty and injustice on his society.

This net of constraining and defeating ideas encumbers our vision and action wherever we find ourselves. Whether on the island or in New York, breaking out of this confining encirclement is a first step toward that space in which we may take a liberating breath. Oppression lies wherever these ideas reign; our freedom is to be found wherever they can be exposed as a mere rationale for denying a people full manhood. What then stands between ourselves and freedom? Chiefly the difference between recognizing the repressive content in ideas and fully understanding what gives them power over us and lends strength to those who wield them against us. More specifically we have before us

the unfinished work of sorting out that part of our oppression
that is subjective and that which rests on more material factors
and therefore requires more than a cleansing of minds in order to
be overcome.

The pervasiveness of the notion of Puerto Rican passivity and
submissiveness is not to be denied. ". . . There is hardly any area
of Puerto Rican society," we have been told by René Marqués, "in
which just a light scratching will not reveal docility as a constant
and determinant feature."[8] Marqués certainly demonstrates that
the theme is a recurrent one in Puerto Rican literature and that
the Puerto Ricans have generated a rich and graphic vocabulary
to express their consciousness of being a subjected people. His
essay is at once a scathing, pained, and painful exposé of the
colonized mentality and the devices by which the oppressed seek
to live with the humiliation of long-felt powerlessness. This fact
lends added weight to his argument. His is an authoritative and
literarily informed view from the inside. Therefore, it not only
collects and echoes but sets off reverberations of its own. Marqués's thesis has to be taken seriously not only with respect to the
psychological and literary ground that he defines for himself but
with respect to the many political inferences that he makes along
the way.

The official rhetoric has come to celebrate Puerto Ricans as a
democratic, tolerant, and peace-loving people. In days when we
were more honest and more candid with each other, affirms
Marqués, we acknowledged that these terms mean fatalistic,
resigned, supine (ñangotado, i.e., content to remain on our
haunches as regards matters of the spirit). The commonwealth is
a perfect political expression of this mentality. A Puerto Rican
solution is one in which what looks inevitable is transformed into a
national project. Our political violence, he affirms, is not revolutionary or revealing of heightened political consciousness but a
heroism of despair. The nationalist movement is the maximum
expression of a deeply ingrained suicidal impulse (the island, in
fact, has a very high suicide rate). The statehood option reflects
an equivalent impulse to extinction on a cultural plane. The rebel,
middle-class writer and intellectual is celebrated but absorbed; he
relieves tensions but changes no one. In this bleak panorama
Marqués provides a single ray of hope, his suggestion that the

Puerto Rican in New York, as he loses the stain of his tropical origins (*la mancha del plátano*) may eventually throw off the impulse to self-effacement and obliteration.

What Marqués chronicles with considerably more effect and detail than the sketch just given reveals is the psychological damage and cultural mayhem worked on Puerto Ricans by centuries of exploitation. He exposes the violence of colonialism but falls short in the apparent presumption that the colonized will indefinitely turn the destructive forces thus generated against themselves. The dialectic of impotence and stubborn resistance, however covert and diffuse, is perceived as a grinding friction shredding individuals and social ties but is denied any prospect of political resolution. We are, perhaps, developing a dangerous virtuosity in documenting the prostration, insecurity, ambivalences, and ideological bafflement within our ranks and assigning too little value to the contrary signs that point to a remarkable capacity for survival in a context of prolonged and radical ambiguity. Few people have been forced to move about the world for so long under such false (externally imposed), discordant, and provisional (incompletely realized) identities. What can Puerto Ricans anywhere, most of us still passing through this mindrending experience, ask or expect of each other?

This is a permanent, underlying question in most of what I want to review here with you today. It is, of course, a question that never arises in the observations of the Dentlers, Blunts, and their successors with more scientific pretensions. They are not searching passionately for meaningful commitments and viable paths to the advancement of Puerto Rican goals. They are content to document what they perceive as political bankruptcy, the fantasied superiority and invincibility of mainland political designs and the need, therefore, of extending U.S. tutelage indefinitely, however it may be mediated. Yet what kind of political bonds, commitments, and thrust can in fact be maintained in such adverse contexts? When individual lives on a massive scale are blasted by the impossibility of living up to the most private commitments to loved persons, where is the work of social reconnection to begin? If it is within a man's reach only momentarily and with great sacrifice to create and mount an idealized situation of abundance of conviviality for his family or friends, does he need a

psychologist to tell him he is giving in to impulses or an anthropologist to inform him he is caught in a fiesta complex? When
stability can be found in a galling accommodation to a low-keyed,
routinized existence, will some not lash out rebelliously against
something they know needs to be destroyed? When the enemy is
elusive and a fantastic price is paid for striking out against him,
will not bizarre modes of copping out be invented or more accessible victims be found to be immolated in his place?[9] This of course
will only certify a proneness to erratic behavior and more serious
mental disturbances. Then, of course, intellectuals will reproach
the mass for being politically inert and unresponsive to political
ideals. They will credit to the exemplary action of a few leaders
the survival of the independence ideal and the stubborn resili-
ence of a culture surviving against tremendous odds.[10] By contrast the politics of personalism, of social work, of the poverty
warriors, and of the bootstrap will be seen to flourish. On the
island and in mainland ghettoes the practical politicians, who
understand how to manipulate "bread and butter" issues, will
announce that they have saved their people from a corrosive
nationalism and taught them to place economic solutions and
speedy assimilation before vague political aspirations or the survival of cherished lifeways. With this they round out and hammer
home the legend of Puerto Rico's conformity and purchased
submission to an externally defined second-rate status.[11] While
the subculture of prostitution and sexual exploitation flourishing
in the island backwaters of dependent capitalism and New York
slums is minutely recorded as a prototype of what is Puerto Rican,
political leaders speak of Operation Serenity. While Puerto Rican
young men are conscripted to brutalize others and give their lives
in the undeclared wars of another nation, island statisticians tally
the value of economy of the remitted earnings and the social
benefits that accrue on the island as the price of this military
service. No wonder then that the legend comes back to mock us,
as in the words of an acute observer, the historian Richard Morse.

> Within this longer perspective, Puerto Rican political formulations
> take on a hollow ring. They seem designed for a people which is
> "shopping" for status. . . . No one would deny that voluntary politi-

cal change should obey, among other things, broad economic considerations. But it is surprising that a people which prides itself on a Hispanic "soul" should translate them into dollars-and-cents reckoning carried to the last decimal point.[12]

Such a remark may be intensive and characteristically omits any details concerning the nature of the market in which a nation is brought to trade its pride and integrity for survival. Still, it captures a fragment of truth of which we are all painfully conscious. On another plane altogether is the main conclusion of a more recent and professedly "sympathetic" study of student politics at the University of Puerto Rico.

> Contemporary Puerto Rican students, the children of their fathers, have disproved a maxim that has characterized nationalist movements in many areas of the world. Puerto Ricans, including their fathers, have shown that man *can* live by bread alone. (Italics in the original.)[13]

This young political scientist forgot to mention that the bread used to fill the mouths of Puerto Ricans has been minimal, hard, and dearly paid for.

The Politics of Migration

Migration itself is thus transformed into a suspect act. Does it represent a massive capitulation, a sellout, escape, or suicide? Is there really no alternative open to Puerto Ricans, whether here or on the island, except full Americanization, a slow extinction and absorption into the underclass of decaying cities? Under what conditions can Puerto Ricans not merely survive but grow affirmatively as a culturally integrated and distinctive collectivity in the mainland context? If we are trying to throw off one set of destructive lies or partial truths, we gain nothing by simply improvising a more congenial set of premises about ourselves or our future prospects. Let it be clear that we are talking about an unprecedented job of psychological and cultural reconstitution and construction that must rest on a very special political and economic infrastructure. If we are unable to imagine outcomes that would satisfy our aspirations, how can we know when we are making or losing ground?

Between 1960 and 1970 the Puerto Rican population in New York shot to over a million. Over that decade the numbers of New York-born Puerto Ricans grew by 150 percent while those born on the island and living in the States grew by only 19 percent.[14] This population overall is extremely young, averaging about twenty-one years in 1960. The eventual predominance of the mainland-born is a significant fact, for the way in which they relate to their putative Americanness will prove decisive in terms of the community's future. As one of the older members of this so-called second generation, I feel a special responsibility to make explicit some of the political implications of choices that lie before us. There are certain core realities that we need to face up to and that we ourselves often conspire to mask or dissemble.

In the first place we are a captured people and remain captives. Formal rights of citizenship and apparent freedom of movement within the country's borders notwithstanding, we remain in a situation that is alien and not of our making. Our parents could not give us any citizenship other than that which, in a watered-down form, was imposed on them.

Secondly, the amalgam of U.S. and island cultures and its mainland transplants has, from the Puerto Rican side, never been seen as a simple fusion. Puerto Ricans are not culturally Americans, and we must have the courage to speak up and affirm that we do not wish to be Americans if we are honestly committed to building on our Puerto Rican roots. Even the most ardent proponents of statehood or other forms of political association with the United States have been at pains to make clear that the island intended to remain true to its Hispanic and Antillean traditions. This fact has not passed unnoticed, though it has elicited primarily sardonic comment.

> From the Puerto Rican point of view, this eventual society is perhaps not best described as "bicultural." For indeed, it is the Hispanic tradition that will supply the "culture" while the United

States will merely supply methods, technics, organizational charts, money for pump-priming, and a market of 180 million people.[15]

As frequently occurs in such appraisals, the terms here become subtly inverted. Puerto Rico is depicted as ready to exploit the U.S. market while being neurotically standoffish about U.S. culture or unrealistic about the consequences of accepting certain technologies. The economic facts, of course, are exactly the reverse. The tiny island is one of the United States' largest and most lucrative export markets. Puerto Rican exports to the mainland market of 180 million are almost entirely the output of U.S. producers taking advantage of cheap labor and other benefits of the offshore, commonwealth location. As regards the cultural argument, the Puerto Rican position has simply never been, as is insinuated, that U.S. technology could be appropriated without an impact on social organization or lifeways, though defenses have in fact been inadequate.

I think we have to recognize in this long-standing rejection of a quick transfer of identity a profoundly political act that is decidedly life-affirming and nonsuicidal. Within the most recent flow of migrants, a current that now seems to move directly from rural island settings to eastern seaboard cities, this awareness and search for a viable design for survival remains very much alive. Recent research in Boston reports that the most characteristic group accepts neither isolation nor assimilation.[16] This search for a space within which Puerto Ricans may live and grow in full freedom has been a constant in the fifty years or more that we have been a visible presence in U.S. cities. It is the counterpoint to the rejection in U.S. culture of all groups that are racially distinct or racially suspect. Speaking of Blacks, American Indians, Chicanos, and Puerto Ricans, Eduardo Seda has written:

> These groups have failed to adapt to the American melting pot because they are differentiated on the basis of racial criteria and in assimilating into the dominant American culture, these groups internalize the stigma and the self-hatred ingrained in that culture against the people of color. In order to avoid the stigma inherent in the internalization of American culture these groups must maintain their own cultural identity as a separate entity in a pluralistic social scheme.[17]

Over the last decade, as the nature of the U.S. role abroad has been incontestably exposed at home, to become fully American has come to mean as well accepting the stigma and mission of the oppressor of others seeking liberation. To shrink from embracing this identity is hardly to be seen as an act of mere malcontents or cranks, neurotically attached to a failing culture.

The history of the Puerto Rican migration has yet to be written. The 1910 census registered some 1,500 Puerto Ricans born in the continental United States. This number had risen to 53,000 by 1930 and 70,000 by 1940. By 1950 the quarter-million mark was close, and two decades later we number more than a million, nearly a third of all those with identifiable Puerto Rican parentage under U.S. jurisdiction. Because this movement has been chronicled chiefly by demographers and migration specialists, most of what we know has to do with a few characteristics of this population and small changes in these that signal gains in or obstacles to "assimilation."[18] By the late 1960s small "advances" could be documented for second-generation Puerto Ricans as against their island-born neighbors: they were not only more youthful but had more years of schooling, higher-status jobs, larger incomes, married early and more often outside their group, and had fewer children. A newly noted trend was the shift in migration away from New York City which was said to augur a "Diáspora" in which the second generation would spread throughout the nation. The growth of ethnic defense organizations and the penetration by some Puerto Ricans into the higher levels of the local party structure and municipal bureaucracy is also hailed as a sign of accelerating assimilation. The fact that, vis-à-vis other victimized groups, Puerto Ricans remain significantly at a disadvantage on every count (housing, education, income, jobs, health) is rarely mentioned in such accounts. Other groups have paid a similar price of admission for their place in the city and nation. After all, too, Puerto Ricans arrived inopportunely and with some grave handicaps (i.e., ambiguous Spanish-African antecedents, stubborn attachment to a foreign language, a strange variant of Catholicism, what looked like an irregularly bestowed citizenship, and brazenly stated doubts about the wish to be American).

I want to use the rest of my time here to argue further that this kind of celebration of Puerto Rican assimilation or integration is premature and in error. These gains in education skills, earning power, and geographic mobility do not signal a simple siphoning off of tensions and a shearing off of individuals into some imaginary American mainstream. Placed against the backdrop of other events and trends here and on the island, they have to be seen as potentially providing a wholly new level of awareness and leadership arising from the depths of a community still imprisoned in poverty and continuously renewed by newcomers entering at the most exploited level. These small successes are also to be seen against the backdrop of the proportions of this youthful generation who are hostages of the society in other settings—who are in schools that teach nothing, without jobs or in dead-end jobs, fighting a war in which none believe, crammed into the nation's cell blocks. All of these settings—the streets, the high schools and colleges, the prison—have become radicalizing contexts, intensifying awareness, sharpening political skills, stimulating reflection and analysis, generating new commitment.

The present system operates so destructively and arbitrarily that talented and thoughtful youth may wind up as readily behind prison walls as in the college classroom. I want to read briefly from a couple of letters from men in Soledad prison in California. I find these letters remarkable because Puerto Ricans in that prison are few and most have been separated from their community for many years since early adolescence.

> I know that it seems as if people are not able to hold together very long. But we who can get together, must stay together and struggle that much harder for the freedom, justice, and equality which we as oppressed people have never seen. As everyone who recognizes the struggle for what it really is knows, it's time to unite.

> I want to help our people. . . . I've been doing a lot of thinking about forming a Puerto Rican Awareness Group. . . . Our people, Black, Brown, Red, Yellow people (brothers), are in need of unity. I understand that there's always a new idea and new minds that get together for our cause. I sure would love to contribute my ideas and my brotherhood and love to the brothers who are trying very hard to bring in a better life for our people.

As the inmates are the first to say, "not every brother inside the joint is a soldier." Nevertheless, the prisons, like the schools and other institutions that up till very recently had served largely to shake and obliterate individuality and Puerto Rican identity, have somehow been in part turned around. Puerto Rican men in prison are defining for *themselves* the condition for their reconnection to society and doing so in terms of a politically informed concern for their own. The prisons have become a front of concern and action as vital to our community as housing, jobs, or schools.

From this perspective the fact that in the city university system alone there are today more than 8,000 Puerto Rican students will prove significant chiefly to the extent that the colleges and universities are also turned into contexts of liberating work. That liberating work involves not only casting off the blinders of a colonializing education which explains only our inferiority and impotence but developing counter-values that thwart co-optation and elitism. Four-fifths of employed Puerto Ricans are blue-collar workers.[19] We will gain nothing by penetrating the university unless those who enter are an advance party with working lifelines on the street, the community, the prison, the island, and every other setting in which things important to mainland Puerto Ricans as collectivity are occurring.

This may seem like a heavy burden to place on young people going into a new and complex milieu that is unprepared for them and reluctant to accept new definitions of its functions. University administrators are quick to respond to such formulations with charges that we are seeking to polarize, politicize, subvert, and fragment institutions and academic traditions. "What will majors in Puerto Rican studies find to do?" they ask, while cheerfully passing out undergraduate degrees in eighteenth-century French drama and medieval history. This is, of course, a defensive screen, for they would like to be seen as irresponsible radicals, hustlers, and interlopers ready to box our young into a meaningless academic dead-end just to have a base in a corner of the academy. In point of fact our needs are fairly modest though impossible to realize within the framework of the universities as now constituted. We are, after all, not preparing our youth to administer an empire, manage global wars, travel to the moon, or control restive minorities. We do need to undo the work of a deforming education, to vitalize and take command of our own process of cultural construction, and to understand the economic and political requirements for our survival as a community.

One additional statistic concerning the New York Puerto Rican population requires comment. In the 1960 census 96 percent of that population was classified as white. Who is kidding whom? What is the extent of Puerto Rican complicity in this numerical charade? Are Puerto Rican social standards of race really so relaxed that all but a few qualify as white? Are we simply refusing to play the racial numbers game according to mainland rules? I want to repeat here a few remarks I have made often before on occasions like this. We live in a society that knows only black and white. Puerto Rican complacency and equivocation with respect to race and even our more genuine accommodations of racial differences have little place here. As we have discovered, here one is black, white, or a nonsomething. Still Puerto Ricans—white or black—have little comprehension of the deep racial animosities that divide mainland Americans. Many are understandably reluctant to become part of a fight that is to them ugly and meaningless. But we cannot continue to pretend to be an island of civility and racial harmony untouched by the storm of racial conflict that surrounds us. Again we must acknowledge that our culture—like all others dominated by Europeans—has taught us to experience blackness as misfortune. Our escapism and lack of realism with respect to race issues is as much grounded in such fears and self-doubts as in any affirmative principles of equality. If the Puerto Rican approach to race is really more humane, we have to prove it here. And the only convincing proof of moral strength in this connection is to stand up as proudly for what is black in us as individuals and for what is black in our community as we do for our Puerto Ricanness.

Beyond Survival

According to all going theories of history, culture, and collective psychology, Puerto Ricans do not exist or are bound to disappear. We are said to have no real institutions, distinctive

culture, or secure identity. Whatever fragments of such unifying
ideals and sentiments we may have scraped together in the past
are only a weak shield against the overwhelming onslaught of the
dominant culture with its power to penetrate and engulf the
alien. I believe we have to acknowledge the silence, surface submission, and nonmilitancy that has marked much of our past. But
we need also to see beyond that to the tenacity and capacity for
survival contained in the resolute avoidance of a capitulation on
the cultural front. This is part of the mystery to be unraveled and
turned now to surer political purpose. The option to struggle for
full sovereignty in the island and power over our own mainland
communities remains very much alive. Part of the success of the
colonizer lies in having pitted Puerto Ricans against Puerto
Ricans of that contention. But this only accentuates the ultimate
contradictions and heightens our awareness of what threatens;
the powerful have nothing to give us except death and now the
prospect of fratricide.

But what content are we to give abstract ideas such as pluralism
and power in the complex and conflict-ridden context of U.S.
cities? What kind of culture can be built on such shallow economic
and political underpinnings? In the past we have mainly been
offered theories and designs pointing to easily won, bright fu-
tures. The bootstrap image is a case in point; a prodigious feat
defying natural laws but implying a soothing economy of effort.
We have before us the first Puerto Rican generation, an important part of which sees heroic struggle as its destiny. They
correctly insist on keeping attention riveted on the everyday
reality of the deprivation endured by Puerto Ricans. But we do
need some future vision of a state of the world satisfactory to us.
This does not mean a quest for grand theories or scientific truths,
but a systematic probing for politically significant truths. If we
choose life, we have to understand what is life-giving and what
deals death. If we choose to go beyond survival as a community,
then our creativity must be fed by a collective vision that reaches
out to Puerto Ricans everywhere. When people ask in what way
Puerto Ricans differ from earlier immigrants, we must be ready
with the true answer, which is that we are a displaced offshoot of a
people and a land that have yet to be liberated and whose freedom is our own.

Notes

1. *Puerto Rico,* embracing the Report of Brig. Gen. Geo. W. Davis, Military Governor U.S. War Dept., Division of Customs and Insular Affairs, 1899, p. 3.
2. Ibid., p. 44.
3. Ibid., p. 45.
4. Ibid., p. 47.
5. Ibid., p. 45.
6. Among the scores of reviews of Oscar Lewis's *La vida* (New York: Random House, 1968), only that by Barrington Moore, Jr. (*New York Review of Books,* June 15, 1967) deals in a serious way with the political implications of the culture of poverty thesis as it applies to Puerto Rico, even though Moore was among the few to disclaim any special knowledge of the Puerto Rican case.
7. Americans were not the first to attribute docility to Puerto Ricans. Similar observations had been made by Spaniards and Puerto Ricans before the U.S. invasion.
8. René Marqués, " El Puertorriqueño dócil," *Revista de Ciencias Sociales* 7, no. 1-2 (1963), p. 78.
9. The initiated will recognize in these remarks some of the seventy interrelated traits of the culture of poverty in Oscar Lewis, *A Study of Slum Culture* (New York: Random House, 1968).
10. An otherwise highly useful and compact overview of nationalist thought and action in Puerto Rico has been called to task on this score. See Manuel Maldonado Denis, *Puerto Rico* (Siglo Veintiuno, 1969) and his "The Puerto Ricans: Protest of Submission" in the *Annals,* March 1969. The critique appears in *La Escalera* 4, no. 1 (June 1970). (Gervasio Garcia, "Apuntes sobre una interpretación de la realidad puertorriqueña.")
11. On the progressive deflation of the commonwealth idea and its architects, see Luis Nieves Falcón, "El futuro ideológico del Partido Popular Democrático," *Revista de Ciencias Sociales* 9, no. 3 (September 1965).
12. Richard M. Morse, "The Deceptive Transformation of Puerto Rico," paper delivered at a Conference on the Social Sciences in Historical Study, University of Michigan, May 1959.
13. Arthur Liebman, *The Politics of Puerto Rican University Students* (Austin: University of Texas Press, 1970), p. 150.
14. *Puerto Ricans in New York State, 1960-69.* New York State Division of Human Rights, no date.
15. Morse, "The Deceptive Transformation," p. 3.
16. Manuel Teruel, "Puerto Ricans in Transition, Social Relations," Honors Thesis, Harvard University, 1969.
17. Eduardo Seda Bonilla, "Ethnic Studies, Cultural Pluralism, and Power," paper presented at the annual meeting of the Society for Applied Anthropology, University of Colorado, April 1970, p. 1.
18. See especially "The Puerto Rican Experience on the U.S. Mainland," a special issue of the *International Migration Review* 2 (Spring 1968).
19. *Puerto Ricans in New York State,* p. 19.

Selected Bibliography

Acosta Belén, Edna. "Literature and Ideology in the Works of the Puerto Rican Generation of 1950," Ph.D. diss., Columbia University, 1976.

Alegría, José S. *Cincuenta años de literatura puertorriqueña.* San Juan: Academia Puertorriqueña de la Lengua Española, 1955.

Alvarez, Josefina Rivera de. *Diccionario de la literatura puertorriqueña.* Río Piedras: Universidad de Puerto Rico, 1955.

————. *Historia de la literatura puertorriqueña.* Vol. I. San Juan: Editorial del Departamento de Instrucción Pública, Estado Libre Asociado de Puerto Rico, 1969.

Babín, M. T. and Steiner, S. *Borinquen. An Anthology of Puerto Rican Literature.* New York: Alfred A. Knopf, Inc., 1974.

Barbusse, E. J. *The United States in Puerto Rico, 1898-1900.* Chapel Hill: University of North Carolina Press, 1966.

Betances, Ramón E. *Las antillas para los antillanos.* Carlos M. Rama, ed. San Juan: Instituto de Cultura Puertorriqueña, 1975.

————. *Epistolario. Año 1895.* Ada Suárez Diaz, ed. Río Piedras: Ediciones Huracán, 1978.

Bhana, Surendra. *The United States and the Development of the Puerto Rican Status Questition, 1936-1968.* Lawrence, Kansas: Regents Press, 1975.

Blaut, James. "Are Puerto Ricans a National Minority?" *Journal of Contemporary Thought,* nos. 2 and 3; rpt. *Monthly Review* 29, no. 1 (May 1977).

Bravo, E., ed. *An Annotated Selected Puerto Rican Bibliography.* New York: Urban Center of Columbia University, 1972.

Buitrago Ortiz, Carlos. *Los orígenes históricos de la sociedad precapitalista en Puerto Rico.* Río Piedras: Ediciones Huracán, 1976.

Cabrera, Francisco Manrique. *Historia de la literatura puertorriqueña.* New York: Las Américas Publishing Co., 1956; rept. ed.; Río Piedras: Editorial Cultural, 1969.

Canino Salgado, Marcelino J. *La copla y el romance populares en la tradición

372

oral de Puerto Rico. San Juan: Instituto de Cultura Puertorriqueña, 1968.

Caplow, Theodore, Stryker, J., and Wallace, S. E. *The Urban Ambience, A Study of San Juan, Puerto Rico.* Ottowa, 1964.

Castro, Paulino. *Historia sinóptica del partido nacionalista de Puerto Rico.* San Juan, 1947.

Commission on Civil Rights. *Puerto Ricans in the Continental United States. An Uncertain Future.* Washington, D.C., 1976.

Corominas, Enrique V. *Puerto Rico libre.* Buenos Aires: Editorial El Ateneo, 1950.

Corretjer, Juan Antonio. *Futuro sin falla. Mito y realidad antillana.* Guaynabo, Puerto Rico, 1963.

——. *La lucha por la independencia de Puerto Rico.* San Juan: Publicación de Unión del Pueblo Pro Constituyente, 1950.

Council on Social Work Education. *The Puerto Rican People: A Selected Bibliography for Use in Social Work Education.* New York, 1973.

D'Estefano, Miguel A. *Puerto Rico: Analysis of a Plebiscite.* Habana: Tricontinental, 1968.

Dietz, James L. "Imperialism and Puerto Rico." *Monthly Review* 30, no. 4 (September 1978).

Diffie, Bailey, and Justine. *Porto Rico: A Broken Pledge.* New York: Vanguard Press, 1931.

Enamorado Cuesta, José. *Fuera de la ley.* San Juan: Editorial Puerto Rico Libre, 1957.

——. *El imperialismo yanqui y la revolución en el Caribe.* 1936; rpt. ed.; San Juan: Editorial Puerto Rico Libre, 1966.

Espinoza García, Manuel. *La política económica de los Estados Unidos hacia América Latina entre 1945 y 1961.* Habana: Casa de las Américas, 1971.

Fernández Méndez, E., ed. *Portrait of a Society: Readings on Puerto Rican Sociology.* Río Piedras: Universidad de Puerto Rico, 1972.

Figueroa, Sotero. *La verdad de la historia.* Carlos Ripoll, ed. San Juan: Instituto de Cultura Puertorriqueña, 1977.

Fitzpatrick, J. P. *Puerto Rican Americans: The Meaning of Migration to the Mainland.* Englewood Cliffs, N.J.: Prentice-Hall, 1971.

Foner, Philip S. *The Spanish-Cuban-American War and the Birth of American Imperialism, 1895-1902.* New York: Monthly Review Press, 1972.

Fraga Iribarne, Manuel. *Las constituciones de Puerto Rico.* Madrid: Ediciones Cultura Hispánica, 1953.

Francis, Roy G. *The Predictive Process.* Río Piedras, 1960.

Freyre, Jorge F. *External and Domestic Financing in the Economic Development of Puerto Rico.* Río Piedras: University of Puerto Rico Press, 1969.

Friedrich, Carl J. *Puerto Rico: Middle Road to Freedom.* 1959; rpt. ed., New York: Arno, 1975.

García Passalacqua, Juan M. *La crisis política en Puerto Rico (1962-1966).* San Juan: Ediciones Edil, 1970.

González, José Luis. *Literatura y Sociedad en Puerto Rico. De los cronistas de las Indias a la generación del 98.* México: Fondo de Cultura Económica, 1976.

Guerra, Ramiro. *La expansión terrritorial de los Estados Unidos.* Havana: Editorial de Ciencias Sociales, 1975.

Gutiérrez del Arroyo, Isabel. *¿Puerto Rico estado federado? Razones de una sinrazón.* San Juan, 1960.

Hackett, William H. *The Nationalist Party (for the Committee on Interior and Insular Affairs).* Washington, D.C., 1951.

Hernández Alvarez, José. *Return Migration to Puerto Rico.* Berkeley: University of California Press, 1968.

History Task Force, Centro de Estudios Puertorriqueños. *Labor Migration Under Capitalism: The Puerto Rican Experience.* New York: Monthly Review Press, 1979.

Hostos, Adolfo de, *Diccionario histórico-bibliográfico comentado de Puerto Rico.* San Juan, 1976.

Institute of Puerto Rican Studies. *A New Look at the Puerto Ricans and Their Society.* New York: Brooklyn College, 1971.

Jiménez de Báez, Ivette. *La décima popular en Puerto Rico.* México: Universidad Veracruzana, 1964.

Latin American Perspectives. Special issue on "Puerto Rico: Class Struggle and National Liberation," Vol. 3, no. 3 (Summer 1976).

Lewis, Gordon K. *Notes on the Puerto Rican Revolution: An Essay on American Dominance and Caribbean Resistance.* New York: Monthly Review Press, 1974.

————. *Puerto Rico: Freedom and Power in the Caribbean.* New York: Monthly Review Press, 1963.

López, Alfredo. *The Puerto Rican Papers: Notes on the Re-emergence of a Nation.* New York: Bobbs-Merrill Co., Inc., 1973.

Malaret, Augusto. *Vocabulario de Puerto Rico.* 1937; New York: Las Américas Publishing Company, 1955.

Maldonado, Rita M. *The Role of the Financial Sector in the Economic Development of Puerto Rico.* Federal Deposit Insurance Corporation, 1970.

Mathews, Thomas. *Luis Muñoz Marín: A Concise Biography.* New York: R.D.M. Corporation, 1967.

————. *Puerto Rican Politics and the New Deal.* Gainesville, Fla.: University of Florida Press, 1960.

Medina Castro, Manuel. *Estados Unidos y America Latina, Siglo XIX.* Habana: Casa de las Américas, 1968.

Mills, C. W., Senior, C, and Goldsen, R. K. *The Puerto Rican Journey.* 1951; rept. ed., New York: Russell and Russell, 1967.

Moreno Fraginals, Manuel. *The Sugarmill: The Socioeconomic Complex of Sugar in Cuba, 1760-1860.* New York: Monthly Review Press, 1976.

Ojeda Reyes, Félix. *Vito Marcantonio y Puerto Rico: Por los trabajadores y por la nación.* Río Piedras: Ediciones Huracán, 1978.

Perkins, Whitney T. "American Policy in the Government of Its Dependent Areas: A Study of the Policy of the United States Toward the Inhabitants of Its Territories and Insular Possessions," Ph.D. diss., Fletcher School of Law and Diplomacy, 1948.

Perloff, Harvey S. *Puerto Rico's Economic Future.* Chicago: University of Chicago Press, 1950.

Petras, James. *Critical Perspectives on Imperialism and Social Class in the Third World.* New York: Monthly Review Press, 1978.

Petrullo, V. *Puerto Rican Paradox.* Philadelphia, 1947.

Puerto Rico: The Flame of Resistance. San Francisco: People's Press, 1977.

Quintero Rivera, A. G. *Conflictos de clase y política en Puerto Rico.* Río Piedras: Ediciones Huracán, 1976.

————. *Workers' Struggle in Puerto Rico: A Documentary History.* New York: Monthly Review Press, 1976.

Ramos de Santiago, Carmen. *El gobierno de Puerto Rico (Desarrollo constitucional y político).* 2nd ed.; Río Piedras: UPR, 1975.

Rivera, Guillermo. *A Tentative Bibliography of the Belles-Lettres of Porto Rico.* Cambridge, Mass.: Harvard University Press, 1931.

Roberts, Lidia J. and Stefani, Rosa Luisa. *Patterns of Living in Puerto Rican Families.* Río Piedras, 1949.

Rosa Nieves, Cesáreo. *Plumas estelares en las letras de Puerto Rico.* San Juan: UPR, 1967.

————, and Melón, Esther M. *Biografías puertorriqueñas: Perfil histórico de un pueblo.* Sharon, Conn.: Troutman Press, 1931.

Ross, David F. *The Long Uphill Path: A Historical Study of Puerto Rico's Program of Economic Development.* San Juan: Editorial Edil, 1969.

Safa, Helen Icken. *The Urban Poor of Puerto Rico: A Study in Development and Inequality.* New York: Holt, Rinehart and Winston, 1974.

Sánchez Tarniella, Andrés. *Nuevo enfoque sobre el desarrollo político de Puerto Rico.* Río Piedras: Ediciones Edil, 1970.

Senior, Clarence. *Self-Determination for Puerto Rico.* New York, 1976.

————. *The Puerto Ricans: Strangers, Then Neighbors.* Chicago: Quadrangle Books, 1965.

Silén, Juan A. *Apuntes para la historia del movimiento obrero puertorriqueño.* Río Piedras: Editorial Cultural, 1978.

————. *We the Puerto Rican People: A Story of Oppression and Resistance.* New York: Monthly Review Press, 1971.

————, and Nancy Zayas. *La mujer en la lucha hoy.* Río Piedras: Ediciones Kikiriki, 1972.

Steward, Julian, ed. *The People of Puerto Rico.* Urbana: University of Illinois Press, 1956.

Tansill, William R. *Puerto Rico: Independence or Statehood? A Survey of Historical, Political, and Socioeconomic Factors, with Pro and Con Arguments.* Washington, D.C.: Library of Congress, 1977.

Todd, Roberto H. *Desfile de gobernadores de Puerto Rico.* 2nd ed.; Madrid, 1966.

Tugwell, Rexford C. *The Stricken Land: The Story of Puerto Rico.* New York: Doubleday, 1947.

Tumin, Melvin and Feldman, Arnold. *Social Class and Social Change in Puerto Rico.* Princeton, N.J.: Princeton University Press, 1961.

Urrutia Aparicio, Carlos. "Puerto Rico, América y las Naciones Unidas." *Cuadernos Americanos* 1 (January-February 1954): 7-56.

U.S.–Puerto Rico Commission on the Status of Puerto Rico. *Status of Puerto Rico.* Washington, D.C.: Government Printing Office, 1966.

————. *Selected Background Studies.* 1966.

————. *Hearings–Senate Document No. 108,* Vol. I: "Legal-Constitutional"; Vol. III: "Economic."

Vivó, P., ed. *The Puerto Ricans: An Annotated Bibliography.* New York: R. R. Bowker Co., Inc., 1973.

Wagenheim, Kal. *Puerto Rico: A Profile.* New York: Praeger Publishers, 1970.

————, and Jiménez de Wagenheim, Olga, eds. *The Puerto Ricans: A Documentary History.* New York: Doubleday, 1975.

Weisskoff, R. and Wolff, E. "Development and Trade Dependence: The Case of Puerto Rico." *Review of Economics and Statistics* (November 1975).

Zavala, Iris M. "Puerto Rico: Siglo XIX. Literatura y sociedad." *Sin Nombre* 7 no. 4 (1977): 7-26; 8, no. 1 (1977): 37-45.